Life Upgrade: Simple Strategies for Daily Self-Development A Guide to Easy Life Revolution

By: Mustafa Nejem

Table of Contents

Introduction to the Book

Do you ever feel like you could be living life at a higher level of happiness, success and fulfilment? That with just a few tweaks or improvements, you could upgrade your daily routine and optimise your potential? This comprehensive self-development guide holds the key to unlocking a better you through simple strategies designed for sustainable progress, one small change at a time.

Across 8 parts and 40 chapters, "Life Upgrade" provides a structured yet flexible framework for readers to explore multiple facets of self-improvement. From cultivating mental resilience and adopting empowering mindsets, to prioritising physical wellbeing through nutrition, exercise and managing stress – the book equips you with practical tools backed by science. You'll also discover how to maximise productivity through time management, single-tasking and automation.

As social connections are so vital for wellbeing, there is an entire section dedicated to building relationships skills like communication, active listening and empathy. Financial acumen is another cornerstone of security and happiness, with guidance on budgeting, investing and earning supplemental income. Ongoing adaptation and learning are also key themes, as the book encourages embracing lifelong education, learning from mistakes and staying curious.

Rounding out the holistic approach, "Life Upgrade" delves into gratitude, simplicity, giving back to others, and crafting an inspiring environment. With prompting after each chapter and reflective questions to aid implementation, results are meant to be experienced incrementally through sustainable new habits. Rather than vague promises of a "new you", each phase presents attainable steps aligned with your specific goals and lifestyle.

Whether you want to skyrocket your career, improve relationships, boost your health or just feel more in control each day – the wealth of advice provides something for every reader. While ambitious goals may feel overwhelming, this book reveals how even modest tweaks, if maintained, can compound to radically transform your life for the better. Dedicate yourself to just one small suggestion at a time, and unleash your highest potential without feeling deprived or burned out along the way.

With a blend of motivation, science-backed insights and actionable prompts, "Life Upgrade" equips you with everything needed to upgrade your daily routine, optimise your wellbeing and develop the skills, mindsets and habits for ultimate success on your own terms. It's time to commit to the one percent daily improvements that can yield 100 percent results over the long run. Your best life awaits - are you ready to begin?

Chapter 1

Achieving Success through Micro-Goals: Starting Small, Winning Big

The Never-ending Power of Small Wins

Let's look at the concept of small wins. As someone pursuing self-development goals, it's an intriguing idea that can really help you in achieving what you set out to do. Simply put, each time you achieve a manageable goal or make progress towards your larger objectives, your brain releases dopamine, often called the "feel-good hormone." That sense of accomplishment you feel when crossing an item off your to-do list? That's dopamine at work.

The dopamine release following a small win reinforces the behaviours that led to it. This is where motivation comes in. When you achieve these micro-goals, you become more motivated to take on further tasks leading you closer to your ultimate objective. Renowned psychologist Teresa Amabile found in her research that even insignificant forward steps can result in considerable boosts in motivation, especially if they are recognized.

In fact, celebrating these small victories can also propel you to overcome more significant challenges. Every time you acknowledge a small success, it builds your confidence and resilience - critical characteristics for continuous growth and achievement. Small wins aren't just motivating but also empowering. They equip you with the knowledge that you have the potential and capacity to reach your goals, no matter how big they seem.

Role of Micro-Goals in Achievement Pathways

Micro-goals play an integral role across diverse pathways to success. Whether you're chasing a personal goal like being fit or driving towards professional sales figures, micro-goals offer a structured approach for progress. But what makes them so potent? It boils down to their specific and manageable nature. By distilling your big goals into smaller, achievable tasks, you lay the groundwork for consistent progress.

Consider the domain of physical fitness, where setting small, realistic goals is considered one of the best strategies. A report from betterhealth.vic.gov.au recommends setting specific targets like 30 minutes of cardio thrice weekly or reducing your sugar intake by two teaspoons daily over vague goals of "getting fit." Here, micro-goals not only become stepping stones but also create actionable plans to stay on track.

Their significance also translates to professional spheres. For instance, as a sales officer pursuing an annual revenue target, focusing on just that large number can feel overwhelming. But by breaking it into monthly or weekly quotas (micro-goals), it becomes far more manageable.

Practical Implications: Setting Micro-Goals and Celebrating Small Wins

It's great to understand these concepts, but for them to make a difference, you need to apply them effectively. First, 'breaking it down' involves taking your ultimate goal and dividing it into smaller, achievable tasks. To do this, you should refer to trusted sources for guidance on task segmentation.

Your micro-goals must also be clear. Ambiguity won't serve you well when setting goals; they need to be specific and measurable. So don't just say "I want to be healthier," say "I will take a 30-minute walk five days a week." Specificity gives clarity.

Once you set clear, manageable micro-goals, you need to allocate sufficient time and resources to accomplish them. Keeping your schedule realistic is critical for achieving consistent small wins.

Embracing uncertainty is also crucial when setting and pursuing micro-goals. You might not always meet your targets as planned; however, unused potentials shouldn't discourage you. Managing uncertainties demands adaptability - adjusting strategies while keeping your ultimate goal in sight.

Another vital component is celebrating small wins. When you take time to appreciate your progress, you fuel motivation and build confidence for bigger tasks ahead. So whether it's a completed project or hitting your weekly fitness target, give yourself credit for achievements.

Case Studies: Applying Micro-Goals and Small Wins in Your Life

Examining real examples can provide tangible templates for incorporating these strategies into your own journey. Consider the story of Sarah, who set the goal to complete a marathon. By breaking this down into shorter weekly runs and increasing her distances gradually, she managed her training in a realistic way. With every mile and small victory she celebrated, she moved closer to achieving her ultimate dream.

Another inspiring account is of an entrepreneur named Rajesh. His dream was to build a tech startup, but the magnitude was intimidating. However, by setting clear micro-goals like developing coding skills or networking, he chunked down this immense task. Recognizing finished projects as small wins helped him maintain momentum, ultimately reaching entrepreneurial success.

Through diverse cases, we see how micro-goals and small victories can form the backbone of achieving bigger objectives. By "starting small" and "celebrating every win," you empower yourself to bridge the gap between dreaming and achieving.

How to Effectively Set Micro-Goals

Now that we understand the significance of micro-goals and celebrating small wins, the practical question becomes - how exactly can you leverage this approach to propel yourself towards your goals? Here are some tips to help you set micro-goals effectively:

Define your ultimate objective. Whether it's losing 20 pounds or getting a promotion at work, begin by clearly defining your end goal. Having a clear vision of where you want to go is imperative.

Break it down. Examine your goal and identify specific actions or milestones you need to achieve along the way. These become your micro-goals. For example, if your goal is to start a business, some micro-goals could be creating a business plan, finding beta customers, or launching an MVP product.

Set measurable targets. Ensure your micro-goals have quantifiable metrics so you can track progress objectively. Instead of "eat healthier", set a goal to "limit sugar intake to 20g per day". Measurable metrics keep you accountable.

Pace yourself. Micro-goals still need to be challenging but manageable. Work with a trusted coach or friend to determine appropriate target dates for each micro-goal. Don't overload your schedule.

Prepare for uncertainty. Unexpected challenges or delays will arise. Build in flexibility so you can adapt your micro-goals when life happens. Your end goal stays fixed, but micro-goals can shift to reality.

Celebrate all progress. No victory is too small, so acknowledge even incremental wins. Celebrations energise you through challenges and motivate continued progress.

Review frequently. Check in with yourself regularly and objectively assess if your micro-goals are helping you inch closer to your main objective. Adjust your approach as needed.

With a thoughtful process of defining micro-goals, you put yourself in the best position to stay motivated throughout your journey. These small, measurable steps fuel determination that can carry you all the way to achieving big goals.

Using Micro-Goals to Succeed at Work

Achieving aspirations isn't just about personal growth - you also want to thrive professionally. By leveraging the micro-goal approach, you can absolutely excel in your career too. But how?

Develop clear professional goals. Envision your ideal future role, title, salary, etc. Paint a specific picture of where you want to be in 5 years.

Break work objectives into subsets. If you want a promotion, identify specific skills, responsibilities or impact you need to demonstrate to get there.

Set interim micro-goals. Commit to deliverables like completing a certification program, taking on a new client, or developing a presentation.

Track results and metrics. Measure performance criteria that align with what your company values, like income generated or customer satisfaction scores.

Present a 'small win' every quarter. Whether it's increased sales or an innovative new process, celebrate progress against goals each 90 days.

Utilise available resources. Mentors, executive coaching, and company-provided development tools can support you.

Just as micro-goals serve you personally, applying the approach at your job helps ensure professional success by setting mini-milestones towards your long-term career vision.

Here are some additional tips for effectively using micro-goals:

Evaluate Your Micro-Goals

Setting micro-goals is hugely beneficial, but you also need to evaluate them to ensure you're on the right track. Consider these strategies:

- ✓ Set review dates for each micro-goal and assess your progress on those dates. Are you on schedule or do adjustments need to be made?
- ✓ Reflect on what's working well and what could be improved. Keep tracking metrics so you have data to inform needed changes.
- ✓ If external factors shift your circumstances, re-evaluate timelines but don't abandon the goal unless absolutely necessary. Adaptability is key.
- ✓ Micro-goal updates don't always need to be major overhauls. Sometimes a slight tweak to duration or target can get you back on pace.
- ✓ Celebrate achievements but also acknowledge setbacks frankly. Problems ignored will persist, so address issues promptly.
- ✓ Ask for feedback. Get objective input from others on your process to catch any blind spots.

Regular self-assessment ensures you're maintaining accountability and momentum toward your larger goals. With agility and reviews, micro-goals remain effective.

Gain Commitment from others

Sharing your goals with others expands your support system for achieving them. Consider including:

- ✓ Close friends and family you trust for encouragement as you progress.
- ✓ Colleagues if goals relate to work or professional growth. Team success is strengthened by individual excellence.
- ✓ Mentors whose expertise can advise your specific goals and evaluation approach.
- ✓ Accountability partners who check on your progress and keep you motivated.
- ✓ Public declaration of goals via social media can motivate through transparency.

Remember, with others invested, you're less likely to divert from micro-goals during difficult stretches. Their engagement fuels your own determination to succeed.

So in summary, micro-goals enable you to achieve big things through consistent small steps. With effective planning, evaluation, and commitment from others around you, stay dedicated to moving closer to your dreams step by small step.

Chapter 2

Developing your
Personal Values and Purpose

IDENTIFYING YOUR PERSONAL CORE VALUES & CONNECTING TASKS TO A BROADER PURPOSE

Do you ever feel like you're just going through the motions in life, with no clear direction or purpose? You are not alone. Many people struggle to find meaning in their daily activities which can result in a feeling of emptiness and dissatisfaction. But what if we told you there's a simple yet powerful way to change that? For example, what if this routine could be turned into an enjoyable experience and source of fulfilment? It begins with identifying your personal core values and relating them to your tasks.

Personal core values refer to the principles and beliefs that inform your decision-making process, actions, as well as interactions with others. Once you have identified your values you gain an understanding of what really matters most importantly to you and what goals are important in your life. This helps create an alignment between your tasks and gives them purpose thereby stimulating motivation as well as satisfaction.

This chapter will take you through how to identify your core values and link them to a broader purpose. You'll learn tips on how to evaluate your daily tasks against the base of your personal principles, aligning these tasks along with decision-making processes around those values. From the end of this chapter you will have all the tools necessary for living a truly purposeful life.

Understanding Personal Core Values

Personal core values are basically fundamental beliefs or principles that guide decisions individuals make or behaviours they show. These values act as reference points for keeping you focused on what is most important to yourself personally. Defining therefore understanding one's core values is highly essential since it allows one to stay true even when facing tough circumstances. They shape up one's beliefs, characteristics of his or her decision making process hence play a very crucial role in living a satisfying life.

The first step towards leading a purpose-driven life is identifying one's personal core values. By being sure about what really matters most to you it becomes easy for you to align your daily tasks with the broader purpose. The increased fulfilment and satisfaction that come from engaging in these activities will thus drive you closer towards your goal. The significance of core values is such that they create clarity on what one stands for hence making it possible for him or her to remain on the right course alongside his or her goals.

Reflecting on Your Values

Now that you understand why personal core values are important, think about yours. Self-reflection is a key part of identifying what guides the decisions you make and the way you act. To start off, dedicate some time specifically for this activity.

Go to a quiet place where there are no distractions and sit down alone with yourself. Reflect on the following points:

What principles do you hold most dear?

What motivates you into action?

What character traits do you find admirable in others?

Meaning

Take your time answering these questions as honestly and thoughtfully as possible. Consider writing down your thoughts in a journal. This should help clarify your personal core values and how they influence your view of things.

Having established our values, we then have an obligation to articulate them properly. In the next section, we will deal with creating a value statement.

Now you know your core values, it's time to put them into words that are both meaningful and concise. The value statement will therefore help you in decision making and concentrate on matters of ultimate concern.

Think about your three to five primary values and how they interact with each other when developing the value statement. Use simple words that make sense to you and accurately represent your values. Avoid general terms or phrases that have no meaning in relation to these values.

Remember, value statements are dynamic and will change over time due to experiences; therefore, be adaptable to redefine the value statement. This should be reviewed periodically to ensure its consistency with changing values or goals.

When you articulate your core values and come up with a value statement, it is a significant stride towards living a purposeful life.

Evaluating Daily Tasks

Now that you know your core values, evaluate your daily tasks to determine if they are aligned with those values. Task analysis will help identify what among the tasks being done contributes to getting there while others do not.

The first step is making a list of all daily activities regardless of their sizes. Afterwards, scrutinise each activity vis-a-vis core principles upon which one bases his/her entire life around. Does it contribute towards an important goal or satisfy some of your desires? If not, consider whether this task can be eliminated or given out for someone else to do.

It is necessary to note that not all activities carried out will fully agree with one's core beliefs. However, appraising such duties frequently might bring slight changes thereby adding more meaning in life.

Connecting Tasks to Core Values

Matching daily chores with personal principles is vital for enjoying one's existence completely. You may even feel fulfilled and successful doing seemingly monotonous activities if they relate back to something bigger than yourself.

To set out on connecting tasks with core principles: firstly find out which things matter most for you; secondly rate the significance of each single chore in terms of supporting these values. For example, you may decide to use public means of transport or ride a bicycle instead of driving to work alone if environmental sustainability is among your core principles.

It is important for one not to lose sight of his/her core values whenever he/she is planning on the jobs to be done. Be it at work or in personal life, question yourself whether your actions are consistent with your values and support your purposes.

Definitely, there could be stumbling blocks on the way; however, staying true to what you believe and what you are directed towards will keep you focused. You can reward yourself for commendable results as well as trace the progress in order not to forget about the set objectives.

In summary, by connecting your tasks with fundamental beliefs you make life more meaningful. Task alignment therefore must be a priority for any person who wants to go through a transformational process.

Incorporating Core Values into Decision-Making

This process will assist in making decisions that fit into your purpose and values. When you embrace your core values in decision making processes, you can be sure of a choice that reflects what matters most to you. For example, whenever faced with a difficult resolution, it is important to think about one's values and how they relate to each of the given tough options regarding that particular matter. This is how value-based decision-making works; it helps individuals make authentic and fulfilling choices.

Always remember that your values may change over time requiring you to frequently evaluate or reassess them. This is how core values become a part of your decision-making framework. By habitually doing this, incorporating core values into one's decision-making becomes second nature leading to more fulfilment and purpose in life.

Discovering Meaning within the Daily Grind

Do you ever find yourself feeling empty after accomplishing something? Sometimes we feel our work does not hold any meaning or sense. Find new found meaning from relating your daily tasks to personal fundamental beliefs.

When you do this, the meaning of even the littlest things can no longer escape your understanding. You understand how every task contributes towards a broader goal or objective that aligns with what is really important to you. This gradual increase in satisfaction, motivation and joy as one completes duties can lead to significant improvement.

No matter their magnitude, reflect on how these small activities impact on your personal beliefs and help you accomplish a higher cause. Doing these tasks slowly helps people find purposeful lives out of them.

By organising your life around tasks which are consistent with your set of ethical principles, it would be much easier for you to live according to them. Thus task significance is about finding meaning in tasks which have far-reaching effects on one's overall level of satisfaction in life.

Having a Sense of Direction

Ever felt like all days were drifting without direction whatsoever? One way is by finding meaning through aligning daily tasks with broader purpose. It is through relating your daily activities to broader purposes that you can experience changes in your life.

When you align what you do with your personal core values as well as a bigger aim, life becomes clearer. By doing this, one will be more motivated to engage and satisfied with the work done.

Therefore, it is important to take time and think about how your core values could help you live each day to its fullest. Such practices not only build up a life of values but also facilitate intention and meaning in living.

Remember, developing a sense of purpose is not an overnight process. Time and effort are needed. However, by considering one's daily tasks in terms of their value in relation to the larger goals and overall value system that represents who we are as individuals, such a life is achievable.

Dealing with Challenges in Matching Tasks

Determining my personal core values and aligning my daily tasks with broader purposes is something I enjoy. Nevertheless, it can be difficult on occasion. This task alignment may encounter challenges that hinder progress and motivation. Common obstacles to task alignment include:

Being overwhelmed by the scale of what needs to be achieved

Problems brought about by prioritising duties

Self-distrust and vulnerability

The desire to fit into others' expectations

It is essential to overcome these challenges by keeping in mind the future. Reflect on your personal values and the difference you want to make in this world. Split up big tasks into smaller ones. Come up with a program or a list of things that need to be prioritised.

If self-doubt begins to creep in, remind yourself of your values and what you are trying to achieve by doing what you are doing. Reach out to a friend, family member or mentor who can provide encouragement and perspective.

Be good to yourself above all else. Change requires time and effort. Recognize small victories along the way to maintain enthusiasm and inspiration.

Track Progress, Celebrate Successes

An action-oriented approach is needed when linking tasks with core values. It is important that you track your progress throughout as it forms an integral part of achieving your goals. Establish specific parameters that will guide you, assess how far you have come, monitor these figures every so often in order to stay on course.

But pause occasionally and acknowledge success no matter how small. Reaching your goals is something worth celebrating, acknowledging the advances made helps keep one encouraged and motivated all through the process. Write down even minor accomplishments, take time to honour them too amid this list-making activity. The sense of achievement derived from this positive reinforcement can give meaning to your acts while encouraging you not to give up.

By embracing a goal-oriented mindset, monitoring progress, and celebrating successes, one can stay motivated towards living life with purpose.

Developing a Values-Based Life Style

The key to finding meaning and fulfilment within everyday activities lies within one embracing a value-based lifestyle. Your actions should align with what matters most through integrating personal core values into daily living. The following ideas could help foster a values-based approach:

- ✓ Take part in activities in agreement with your principles
- ✓ Associate with people who reinforce your ideal value system
- ✓ Stay centred upon them being mindful
- ✓ Regularly reflect and re-evaluate your values in order to keep things in perspective

Remember, it is a journey to live by your values. You become more content with the activities you undertake from day to day by incorporating them into your daily schedule.

Task Alignment and Life Satisfaction

Aligning tasks with personal core values results in a high sense of purpose, which leads to fulfilment. This not only gives meaning to your daily activities but also provides a direction and focus that can significantly improve overall life satisfaction.

When these duties reflect on your most cherished ideals, the enhanced sense of an objective and significance would translate into raised fighting spirit, efficiency, involvement in all areas of living. It has the potential to enhance self-esteem, deepen joy, as well as make life generally more fulfilling.

A deep sense of satisfaction and fulfilment could be fostered through task alignment which can impact every area of one's life positively. Simply take time out to identify your innermost principles and connect those everyday tasks with broader purposes – you will be amazed at the difference it makes.

Take Action: Implement What You Have Learnt

You now have a better understanding of who you are concerning values and how they can be tied with day-to-day tasks for greater good; simply put everything into action.

Consider your present daily activities and measure them against your innermost principles. Classify some duties as directly related to a larger purpose and others that are not.

After that, find an appropriate concise way to express yourself. This value statement captures your thoughts and helps you in decision-making.

Use your core values and value statement as a framework for making decisions and choosing tasks that align with your purpose. Use value-based decision-making to ensure your behaviour is congruent with your values.

Set doable goals that reflect the core values you uphold and work towards achieving them. Gauge your progress and take pride in your accomplishments along the way.

Lastly, integrate these beliefs into all areas of their day-to-day lives for a values-based lifestyle. When choosing what you will do on every day basis, deliberately select chores which match with one's mission or passions.

Practising these teachings can lead to a more fulfilling life underscored by purpose. Remember: it is essential to act if we want to reach our objectives and live according to our own principles.

Chapter 3

SMART Goals and
Goal Setting Techniques

Has your personal development journey come to a standstill? Is it hard for you to find motivation and stay on track towards your goals? If yes, then this is the moment to set SMART goals.

Personal development is a lifelong process that requires persistence, motivation, and purpose. In order to succeed in your personal growth journey, you should have smart goals which provide clarity and focus.

In this chapter, we will go through what SMART goals mean, how they can help in one's personal development and how to create an action plan that will support the achievement of the intended goals. Therefore, let us deeply look at how SMART goals can change all about your journey of personal growth!

Knowing Personal Development

Personal development refers to the act of learning something new or improving oneself. This means actively doing things that will add value to your life and make you better off than before.

A journey of personal development helps one identify areas that need improvement and set goals and objectives with regard to success in various aspects of their life.

Self-improvement remains as an important part of personal growth because without it you may not grow beyond certain fear zones that hinder progress. Therefore, by learning new skills, acquiring different perspectives and getting out of your comfort zone , people achieve more than even they never thought possible.

Basically, personal development is a continuous process that demands commitment, effort as well as open-mindedness. Through having a mindset of growth and taking actions towards one's goals one can unleash their potential fully hence leading a fulfilling life.

Why Goal Setting Matters

Without clear objectives it becomes tough to make any progress or develop yourself. Goals give direction and help you concentrate on things that really matter most for you. When you set reasonable, achievable aims for yourself, they become something you are working towards every day. Such aims should assist in motivating as well as inspiring an individual toward trying their best in reaching higher levels.

Setting goals also helps you track your progress and measure success. You can break down large goals into smaller manageable tasks, celebrate small wins along the way, and stay motivated to continue on your personal development journey.

Personal growth requires self-reflection, dedication, and a willingness to challenge yourself. Setting and achieving goals can help you stay accountable to yourself and ensure that you are consistently making progress. Therefore, whether it's learning a new skill, improving health or advancing in a career goal setting is necessary for a personal developmental journey.

Introduction of SMART Goals

SMART goals are useful in setting objectives for one's life. In this case, the letter 'S' represents specific while 'M' means measurable, 'A' stands for achievable, 'R' indicates relevant while T denotes time-bound objectives. With all these aspects in place, a person is more likely to achieve their set objectives.

Specific Objectives

It is important that personal development goals be made specific. Specificity gives your goals direction and clarity, ensuring that you stay focused on what you want to achieve. For instance, instead of setting a goal to "be more productive," set a specific goal of "increase your productivity by 20% by the end of the month."

Specific goals also help you measure progress more accurately. You are more likely to know if you are making any progress towards a certain target than when it is just vague. It makes tracking your progress more effective and encouraging. This way, you will also know whether the goal has been achieved or it still needs improvement.

Do not forget that your personal development goals must agree with what you want to do and what matters most to you. Your goals' specifics need to be tailored according to your own values and aspirations. When you set specific objectives that match your development goals personally, it is easier for you to remain motivated and successful.

Measurable Goals

In order to effectively track your progress and hold yourself accountable in personal development, measurable goal setting is important. Measurable goals have specific, quantifiable targets which allow for assessment of success as one moves towards desired outcomes.

To create measurable goals, start by identifying key performance indicators (KPIs) that align with your broader personal development objectives. Set up metrics that can accurately measure these such as timelines, numbers or percentages which show movement in the right direction. These metrics will provide a clear way of tracking results as well as showing if an individual's growth targets are on course.

Through creating measurable objectives, one can regularly evaluate their progress and make strategic adjustments whenever necessary. This helps an individual keep their eye on the ball while closely watching over their growth where tangible results are seen.

When setting measurable goals, it is important to use tools such as spreadsheets or apps or even personal development journals that allow one to track their KPIs against them. These resources provide a concrete way to evaluate your progress and make data-driven decisions.

In summary, making personal development goals measurable is an important step towards achieving success. By incorporating KPIs and metrics into your goal-setting process, you will be able to stay focused, hold yourself accountable, and track your personal growth journey with clarity and purpose.

Achievable Goals

Setting attainable goals is necessary for a personal development journey. When goals are realistic and achievable, it becomes more motivating for you to work towards them resulting in progress and growth. One way of setting achievable goals is by starting small then gradually increasing the targets as one progresses. Moreover, it could be useful to break down bigger goals into smaller steps that are easier to manage for better chances of success. Remember setting achievable goals is all about pushing yourself beyond the comfort zone while being within reach. This way, you can build momentum towards your dreams slowly but surely, leading a more fulfilling life.

Setting Relevant Goals towards Personal Growth Objectives

While setting out on a journey of personal growth, setting goals plays a critical role in achieving personal development; however it's crucial to set up the correct ones too. Relevant goals align with an individual's personal values and aspirations that have a significant impact on their developmental path.

When setting relevant goals, it is important to consider what you value most. What are your interests, passions, and strengths? What are some of the things that you want to achieve in your life? Answering these questions can assist you in creating goals that really matter and mean something to you.

Relevant goals can also help you maintain motivation and focus. Pursuing something that is truly important to you can provide a sense of purpose and determination that makes staying on the right path easier than ever before.

To set relevant goals, one should take time to reflect on what is important and desirable for them. Keep the bigger picture in mind about how your goals fit into your overall vision for your life. This way, setting relevant goals will help you stay true to yourself as well as make progress towards attaining your personal growth objectives.

Time-Bound Goals

Setting deadlines for personal development goals helps one sustain motivation and attain consistent progress towards desired outcomes. In the absence of a definite timeline, it is easy to become distracted and disoriented by competing priorities. By setting time-bound goals, a sense of urgency is created which makes it possible for one to keep focused during their personal development journey or self-improvement plan.

While setting deadlines for your objectives, be realistic about how much time would be needed to achieve them. Consider factors such as goal's scope, availability of resources plus other commitments which might affect the time available for working on it. Indicate exactly when each specific goal will be achieved or over which period with regular checks being done on oneself so as not to deviate off course.

Remember; Deadlines are not supposed to create pressure or stress but rather provide you with a framework and direction for going through your personal development journey. By setting time-bound goals, you direct your attention towards growing personally and becoming a better version of yourself.

Creating a SMART Goal Action Plan

Now that SMART objectives have been formed by you, let's move on to how you can develop an action plan in order to achieve them. An action plan helps you know the steps that you should take in order to reach your goals successfully. In order to create an effective action plan, there are few things that you need to do:

Break down your goal into manageable tasks: Divide your goal into smaller and easier tasks, which will help in ensuring that you do not lose track of progress.

Set deadlines: For each task, state the deadline so as to create a clear timeframe as well as personal responsibility.

Identify necessary resources: Find out what are the necessary inputs for every task such as time, monetary value and people.

Assign responsibilities: Decide who is responsible for doing particular tasks and ensure they clearly understand their roles and the expectations.

Monitor progress: Regularly visit your action plan in order to check whether it is still on course or adjustments are required.

The action plan is also crucial for successful implementation of SMART goals. By breaking down goals into manageable tasks, setting deadlines, identifying necessary resources, assigning responsibilities and monitoring progress; one can set themselves up to win!

Overcoming Challenges and Obstacles

Personal development journeys do not always go smoothly - there will be obstacles along the way. It's therefore essential to have strategies for dealing with these challenges while staying motivated towards your own growth objectives.

Breaking down challenges into smaller, more manageable steps is one of the most effective ways to overcome them. Instead of looking at the big picture, look for specific obstacles in your path and work through them one at a time.

Another approach that can be helpful is to be answerable to goals. Share these with a trusted friend or mentor who can provide support and encouragement during difficult times. Creating a community of individuals with personal development objectives similar to yours can also provide motivation and foster accountability.

It is important to recognize that failure and obstacles are part of our transformative path. They should not discourage you; rather, they should be used as stepping stones for learning, growth and becoming a better and stronger person.

Celebrating Milestones and Progress

While it's essential to track your development progress, remember also to celebrate milestones along the way. By celebrating your achievements, you will feel proud about what you have done so far, reinforce good habits and remain motivated.

Apart from being simply joyful experiences, celebrating milestones allows us to pause for reflection on our journey towards our goals. It is important that we acknowledge the work we put towards personal growth. Perhaps giving yourself something that makes you happy like a day off or buying something that you have always desired.

Just remember that milestones come in all shapes and sizes – both big and small. No matter how trivial, ensure each is celebrated. You will see how far you have come when you take time to acknowledge your accomplishments on this journey of personal development.

Adjusting and Refining Your Goals

As we move forward in our personal development journeys, we may find it necessary to change or refine our goals. The circumstances may change; new information may come up; what was once relevant could become unattainable for your own growth. All this is normal as far as self-improvement is concerned.

To effectively refine your goals, start by assessing your progress and identifying areas where you may be falling short or exceeding expectations. Recall any setbacks and problems you might have experienced and take a lesson from them. Be honest with yourself as to whether your target still matters if it is meaningful to your personal growth.

The SMART framework can guide you in case you need to adjust your goals. Can the goals be specified, measured, attainable, relevant and time-bound? Remember that the whole purpose of goal refinement is to ensure that your goals are still growing with you and continue guiding your personal development path.

Stay Accountable with SMART Goals

For anyone to achieve success in personal development, accountability is very important. The other half is sticking to these goals once you set SMART goals. One good way of being accountable to yourself during this process is evaluating how far you've come. Use a journal or an app to document your journey so that it remains on course.

The other option is sharing your aims with someone who can be trusted. It helps one feel responsible enough and motivated towards fulfilling them. Moreover, setting deadlines and benchmarks can help keep track of progress and identify areas for improvement.

Remember, setbacks and challenges are inevitable along the way. Do not let them throw you off course, instead keep yourself motivated, adaptable and most importantly responsible to your SMART goals. It will amaze you how much you can achieve when you remain answerable.

Reviewing and Revaluating Your Personal Development Journey

Whenever you are moving towards the attainment of your SMART objectives, it is necessary that you periodically assess your progress and rethink your approach. It enables one to know if they have made any mistakes or if they need to change their goals as well as the action plan.

In this process self-reflection is very essential. Take a moment to evaluate your progress, what is working and what is not. The following queries may be asked during this time:

Which achievements have been realised until now?

What difficulties have been encountered?

What has one learnt so far?

Need for changes in the goal-setting strategies?

Truthful answers to these questions enable individuals to understand their personal growth journey as well as inform their next steps.

Remember that personal development is an ongoing process, and it's okay to make changes to your goals as circumstances change and as you gain new insights. This means refining objectives so that they can still be attained while remaining on topic.

This will help increase motivation and drive because when milestones are celebrated and accomplishments acknowledged by others along this path of personal development it enhances somebody who wants more from life.

If people can remain accountable by sticking with their SMART goals then review them regularly in order to understand where they are in their personal development journey; then they will definitely achieve their end objective of self-growth.

Chapter 4

Understanding Personal Habits, Triggers, and Routines for Self-Development

Do you ever struggle to make necessary positive changes in your life? Or do you find yourself repeating the same negative behaviours despite attempts to stop them? Understanding personal habits, triggers, and routines is crucial for self-development and personal growth.

We will explore how our habits, triggers, and routines influence our actions and outcomes. This science-based exploration of these mechanisms can help you better comprehend your behaviours and make effective changes, enabling you to achieve your goals.

As we embark on this journey of discovery, the topics covered include the power of habits, identification of triggers, breakdown of routines, building good habits, defeating bad triggers, optimising routines for enhanced productivity, adding self-care to daily routines, accountability in habit-building, adapting habits to changing lifestyles, being mindful about habit formation, using visualisation as a catalyst for habit change, tracking progress, and enjoying successes (milestones).

Join us on this quest for self-improvement as we unveil the secrets to understanding personal habits, triggers, and routines for self-development.

The Power of Habits

Our daily lives are more influenced by our customs than we might think. How often do we realise that the power behind these traditions is enough to determine the course our lives will follow?

Habit formation starts with a cue or trigger that prompts behaviour or routine leading to a reward or outcome. This cycle has led some people to believe that breaking free from such shackles is impossible.

By understanding how habits are formed scientifically and studying habit loops, it becomes possible, even at an individual level, to align one's habits with specific personal goals. In other words, new practices need to be cultivated through deliberate practice and repetition to contribute to positive change in one's life.

However, it is worth noting that not all behaviours are created equal, as some can have detrimental effects on our lives and well-being. Therefore, by appreciating the significance of habits, we can start controlling our behaviours and bring about positive changes that enable personal growth.

Identifying Triggers

Do you ever feel a very strong reaction to some event or person without understanding why? Triggers are stimuli that cause a particular response or behaviour. They could be both external, like sounds, smells, and sights, as well as internal, like thoughts and emotions. Through trigger awareness, which is the ability to recognize when you are being triggered and how it affects you, you can identify triggers.

Emotional triggers, on the other hand, can be highly influential in changing how we behave. Often based on our past experiences, they frequently result in feelings of anger, sadness, or anxiety. By understanding your emotional triggers, you can find ways to manage your reactions constructively and reduce negativity.

The first step toward personal development is becoming aware of my triggers. The process includes identifying the causes of my trigger points as well as their respective implications on my life.

Breaking Down Routines

Your everyday routines define who you become throughout the day. To accomplish your desired results and improve self-development, you have to find areas for improvement and optimise your daily routines accordingly.

Doing a routine assessment is one effective way to achieve it, where you break down your normal day by evaluating every activity and identifying all the components that contribute to your actions and behaviour.

List down all your daily routines from the moment you wake up until when you go to sleep. For each activity, write the emotions, thoughts, and behaviours associated with it. This will show areas where changes may be necessary for bettering your daily routine.

For example, if you find yourself feeling overwhelmed and stressed while checking emails each morning, maybe a change in schedule would help minimise the negative impact of such an experience.

By breaking down daily routines, you gain an understanding of what makes habits and behaviours that you usually do each day. These insights can be used to optimise your daily routines for self-development so that you can achieve your goals.

Developing Positive Habits

To foster personal growth and development, creating positive habits is one of the most effective ways. When establishing new habits, one approach is habit stacking, linking a new habit to an existing one already practised. For instance, if you want to start meditating for 10 minutes every morning before work, this could be part of your morning routine after brushing teeth.

Also, tracking habits helps in developing positive ones. The use of any app, journal, or other means that can track progress will always motivate and enable you not to lose direction about your goal.

Remember that developing positive habits takes time and dedication, as well as patience towards yourself because they are small but meaningful adjustments reflecting upon your personal values and aspirations. This way, you will start building a strong foundation for sustainable success leading to self-improvement through habit stacking and habit tracking.

Overcoming Negative Triggers

Negative triggers are caused by various things like stressors or anxiety, even from negative self-talks. These prevent us from growing while leading us into unwanted actions that are bad for our personal development. To overcome negative triggers, one must be self-aware and possess effective trigger management techniques.

One way of managing triggers is identifying the situations or contexts that cause negative behaviours to manifest themselves. This will help individuals in coming up with ways of avoiding or adjusting such situations so that their influence is minimised. Furthermore, becoming self-aware would enable someone to identify negative triggers by observing patterns and thoughts they follow.

In addition, another means of overcoming negative triggers is participating in activities that promote positive emotions and behaviours. Physical exercise, mindfulness, and socialising can change your mood, leading to a reduction in the effects of negativity.

Therefore, if you want to deal effectively with negative triggers, take a proactive approach towards addressing them. When you put in place practices for managing the triggers and become self-aware, the impact of these triggers on life will diminish, paving the way for a shift from detrimental habits towards growth-oriented ones.

Making Routines More Productive

Are you unable to complete everything needed every day? Do you want to enhance your daily productivity levels? Enhancing routines helps maximise time-use and create a balanced lifestyle.

You can start by analysing how your daily routines are performed to determine the areas that require improvement. Consider the activities that consume a lot of time and energy and find ways to simplify them or delegate them. You can also set specific targets for each day to ensure that you remain focused and motivated.

Alternatively, another efficient technique for dealing with this challenge is developing a schedule every day that prioritises your most important things. This also ensures that you do not get distracted by other things but rather make progress towards what you want in life.

Moreover, habit stacking is another method that may alter your routines. By connecting new positive practices with those already established, it forms a framework for sustainable success and effective management of time and energy.

Lastly, always remember to take breaks and pay attention to self-care throughout the day. This would help you recover and not feel tired too soon, making you more productive in the long term.

Optimising Daily Efficiency Through Routines

Integrating Self-Care into Daily Routines

Self-care is usually overlooked, yet it is crucial in maintaining a balanced and healthy lifestyle. By integrating self-care into your daily routines, you can prioritise your well-being and enhance your mental, emotional, and physical health.

Start by identifying the areas of your life where you need to prioritise self-care. It could be as simple as incorporating a five-minute meditation into your morning routine or taking a break to stretch during the workday.

Another way of prioritising self-care lies in taking care of yourself. Take part in activities that make you feel good

such as yoga or walking around nature. Make sure you eat healthy food that provides all the nutrients required for the proper functioning of your body.

Finally, engage in activities that bring joy into your life or help calm down after a hard day at work. Whether it means reading books, taking baths, or spending time with friends or family, self-care should be considered an essential part of your daily routine. You will be more energised, focused, and ready to face all the challenges that come your way.

The Role of Accountability in Habit Formation

Creating new habits can be difficult, but their adoption can be greatly facilitated by seeking support from other people. Accountability is one aspect of habit formation that helps you stick to your goals. By being answerable to yourself, you create a sense of responsibility and dedication towards these habits.

One way to include accountability in your journey towards habit formation is by finding a partner or support system for this purpose. Regular check-ins with a person who shares both your and their goals will keep you motivated as well as accountable. Additionally, joining a group or community that has similar objectives can make you more responsible and hence keep you on track.

Another way to enhance the level of accountability is monitoring progress. In this case, keeping a journal on habits or utilising an application that tracks them plays a significant role in helping one look back upon what they have accomplished and hold themselves accountable if they fail. By being honest with yourself about where you fell short, it is possible to regain control and maintain your habit-forming process.

But remember that establishing such patterns takes time and effort; nevertheless, proper support and accountability would enable one to meet set targets and maintain positive changes in their life.

Adapting Habits to Life Changes

Life, a continuous process that requires one to adapt their habits, is subject to change. Whenever your work schedule varies, you relocate or experience a huge transition in life, aligning your habits may be the way to go.

Another important thing in adapting one's habits to life changes is building resilience. Resilience helps in bouncing back from challenges and setbacks; it is a skill that can be learned through practice. It will enable you to maintain a positive attitude and keep growing even when the unexpected happens.

One good way to change your routines for adapting yourself to life again is assessing them and determining areas that require adjusting. Analyse how you're going to manage your new routine on an everyday basis and decide which practices are still valuable and which ones must be changed.

Also, remember that it would not hurt to be flexible enough to consider new habits that fit into one's new condition better. Take this moment as an opportunity for growth while accepting change; do not be afraid of testing new timetables and rituals until you find one that works best for you.

Changing your habits according to the changes in life takes time and practice; hence, be patient with yourself on this journey and celebrate small achievements accomplished. By remaining committed to personal development goals while developing your habits according to your ever-changing circumstances, this will enable you to live a satisfying life.

The Benefits of Mindfulness in Habit Development

Positive habit formation is essential in personal development with preferred outcomes. Habit development may be deeply influenced by mindfulness, leading us towards present moment realisation. Being mindful is living within the present moment so conscious choices become available for our decisions.

Being more aware of our habits, triggers, and routines through mindfulness enables positive changes to happen, thus breaking negative patterns. You can tell when you are about to perform the same act that needs some changing by staying present and then choose differently every time. This enables self-awareness fostering deeper understanding of the reasons behind certain behaviours.

Additionally, mindfulness can provide many other benefits for personal growth. For instance, it can help in reducing stress and anxiety, increase focus and productivity, while raising well-being overall. It has the capability of improving your mood, enhancing resilience levels, and promoting a more positive view of life.

If you want to develop good habits leading to personal growth, then try blending mindfulness into your everyday life. Be it through meditation, mindful breathing, or other practices of mindfulness, you start envisioning the power of mindfulness, hence achieving your peak point.

Harnessing the Power of Visualization for Habit Change

Visualisation is a powerful technique that can accelerate habit change and goal setting. Through creating vivid mental pictures of what we want to achieve, we are able to retrain our brains, thus forming new habits.

When visualising, use all your senses so that things seem more real. Imagine the sounds, smells, and feelings associated with reaching your goals. Hence, the emotional bond established with such dreams would enable one to remain motivated while committed to their newly formed lifestyles.

Overcoming blocks and obstructions on the way by using the mind-eye is another use of visualisation that can help you. Imagining different situations in your mind beforehand can assist you in being focused and easily moving forward even when things do not work out as expected.

For instance, the next time you set a new habit or goal, include visualisation practices in your standard operating procedures. Try to visualise as much as possible when doing this so that with time, you will be able to improve your rate of personal growth.

Track Progress and Milestones Compliment

In order to make strides in personal development, one needs to track their progress. This can only be measured by understanding where one is at present as compared to where they started from. It is easy to keep a journal or use an app for this purpose.

Self-reflection also comes in handy when tracking your progress. Therefore, whenever you have free time, take it and think about the things that you have done well and those that you have not done well enough. With such information, you will be able to adjust your routines accordingly.

Apart from tracking progress, celebrating milestones can serve as a great motivation and confidence booster. It is such an amazing thing to do when you achieve a long-term goal or even just finish a small task that has been strenuous for you.

There are several ways through which these milestones can be celebrated. Some people love indulging themselves with something special while other individuals prefer sharing with their close ones about their achievements. However, whatever way in which these celebrations are made is always important so long as it entails noticing the advancements that you have made in life from your hard work point of view.

Always remember that personal development is a journey; therefore, celebrate every step of the journey. Track progress, reflect on successes and challenges, and celebrate milestones: these steps will keep you motivated towards positive change.

Cultivating Personal Development through Growth Mindset

A growth mindset is essential when it comes to personal development. It involves perceiving setbacks as opportunities for learning, embracing challenges, striving towards improvement, and believing that abilities can be developed through effort.

Individuals with growth mindsets are likely to approach problems confidently and take risks more frequently than those who don't possess such an attitude. They see mistakes or failures as a chance of learning rather than being reluctant to seek assistance or feedback.

It's necessary to change focus from fixed traits into growth potential if one wants to develop a growth mindset. Furthermore, practise positive internal dialogue by countering negative thoughts with positive ones that reinforce your ability to learn and improve.

Another way of cultivating a growth mindset is by embracing challenges and understanding them as learning opportunities. Celebrate your progress, focus on the journey rather than the final outcome.

Surrounding yourself with positive influences and seeking feedback from mentors or peers can also support the development of a growth mindset. As such, personal development is a lifelong journey; thus, embracing challenges, forming new habits.

Chapter 5

Reviewing How You Currently Spend Your Time & Energy and Realigning Priorities

WELCOME to our chapter on the subject of time and energy management. It may be hard these days in our fast-paced world to keep track of how you and I spend our time as well as where we put our energies. This is why it is not unusual to find ourselves working on tasks that are only aimed at giving us immediate solutions while ignoring long-lasting goals, which means that at the end of it all, we fail to get what we wanted. Nevertheless, one can only achieve success and fulfilment by setting his or her priorities right.

In this section, we will explore techniques that can help you evaluate your present use of time and energy. The goal is to enable changes that will align your priorities with your future ambitions/ethics. Once you have this mindset and tools for it, you can then make deliberate decisions that sustain your objectives and push you closer to what you desire in life.

So follow us along on this journey where we learn how to optimise time & energy management while taking control of life itself.

Comprehending How Important Time and Energy Management Is

Efficiently managing your time and energy can make a huge impact on different aspects of your life, both personally and professionally; it is what enables one to succeed while still having a healthy life.

Proper time/energy management involves prioritising tasks. This entails taking charge of your schedule to manage every day's activities efficiently, giving oneself full concentration on things that matter most, avoiding distractions, and minimising unnecessary pressure.

Having good time management skills ensures things are done faster, providing more free hours for leisure activities or attending other important activities in one's life. Effective energy management allows one to possess adequate physical endurance as well as emotional stability, ensuring successful productivity during challenging times.

You might be surprised at how much more time & energy you'll have for doing things you love if only you manage them effectively. After all, meeting your goals quickly, maintaining a healthy work-life balance, and living happily ever after.

Analysing How You Allocate Your Daily Time and Energy Resources

It is important to understand how you presently spend your time and energy before you can make any changes in your time and energy management. This calls for an evaluation of the daily activities undertaken so that you know which ones need to be worked on.

To begin with, assess your daily time expenditure. Note how much time you spend at every hour of the day plus rate the level of energy used on a scale of ten. Be honest with yourself, and then you will see patterns & identify areas where improvements could be made.

Once a clear understanding of what consumes most of your time and energy is known, it is possible to tell when there are imbalances or heavy physical strain without adequate rest as well. This information helps formulate a sustainable plan for managing one's time/energy to achieve their goals while keeping them healthy.

Remember that analysing your daily expenditure on both time and energy is not a one-off occurrence but rather an ongoing process that has to be continuously reviewed depending on new priorities or situations. Thus, if people continue working towards this direction, they can develop favourable strategies for managing their time & energy necessary to succeed while maintaining good health.

Identifying Your Most Important Priorities

Managing your time and energy well requires knowing what you are most concerned about in any case. Hence, this helps establish good decision-making opportunities so that one can allocate resources properly. If you want to accomplish your core priorities, the first rule is to think about what means a lot to you. Reflect on the things that make you very happy, satisfied and fulfilled as well as your life objectives and values.

What would your ideal life look like? The kind of people that you would be hanging around with and what activities would you do? It can help us understand our goals and what truly counts for them.

Another helpful way is to determine how much time and energy goes into different things for now. Do resources go where they are mostly wanted by us? What could have been done differently if this doesn't happen?

By having defined our core priorities, we can focus on those things which really matter so that we could lead more purposeful lives.

Analysing How You Are Using Your Time and Energy Right Now

It is vital to look into how much time and energy we dedicate towards different areas in life. For example, it gives an impression of where we are now so that little changes may be made for better daily schedules as well as long-term goals.

Begin by checking the amount of time and effort spent on employment, self-improvement, relationships as well as self-care. Is enough time or energy being given to each area or do some adjustments need to be made?

It's easy to overwork oneself, disregard friends or ignore yourself, but when one looks at where they are right now, lay emphasis on areas needing attention and focus only on matters that count.

For a holistic view of a daily routine, use methods such as time tracking or energy mapping. Through this awareness, one can make informed decisions to create actions towards sustainable and happy living.

Matching Priorities with Goals and Values

When making deliberate choices that align with your ambitions, it is imperative to ensure that priorities are in line with your goals and values. You should, therefore, first identify what matters most to you, the things you value the most in life, and where you want to go. Think about your personal and professional goals and see if they match with your current priorities.

At times there may be some inconsistencies between the two hence calling for a review or even adjustment. In other words, to prioritise what really matters a person might need to change their focus, schedule, or delegate some tasks.

First of all, when we align our priorities with our personal values, this becomes possible. For example, family relationships, self-development, or career can be on this list. Such an approach guarantees a purposeful existence as well as joy-filled experiences because one lives by his/her values that match their main objectives in life.

Always remember that priorities change from time to time and goals and values should be matched to them. Individuals must, therefore, review their decisions regularly and if need be, change them to remain relevant. Live this way, and your plans will eventually come true while still leading a purposeful life.

Time and Energy Optimization Strategies

Proper handling of time and energy plays a critical role in personal aspirations, professional future, and general well-being. The following are some strategies or techniques that can help you optimise your time as well as energy allocation:

1. **Create a schedule for each day:** Have a plan for tomorrow that will ensure enough time is allocated to those activities which are more important.
2. **Keep a list of things you have to do:** This helps you set out the most important jobs first.
3. **Do not multitask:** This lowers the level of productivity, thereby increasing stress levels. So be sure to concentrate on one task at once all the time to enhance efficiency.
4. **Take breaks:** They are capable of making someone rejuvenated to produce better generally.
5. **Differentiate tasks according to energy levels:** Do difficult ones when highly energetic, then undertake simpler ones when low.
6. **Eliminate Distraction:** Identify certain things like email notifications or social media which may distract you while you are busy working.

Once put into action, these strategies would go a long way in optimising time management, resulting in increased productivity rates while avoiding unnecessary stress. Additionally, one needs to evaluate frequently what works best with her/his life without affecting other areas such as work-life balance, among others.

Prioritising Self-Care and Well-being

No matter how tight

your schedule may be, it is important that you allocate a significant amount of time for self-care. Taking care of oneself does not mean selfishness but rather a necessity to keep a healthy work-life balance.

It refers to any activity done by an individual aimed at maintaining good health either physically, mentally, or emotionally, for instance, exercise or meditation where one can spend his or her time with loved ones or any other joyous and rejuvenating activity.

On the other hand, well-being involves taking good care of one's health and happiness in general, encompassing emotional, physical, and psychological aspects. This involves; being mindful; eating right; getting enough sleep as well as consulting when need be, to mention but a few stress management techniques.

Your life overall gets better when you give your well-being and self-care first priority; you end up increasing performance levels while also reducing stress. These activities should therefore be allocated sometime within either the daily or weekly routine.

Creating a Sustainable Time and Energy Management Plan

Now it is high time you made a personal plan of time and energy allocation that corresponds with your priorities. Thus, one can be able to effectively utilise their time in addition to energy without feeling overwhelmed with fatigue.

One of the first steps is to create a sustainable time management plan that prioritises tasks based on importance, so that energy allocation is done accordingly. Moreover, identify those things that totally drain you. This can help you reduce their frequency so that they are minimised.

While creating your plan, consider how much time you can actually put into it. Realise that there is a limit to the amount of work you can do without jeopardising your health and well-being.

Another main point is that of maintaining a time and energy management plan that works for you as an individual, one that fits in with your values and lifestyle at any given time. You should periodically evaluate its effectiveness to ensure it is still useful.

In conclusion, for you to achieve your goals and take care of yourself in general, it is important to develop a personalised and sustainable time-energy management program. Take some time to thoughtfully prepare this document; assess and tailor it for long-term success and happiness.

Maintaining accountability through continual evaluation

Congratulations! You have created a personal time-energy management system which corresponds with your priorities. However, it doesn't mean the journey towards the best time-energy management ends here. Regularly evaluating one's practices will help him or her remain answerable since there are chances of continuous success.

To stay answerable, create a way on how far you have come from. Plan daily routines by using any means such as an organiser or phone application in relation to essential jobs. Further, having someone responsible for holding one up-to-date guarantees persistence towards set goals.

Continual evaluation identifies weak areas where corrective measures should be applied. Thus think back regularly over what has been happening so far about efficiency of your operations? Ascertain factors that hinder progress in either way hence facilitating changes on how energy and time are utilised.

Moreover, change the way you manage time and energy whenever personal objectives change. There may be adjustments within the plans made out of new demands in life that individuals should not hesitate adopting.

Remember, accountability plus continuous assessment are two mainstays behind sustainable time-and-energy-management practices. Frequently measure rates while adapting them accordingly so that successes continue without pressure.

Chapter 6

Unlocking Resilience: Building Mental Strength with a Growth Mindset

To successfully navigate the unpredictable waves of life, it is necessary for you to develop mental toughness. However, what is resilience, and why does it matter to you? Resilience refers to your capacity to bounce back from hardship or failure, to recover quickly from setbacks and adapt well to changes or pressure. It doesn't mean getting rid of stress but managing it and gaining strength from prior experience. In other words, it's your psychological fortitude against challenges.

In relation to resilience, you cannot ignore the vital role of a growth mindset. The theory of a growth mindset was first posited by Dr. Carol Dweck after decades of research; this suggests that individuals who believe their intelligence and abilities can be developed are more likely to attain greater levels of success compared to others. This is in contrast to a fixed mindset where people think that their skills are unchangeable, thereby limiting their potential.

But why does a growth mindset matter to you? The answer lies in its effects on your behaviour. With a growth mentality, learning and overcoming challenges become a continuous process rather than stopping at failure. You learn not to see failure as a reflection of your capabilities but as another opportunity for learning and effort because you view struggle not as condemnation but as an incentive for improvement. As per Dweck's findings, one with a growth mindset shows greater resilience by viewing difficulties as temporary hurdles rather than insurmountable obstacles.

A growth mindset is not just about praising your efforts or having an unbreakable spirit; it's about adopting a constant evolution perspective for your capabilities and understanding that your aptitude can be developed over time. When armed with this thought pattern, setbacks are seen as opportunities for growth rather than discouragements. This, therefore, means that such an attitude becomes vital when building your mental toughness because it enables you to remain positive despite challenges and eventually achieve your objectives.

The value of connecting a growth mindset, learning, and challenges together is priceless in your daily life. Learning isn't about knowing; it's about growing. You with a growth mindset aren't deterred by difficulties; instead, you see them as opportunities to learn and grow. You know that struggle is part of the process as much as it is a necessary evil.

Adopting such a growth mentality has multifaceted benefits - from overcoming setbacks and difficulties to fostering a fondness for continuous learning. This section will, therefore, delve deeper into the subject matter of resilience, discuss how you can develop a growth mindset, and finally examine their implications in education, leadership, personal growth, health, and learning styles.

Resilience Building through Failure, Setbacks, and Challenges

Usually, failure is looked down upon together with setbacks in popular culture. However, these experiences often serve as the bedrock for your personal growth and learning, leading to enhanced resilience. But when you quit seeing failure as a defeat but rather an integral part of the journey of success, then you start to build your resilience. At its core, a growth mindset is simply the understanding that setbacks and challenges are opportunities rather than obstacles.

Another post on betterup.com discusses this idea further in relation to embracing failure. What it means is that admitting your mistakes shows who you really are and at the same time makes you more resilient. Therefore, as long as you analyse what caused the setback and use the experience for future endeavours, you come out stronger in the end.

However, it should be noted that developing resilience is not enough to overcome setbacks. In so doing, it implies coming up with specific methods or approaches that will help you deal effectively with difficulties experienced. Angela Duckworth's concept of grit refers to maintaining effort and interest over years despite failures, adversity, and plateaus in progress. In other words, while grit may sound like a rigid approach towards life, adopting a growth mindset will foster perseverance even when there are significant obstacles ahead.

To achieve this aim, psychological resources such as optimism, self-esteem, and control beliefs are important in building your resilience. In this context, they envision how things can get better regardless of immediate roadblocks or disappointments by focusing on long-term goals and possibilities instead.

Developing resilience also involves nurturing emotional skills like empathy, patience, humour, flexibility, etc., which help to sustain your morale when times are hard. You can create a strong mental toolbox to survive subsequent failures by building these psychological resources and resilience strategies systematically.

An organisation is made up of individuals, and as each individual is given a growth mindset, the organisational capacity becomes increasingly resilient. In this way, organisations can have a workforce that is more resilient and better able to cope with inevitable crises on the road to success by creating an environment where mistakes are learning opportunities that contribute to learning from failure rather than being threats.

At its heart, the construction of mental toughness consists of redefining your understanding of disappointments and challenges. Instead of perceiving failures as obstacles towards the development process, you need to consider them part of it. This change in view turns backwardness into stepping stones for personal development, promoting self-improvement as well as resilience over time.

Impact of Growth Mindset on Personal Growth, Health, and Learning Style

But a growth mindset goes beyond improving academic performance or increasing resiliency; it has implications for your personal development too, as well as for mental health and learning styles. Those who possess a growth mindset view their brains as flexible enough to be developed over time, hence experiencing personal developments more often than not.

In terms of personal development, a growth mindset allows you to see possibilities where others might only see limitations. This means doing away with fixed abilities and recognizing that through effort, your abilities can improve.

People who embrace a growth mindset continuously transform themselves. They seek challenges; they learn from their mistakes, and they persistently move toward their goals so as to be better versions of themselves. This makes them fearless enough to take on challenges since they see failure as a doorway for progress rather than anything else in the personal development journey.

A growth mindset also significantly affects mental health. For example, many studies emphasise the importance of adopting a growth mentality towards different aspects of emotional well-being. Embracing this disposition helps you maintain positivity in the face of adversity, fosters determination in overcoming setbacks, reduces anxiety through better stress management techniques, and ultimately promotes healthier psychological outlooks.

Moreover, when looking at learning style, considering intelligence and talent as fluid instead of fixed traits can have far-reaching implications. This allows you to enjoy learning without being stopped by difficulties or failures along the way. The realisation that each problem overcome or concept grasped makes you smarter, more competent, and better learners takes away the drudgery from learning.

With such an understanding that there is always room for improvement and an eagerness to embrace challenges as opportunities for growth, you are likely to display an insatiable curiosity and thirst for knowledge. This also increases your capacities but it also helps you become lifelong learners who are constantly seeking new experiences through learning.

In conclusion, if you integrate a mentality of growth into your lifestyle, it will go a long way in helping you get the best out of personal development, mental health, learning style, and so on. While we are all growing stronger and tougher people, it is important to remember that being able to learn and grow is what matters. The road ahead may not be easy but embracing this perspective will certainly make it worthwhile.

Tips for cultivating a growth mindset in your life

To promote mental toughness, personal growth, and transformation in learning styles, nothing could be more effective than having the right mindset. However, how can you successfully fit this approach into your lifestyle? Here are some tips about how to develop grit drawn from Better Up's 13 Tips to Develop a Growth Mindset and Positive Psychology's 5 ways to develop grit.

Embrace Challenges: Instead of avoiding new experiences or challenging tasks due to fear of failure, embrace them as opportunities for education and personal advancement. Just understand that making mistakes or experiencing hardship does not mean that you are dumb but they are just parts of the learning process.

Persist in the Face of Setbacks: Don't allow failure to stop you; sometimes failure is actually progress. When faced with setbacks, instead of giving up, use them as information to refine your strategies and try again.

Develop a Passion for Learning: Cultivate an insatiable curiosity and enthusiasm for gaining knowledge. Rather than focusing solely on outcomes, enjoy the process itself. This shift in perspective transforms learning from a chore into something enjoyable.

Foster Grit: Angela Duckworth describes 'grit' as passion plus perseverance for very long-term goals such that you do things until you become perfect at them. Building grit requires practice and patience but it pays off – research shows that individuals with higher levels of grit achieve more success in their chosen fields.

Emphasise Effort over Talent: Rather than attributing achievements solely to natural ability, acknowledge the effort and hard work that goes into success. This fosters belief in continuous improvement and growth.

Encourage Constructive Feedback: Actively seek feedback and consider it to be developmental rather than critical. Additionally, this can help you identify areas for improvement as well as provide an opportunity to learn from other people's viewpoints and experiences.

Cultivate Positive Self-Talk: Our mindset is significantly affected by how we talk to ourselves. Practice talking to yourself with kindness, patience, and encouragement especially during challenging times or when faced with setbacks.

Developing a growth mindset doesn't happen overnight; it requires ongoing effort, patience, practice, and most importantly, the desire to keep learning and improving. In your journey of personal development, embrace the following principles to cultivate a growth mindset:

Acknowledge Mistakes as Learning Opportunities: Rather than seeing mistakes as failures, view them as valuable lessons. Analyse what went wrong, learn from the experience, and apply those lessons to future endeavours. This mindset shift helps in continuous improvement.

Celebrate Effort and Progress: Instead of solely focusing on end results, celebrate the effort you put in and the progress you make along the way. Recognize that improvement is a continuous journey, and each step forward is a success worth acknowledging.

Set Realistic Goals: Establish goals that challenge you but are achievable with effort and perseverance. Setting realistic goals provides a sense of direction and purpose, contributing to the development of a growth mindset.

Surround Yourself with Positive Influences: Engage with individuals who embody a growth mindset. Positive influences can inspire and motivate you to overcome challenges, fostering a supportive environment for personal and collective growth.

Embrace the Power of "Yet": When faced with difficulties, incorporate the word "yet" into your thoughts. For instance, instead of saying "I can't do this," say "I can't do this yet." This simple linguistic shift implies a belief in the potential for improvement over time.

Learn Continuously: Cultivate a love for learning by seeking out new knowledge and experiences. Approach challenges with a curiosity-driven mindset, understanding that every obstacle presents an opportunity to acquire new skills and insights.

Remember, developing a growth mindset is an ongoing process, and consistency in applying these principles will contribute to its gradual integration into your daily life. Embrace the journey of continuous learning and self-improvement, and you'll find that challenges become stepping stones toward personal and professional success.

Chapter 7

Identifying and Challenging
Limiting Beliefs to Unlock Your Success

Chapter 7: Identifying and Challenging Limiting Beliefs to Unlock Your Success

Welcome to Chapter Seven of our personal growth and success series. This chapter focuses on limiting beliefs and how they impact our journey toward our goals.

Limiting beliefs act as concealed barriers that hinder our progress towards our desired destinations. They often stem from an individual's background, upbringing, or self-doubt. For instance, these beliefs can influence relationships, careers, or personal development.

Fear not! You can lead a fulfilling life by identifying and taking action against these limiting thoughts. Throughout this chapter, we will guide you in acknowledging and confronting them head-on, empowering you to pursue your dreams for success.

Are you ready to unveil the limitations that have been holding you back? Let's initiate this transformative process together, aiming to adopt a mindset of growth, resilience, and boundless possibilities. It's time to dismantle what no longer serves us and pave the way for genuine achievements.

As we embark on this journey to uncover limiting beliefs, we discover clues that unlock your full potential. Together, let's explore self-discovery and personality development, breaking free from the barriers set by limiting beliefs and leading lives filled with meaning, accomplishments, and fulfilment.

What do limiting beliefs mean?

Limiting beliefs are incorrect mindsets that hinder someone from realising their full potential in life. They create invisible boundaries, making it challenging to achieve dreams in various aspects such as careers and relationships. These perceptions are often shaped by past experiences, like traumas or societal conditioning.

In relationships, career development, or personal growth, one may harbour limiting beliefs. Some individuals fear taking risks, believing they cannot perform well due to a lack of opportunities or fear of failure. These deep-seated ideologies shape how we think about everything, influencing our choices, behaviours, and overall perspective.

To break these beliefs for personal growth and expose your true potential, you must step out of your comfort zone. By acknowledging and confronting the limiting beliefs that hinder your thoughts, you can lead purposeful, successful lives.

Examples of Common Limiting Beliefs

Limiting beliefs come in different forms, preventing individuals from reaching their potential and achieving success. To overcome self-doubt, fear of failure, and other obstacles, it's essential to recognize these typical limiting beliefs.

One of the most common limiting beliefs is self-doubt. Many people underestimate their abilities and feel unworthy of success, often due to past failures or negative comments discouraging them.

Fear of failure is another major type of limiting belief. This fear prevents people from taking risks and making mistakes due to expectations, often stemming from perfectionism and the fear of judgement.

Moreover, some people believe they lack abilities or talents. This belief discourages individuals from making efforts toward personal and career development.

Imposter syndrome is a common limiting belief that affects many high-achieving individuals. Even when there is evidence of accomplishments, this thinking causes continual inadequacy.

Scarcity mindset is a limiting belief that arises from the idea that resources, opportunities, and success are scarce. This mindset fosters a sense of lack and competition, hindering individuals from embracing abundance and discovering new possibilities.

These everyday limiting beliefs significantly impact people's lives through self-sabotaging behaviours, missed opportunities, and unfulfillment. Overcoming these beliefs is crucial for personal growth and developing a positive mindset.

The Impact of Limiting Beliefs on Success

One's ability to succeed is greatly hindered by limiting beliefs. These negative thought patterns create boundaries, hindering individuals from acting or seizing available opportunities.

Feelings of inadequacy and low self-esteem often accompany these self-limiting thoughts, creating a belief that success is impossible. This results in a reluctance to take risks, avoidance of challenges, and a life below one's true capabilities.

"Limiting beliefs are invisible walls around us that keep us from moving beyond our comfort zones." - Dr. Carol Dweck, Psychologist

As a result, individuals miss out on many opportunities for growth and success. Some may delay decision-making processes, while others may hesitate to pursue their passions, leading to self-destructive behaviours. This creates a vicious cycle of self-doubt and fear, limiting oneself from reaching full potential.

"You're Right" - Henry Ford, American Industrialist

However, recognizing and challenging these limiting ideologies can break free from self-imposed barriers, opening up new opportunities that were not visible before. It starts with changing perspectives to view negative thoughts positively by replacing them with empowering beliefs. This adaptive process allows one to develop into a goal-oriented person who appreciates challenges and takes steps toward achieving their desires.

"When you believe in yourself and possess the right mindset, you have the power to accomplish anything you set your mind to." - Les Brown, Motivational Speaker

Overcoming limiting beliefs is crucial for personal development and success. Challenging these beliefs allows individuals to move beyond imposed restrictions and live accomplished lives.

Identifying and Challenging Limiting Beliefs

The first step toward overcoming limiting beliefs is recognizing them. This involves observing negative thoughts and patterns that manifest in various aspects of your life, such as self-doubt or the perception of lacking.

"Our beliefs create our reality. It is essential to question thoughts that hold us back."

Ask yourself if these beliefs hold any truth or if they are based on past events or societal teachings. Often, these beliefs lack evidence or rely on stereotypes that do not withstand scrutiny.

Rephrase these beliefs positively to align with your growth and prosperity. For example, transform the statement "I am not talented enough to follow my passion" into "I have unique strengths and abilities that I can develop to achieve my goals."

"By challenging and reframing our limiting beliefs, we open ourselves up to new possibilities and create the path toward personal growth and success."

Remember that transforming deeply rooted beliefs takes time and practice. Continuously question and reframe negative thoughts to strengthen new empowering beliefs. Gradually, you will change your mindset and develop the capacity to overcome self-imposed constraints.

Creating a Positive Affirmation

Dealing with limiting beliefs can involve having positive affirmations. These brief statements capture empowering beliefs that you want to adopt. Write down your affirmations and repeat them daily.

"A gradual shift in mindset towards success results from positive affirmations, like seeds of empowerment."

For example, if you believe you don't deserve success, create an affirmation like "I am supposed to be successful and rich." Repeat this affirmation daily, especially when standing in front of a mirror, to internalise this empowering belief.

Remember, identifying and challenging limiting beliefs is an ongoing process. Stay committed to your personal growth journey and seek support from professionals or mentors who can guide and hold you accountable.

Replacing Limiting Beliefs with Empowering Truths

Once you have identified and challenged your limiting beliefs, it's time to replace them with empowering truths. This crucial step involves cultivating positive affirmations, creating a new narrative, and shifting your focus toward your strengths and abilities.

"Positive affirmations are powerful tools that can reshape your mindset to become more positive, reinforcing empowering beliefs. You can train yourself into more positive thinking by deliberately repeating affirmative words about yourself."

Empowering truths counteract limiting beliefs by reflecting your true capabilities. They enable you to think differently, challenge self-doubt, and boost confidence after realisation.

"Empowering truths provide a solid foundation for personal growth and success by breaking free from self-imposed limitations and achieving goals and dreams."

Instead of focusing on limitations, concentrate on your strengths and what you can do. Recognize your uniqueness and understand that nothing limits your potential.

Reinforcing empowering truths requires consistent practice and repetition. Identify a few empowering affirmations, write them down, say them aloud, or create visuals to remind yourself of these empowering truths daily.

"By continuously affirming your strengths, abilities, and potential, you will gradually rewire your brain to embrace these empowering truths as your new reality. This shift in mindset will be accompanied by increased confidence levels and a stronger belief in your capability to handle challenges."

The journey of replacing limiting beliefs with empowering truths is transformative. It demands dedication, self-compassion, and determination. Celebrate every small step and be patient as you work toward creating a new, empowering narrative for your life.

"Remember, you have the power to shape your beliefs and rewrite your story. Embrace the empowering truths that propel you toward success and live a life that reflects your true potential."

Strategies for Overcoming Limiting Beliefs

Overcoming limiting beliefs is a crucial step toward personal growth and success. Numerous helpful strategies can challenge and overcome these beliefs, enabling you to reach your full potential and achieve your objectives.

"There are no limits but those we impose on ourselves."

1. Self-compassion as a strategy

One of the initial techniques in conquering limiting beliefs is self-compassion. Be gentle with yourself, knowing that everyone faces trials and self-doubt at times. Show yourself compassion when negative thoughts arise, reminding yourself that you can grow and change.

2. Seek Support from Others

If necessary, do not hesitate to ask for assistance from people you trust, such as friends, relatives, or professionals like coaches or therapists. Sharing your challenges with others provides a new perspective and encouragement, making it easier to resist limiting beliefs. Surround yourself with positive and supportive individuals who can facilitate personal growth.

3. Establish Realistic Objectives

Set realistic goals when overcoming limiting beliefs. Break down major objectives into achievable smaller parts to build confidence and momentum. Celebrate every milestone along the way, reinforcing belief in yourself and inspiring further growth.

4. Make Small Moves Towards Your Goals

Taking small steps toward your goals helps dismantle limiting beliefs. Gradually stretch your comfort zone by taking manageable steps forward. Start with simple tasks and progressively add more challenges as confidence grows.

5. Visualise Success

Visualisation is a potent tool to defeat limiting beliefs. Take time each day to see yourself succeeding or achieving your desires. Mentally picture overcoming any barriers that arise. By visualising success, you create a constructive imagination that reframes your beliefs and motivates you to take steps toward your dreams.

6. Keep Challenging and Reframing Negative Thoughts

To overcome limiting beliefs, continuously challenge and reframe negative thoughts. Whenever a negative belief arises, question its veracity and look for evidence to the contrary. Replace negative thoughts with positive affirmations that remind you of your capabilities.

By following these strategies, you can effectively put an end to limiting beliefs and experience personal growth. Always remember that your beliefs shape your reality, so choose to believe in yourself and recognize your potential.

Developing a Growth Mindset

Establishing a growth mindset is vital for overcoming limiting beliefs. A growth mindset involves embracing the idea that capabilities and intelligence can be cultivated through effort and practice. This mentality encourages exploration of new opportunities for personal development and success.

"The growth mindset allows people to value what they're doing regardless of the outcome."

With a growth mindset, challenges become opportunities for growth and learning. Instead of fearing failure, it becomes part of the learning process. Embracing challenges as growth opportunities is a fundamental aspect of a growth mindset.

"In a growth mindset, your mistakes are your friends; they are NOT your enemies."

A growth mindset means your potential is not fixed. You develop resilience and perseverance, understanding that hard work and dedication can lead to improvement in any area of life.

"When you have a growth mindset, there is no limitation of oneself because of inherent abilities. Instead, you consider the power behind trying, learning, and practising as sources of new skills development and breaking down obstacles."

By thinking this way, you step out of your comfort zone, explore new opportunities, and become more successful than before.

The Path to Empowerment and Success

By developing a growth mindset, you gain control over your own development and success. Self-imposed limitations are relinquished, making room for the possibilities associated with a change in attitude. Believing in your ability to grow, adapt, and achieve greatness is the key to each step in this process.

"With a growth mindset, you have the power to transform your life and create the success you desire."

Embrace a growth mindset, question limiting beliefs, and unlock your true potential. Understand that with effort and dedication, learning anything is possible, regardless of what lies ahead.

The importance of self-reflection and self-awareness

Self-reflection and self-awareness are fundamental elements for personal development in every individual's life. They play a significant role in realising and challenging our constrained opinions about ourselves. By analysing our thoughts, emotions, and behaviours, we gain insights into patterns that limit us from achieving our goals.

Thus, cultivating self-awareness matters a lot, where practices such as journaling, meditation, and mindfulness help us establish a more intimate relationship with ourselves. These techniques enable us to tune into our inner dialogue and identify instances when we engage in limiting thinking.

"Self-reflection is the mirror through which we gain clarity and insight."

Recognizing limiting beliefs

During moments of self-reflection, we can shine a light on the limiting beliefs that have been shaping our lives. We can identify the thoughts and beliefs that hold us back and hinder our personal growth. It is only by becoming aware of these beliefs that we can begin the process of challenging and overcoming them.

"In the journey of personal development, self-awareness is the compass that guides us toward growth and transformation."

Taking proactive steps

Once we have identified our limiting beliefs, self-awareness empowers us to take proactive steps to challenge and overcome them. With knowledge gained from self-reflection, one can question their own beliefs, turning down any evidence in support of them.

As a result, through the affirmation of positive thinking and related reinforcement, over time, your perspective changes while walking away from self-imposed limitations.

Unlocking personal growth

Self-reflection and self-awareness are essential tools in our personal growth journey. They enable us to navigate the inner landscape of our minds, understand our thought patterns, and transform our beliefs. By developing a deep understanding of ourselves, we can unlock our true potential and create a life aligned with our aspirations and values.

"Self-reflection and self-awareness are the keys that unlock the door to personal growth and self-transformation."

Seeking Professional Help

If limiting beliefs seem challenging to overcome on your own, do not hesitate to seek professional help. This could be a therapist or coach who can guide you, provide support, and offer tools to manage through your limiting beliefs for personal growth and success.

"We all need a bit of a helping hand at times to bring out our true potential and free ourselves from the chains of self-limiting beliefs."

Professional assistance, such as therapy or coaching, offers valuable external perspective and expertise, illuminating blind spots and providing customised techniques for unpacking and overcoming limiting beliefs. These professionals can assist you in recognizing negative thoughts, changing the way you think about things, and helping you make empowered decisions toward your goals.

Therapists or coaches can create an environment where you can explore yourself during personalised sessions, allowing more in-depth investigations into the roots of those limiting beliefs while guiding the process, never shy away from accepting help when needed.

Chapter 8

Understanding Your Own and Others' Emotions: A Guide to Emotional Intelligence

Welcome to Chapter Eight, where we shall be examining Emotional Intelligence – a vital tool in navigating diverse personal and professional relationships. By gaining a deeper understanding of Emotional Intelligence, you will master how to better control your emotions and comprehend the feelings of those around you. Developing your Emotional Intelligence offers opportunities for richer relationships, improved mental health, and professional success. Therefore, let's get started and discover what Emotional Intelligence has in store for us!

In this chapter, however, we will discuss the five components of emotional intelligence, namely: self-awareness, self-regulation, motivation, empathy, and social skills. We can explore how each component plays an essential role in developing your emotional intelligence, as well as its impacts on your life.

So, are you ready to commence the journey toward becoming a more emotionally intelligent person? Let's do it!

Keyword: Emotional Intelligence

What is Emotional Intelligence?

Emotional Intelligence (EI) is the ability to identify and comprehend one's own emotions, as well as others' feelings. It entails managing one's emotions effectively while also being able to empathise with others and foster positive relations with them. These days, emotional intelligence is considered a key determinant of success in all areas of life by many experts.

Emotional Intelligence has five key components, which include: self-awareness, self-regulation, motivation, empathy, and social skills. The development of EI involves all these components, leading to improvement in emotional well-being among individuals. Knowing about Emotional Intelligence (EI) itself and its various constituents would help gain insights into differing personal and professional relationships, thereby attaining success in diverse spheres.

The Five Components of Emotional Intelligence

Emotional intelligence (EI) is made up of five parts that influence our ability to understand or manage our own emotions, as well as those of others close to us. Hence, they include:

Self-awareness: Recognizing one's emotions and their impact on thoughts and actions.

Self-regulation: Keeping control of your emotions and impulses so as not to overreact or make hasty decisions.

Motivation: Channelling emotions to accomplish objectives and pursue interests.

Empathy: Understanding how others feel by putting oneself in their shoes.

Social skills: How to communicate effectively, build connections, and resolve differences with other people.

Developing these components of emotional intelligence is important for improving our emotional intelligence, influencing both personal and professional relationships. By strengthening your EI, you will be better equipped to navigate the complexities of daily life with greater success and fulfilment.

Enhancing Self-Awareness

Emotional intelligence starts with self-awareness. If you realise and accept your feelings, you will be able to control them better, thus improving relationships. Start by reflecting on your emotions and behaviours. Take notice of your thoughts and feelings in response to different situations.

Through journaling, meditation, or confiding in a trusted friend, you can figure out why you feel the way you do. Assess yourself using tools like personality tests or Emotional Intelligence assessments to have a better understanding of your strengths as well as your weaknesses.

To improve self-awareness means one should be honest and expose oneself. Other than that, let others give their feedback on issues you might have that are limiting you. This way, we can grow emotionally intelligent because it enhances our interpersonal relations, mentally transforming us in the process.

Cultivating Self-Regulation

Developing emotional intelligence requires the ability to manage and control your emotions and impulses. This is where self-control comes in. You can enhance your decision-making skills as well as improve your relationships with other people by growing self-control.

One effective technique to develop self-regulation is through mindfulness and meditation practices. These exercises can help you better understand your thoughts and feelings, allowing you to respond to them in a more thoughtful and intentional manner.

Another strategy is to practise self-reflection regularly. Set aside time each day to evaluate how you responded to certain situations and how you could have responded differently. This builds emotional intelligence through self-awareness.

Self-regulation skills enable individuals to control their emotions and impulses, thereby improving decision-making, relationships, and emotional well-being.

The Role of Motivation in Emotional Intelligence

Motivation is a critical aspect of Emotional Intelligence and plays a significant role in achieving success and fulfilling personal and professional goals. When you are highly motivated, you are more likely to be resilient, proactive, and focused, which enhances Emotional Intelligence. In contrast, however, no motivation hampers an individual's ability to regulate his/her emotions, understand others' feelings, or navigate through complex relationships.

To increase motivation, it is important that one sets clear, attainable objectives. Divide long-term ambitions into smaller, realistic milestones that serve as stepping-stones toward the achievement of these goals. Moreover, finding purpose in whatever we do can increase our motivation levels, hence driving us towards what we need.

Motivation also includes having a growth mindset as a crucial part of it. By considering challenges as chances for growth while taking failures as lessons learned, one can create a resilient spirit within oneself. Additionally, learning from mistakes or setbacks can provide information regarding one's thought process or behaviours, which eventually leads an individual into attaining a higher level of EI.

Overall, motivation has fundamental importance in developing EQ; by setting goals for ourselves, finding meaning behind them, maintaining the right attitude toward life; intrinsic motivation can be achieved, building a strong foundation for emotional well-being.

Developing Empathy Skills

Empathy is one of the components of Emotional Intelligence. This means understanding and sharing other people's emotions. Developing empathy skills helps to improve relations with family, colleagues, and friends.

Try perspective-taking – putting yourself in someone else's shoes and imagining how they feel – as a way to enhance your empathy skills. Active listening is another technique to strengthen empathy. Asking clarifying questions shows that you care about their feelings: this means paying close attention to what the other person is saying.

Improving your empathy skills will enable you to become a better communicator and form stronger bonds with others. Furthermore, empathy leads to a better understanding and acceptance of diverse perspectives, which is important in modern society.

Mastering Social Skills

Developing social skills is a major part of Emotional Intelligence. It implies our abilities to have effective communication, handle conflicts, as well as establish and maintain positive relationships with others. Mastering social skills will help us improve personal and professional relationships in our lives.

Social skills development requires effective communication strategies. With active listening, one may listen to other people, respect their opinions and ideas. When things go wrong, it is good to realise that some conflict resolution strategies, such as compromise and negotiation, can be helpful.

An important part of social skills is building positive connections with others. Empathy, supportiveness, and appreciation contribute to the cultivation of positive relationships with others. By conquering social skills, you will enhance your Emotional Intelligence, which, in turn, will lead you into fulfilling relationships in all dimensions of your life.

Leadership and Emotional Intelligence

Effective leaders have strong Emotional Intelligence abilities that help them motivate and inspire their teams, thereby creating a conducive working environment for everyone. Leaders who are emotionally aware also possess excellent communication capabilities, handle conflicts well, as they make decisions based on an insightful view of individuals' feelings and perspectives.

On the flip side, leaders without Emotional Intelligence find it hard to build teams, engage workers, or complete successful projects. A leader must become more emotionally intelligent so as to enhance the relationship within his or her team members, make better decisions, and hence achieve higher performance at large. Institutionalising Emotional Intelligence in a business atmosphere that is prevalent among team members can enable you to empower employees to succeed in their tasks.

Emotional Intelligence's Effect on Relationships

Emotional intelligence helps create and nurture personal relationships, including family ones, friendships, and love relations. Better understanding not only for oneself but also for others enhances emotional attachments while helping solve quarrels.

Empathy building enhances communication skills or self-awareness training are part of Building Emotional Intelligence. Understanding what emotions other people are going through by listening actively gives rise to strong emotional bonds between two individuals because of responding appropriately to those emotions. In addition, expressing emotions clearly through active listening fosters emotional connections while alleviating miscommunication during conversations.

Furthermore, when developed self-awareness/self-regulation/social skills lead to healthier personal relationships, they become more productive in life too. For instance, if your social skills are great, hence you can handle your own emotions and feelings effectively; it is possible to form bonds, cooperate, and ensure a conducive atmosphere between you and others.

Generally, when Emotional Intelligence is practised in personal relationships, they become more meaningful and fulfilling. It is, therefore, appropriate to apply the teachings herein for better interpersonal relationships and the establishment of stronger connections with people around us.

Emotional Intelligence at Work

In today's competitive job markets, Emotional Intelligence is an essential skill that distinguishes you from other candidates. It requires understanding one's own feelings as well as those of others through emotions management.

With increased Emotional Intelligence, individuals are able to cope with stress effectively, communicate properly while building good working relationships with peers and superiors. This may result in higher job satisfaction levels, improved productivity, and eventually career growth prospects.

To further develop your emotional intelligence in the workplace, consider attending courses focused on emotional regulation, conflict resolution, or team development. While colleagues are presenting their ideas during meetings, look at how they move their bodies too in response to what they say. Think about what it would be like if it was you who was undergoing their current experience.

By practising the skill of Emotional Intelligence at work, not only will you become better at what you do, but also shape a vibrant workplace culture which, in turn, benefits both you and your organisation in the long-term.

Developing Emotional Intelligence among Children

Emotional Intelligence is a vital skill that children need to develop since it shapes their overall well-being and how well they succeed in life. Parents as well as educators play a crucial role in fostering Emotional Intelligence in children from an early age by providing them with activities and tools that are age-appropriate.

To improve emotional awareness and regulation between children, have discussions about feelings, be an active listener, and promote empathy and understanding. Utilise books alongside games focusing on emotions together with their expressions, thus enabling kids to recognize and explain their sentiments. Encourage problem solving by teaching children how to brainstorm solutions and how to adapt to unforeseen challenges and disappointments.

Supporting kids' emotional growth equips them with the necessary skills they require for navigating relationships, managing setbacks and stress, as well as achieving improved social as well as academic outcomes. If we invest in building Emotional Intelligence through children's lives, then it leads to more joyous lives that are more successful generally.

Emotional Intelligence (EI) is key in maintaining good mental health as well as emotional well-being. Better management of stress, anxiety, or other related mental health challenges is possible when you enhance your EI skills.

Research has shown that those with higher EI levels cope better with stress than others, hence they can handle anything life throws at them. This is because EI fosters self-awareness, self-regulation, empathy, and social skills, which are all important for managing emotional reactions towards developing healthy relationships.

When you build up your TalentSmart EI Toolkit™, you will know just what emotions these are and be able to manage yourself, which can prevent or help manage disorders such as depression or anxiety. In addition to this, being able to understand others' emotions helps in building strong relationships that are more satisfying.

Meditation, mindfulness, and journaling can positively affect your mental health if they are built into your routine. Alternatively, professional support is important since it enables one to identify areas of improvement as far as emotional intelligence is concerned and develop strategies for enhancing these skills.

In summary, establishing as well as maintaining high levels of Emotional Intelligence could contribute towards improved mental health outcomes and enhanced emotional well-being.

The Future of Emotional Intelligence

Emotional intelligence is becoming even more critical than ever before, as the world moves further into a digital era. As automation and artificial intelligence become more prevalent, there will be an increased need for emotional skills. In the future, experts predict that EI will become a core competency that will be essential to success in both personal and professional contexts.

Technology also plays an important role in the development and application of Emotional Intelligence. Virtual reality alongside AI-powered tools is being employed to train people on emotion regulation, empathy, and social skills. These technologies have the potential to change emotional learning entirely and contribute to making Emotional Intelligence democratic.

As we look forward to what lies ahead for us, Emotional Intelligence will continue to grow with us in new ways than can be imagined today. It is left upon us to focus on these skills that grow with the changing times so we do not fall behind.

Having gained a deeper understanding of Emotional Intelligence and its constituents, it is important to put it into practice in your everyday life. Here are some ways in which you can improve your Emotional Intelligence:

Self-Reflection: Allocate some time each day for considering emotions, thoughts as well as actions. This will enhance your self-awareness and how you react in different situations.

Positive Self-Talk: Use positive self-talk when you talk to yourself, make an intentional decision to this effect. Largely concentrate on the good things about you rather than focusing so much on perceived weaknesses.

Active Listening: While communicating with others, be empathetic and listen actively to the words they say.

Emotions Awareness: Pay attention to your feelings and try to figure out what triggers them. Through this, managing feelings becomes easier and appropriate responses can be made in different circumstances.

Set Targets: Set goals that are attainable for yourself with a plan of accomplishing them thus; this will help maintain your desire as well as focus.

Thankfulness Practice: Take a moment every day to think about what you are grateful for. This helps develop a positive attitude towards life hence better emotional health in general.

Always remember that developing Emotional Intelligence is not something that happens overnight; it requires commitment and practice. You may improve your personal as well as professional relationships by following these practical tips and honing your Emotional Intelligence skills thereby enhancing the overall quality of your life.

Chapter 9

The Benefits of Mindfulness
in Your Daily Routine

Mindfulness has been a 'buzzword' phrase in recent years, and deservedly so. This age-old approach offers many advantages for our mental and physical health. If you introduce mindfulness techniques into your everyday routine, then there are improved overall health outcomes, including an increased sense of well-being.

So what exactly is mindfulness? It is the state of being aware or paying attention to one's own thoughts, emotions, and experiences as they occur now. This implies focusing on our thoughts and emotions without judging them. Mindfulness research has found that it can significantly improve psychological state by reducing rumination and stress while also boosting cognitive abilities, emotional regulation, and resilience.

Mindfulness does not only have an effect on our minds; its effects go beyond that. According to neuroscientists, it has the ability to change the architecture or function of human brains through mindfulness practices. It can increase the thickness of the prefrontal cortex (responsible for attention and decision-making) while simultaneously reducing amygdala volume (where fear and stress responses occur). Moreover, mindfulness increases grey matter production as well as activating the insula that is associated with self-awareness and empathy.

Nonetheless, mindfulness has many more benefits than we think. Studies have shown that mindfulness exercises have positive implications on physical well-being as well.

Inflammation can be reduced through this approach, which will also bolster immune system functioning apart from lowering blood pressure levels as well as improving sleep quality among others. By alleviating anxiety and aiding relaxation processes, these practices foster good health from every angle.

So how do you bring mindfulness into your daily life? There are different ways one can do this such as breathing exercises, body awareness exercises, meditation, etc. Breathing exercises like the 4-7-8 technique are simple yet effective means of beginning to practise mindfulness. Body scans together with mindful walking enhance the mind-body connection. Also, meditation, whether it may be focused attention or open monitoring, assists in increasing awareness and diminishing the force of negative thoughts and feelings.

However, it is important to note that while formal mindfulness practices are a priority, so is living mindfully. This refers to being aware of each moment as it unfolds and engaging with the world in a way that shows one's mindfulness. Mindfulness, therefore, pervades your whole existence through heightened awareness and presence in all your daily activities.

The future of mindfulness is bright, as ongoing research continues to explore its mechanisms and applications. Many institutions are incorporating mindfulness into their programs, and it's becoming more widely adopted in various sectors. As mindfulness continues to expand, it has the potential to positively impact individuals and society as a whole.

So why not start reaping the benefits of mindfulness yourself? Incorporate mindfulness techniques into your daily routine and experience the transformation it can bring to your mental and physical well-being.

Research on Mindfulness

"Mindfulness" encompasses both a psychological state of heightened awareness as well as practices towards achieving this end. Numerous studies have shown that there are many positive effects of mindfulness on our mental health.

Many studies have established that practising mindfulness can reduce rumination, stress, and anxiety levels in general. By embracing mindfulness, people can enhance their cognitive abilities, improve emotional regulation as well as increase resilience while facing challenges in life.

Accordingly, research has shown that mindfulness is effective in cultivating psychological health and lowering stress. It has the potential to revolutionise our lives with its practical techniques for dealing with stress and enhancing inner peace. Mindfulness practitioner, Dr. Rebecca Johnson.

Through mindfulness practices, people can have a chance to shift attention to the present moment as well as adopt a non-judgmental attitude towards their thoughts and emotions. This promotes better regulation of psychological states, hence lessening stress levels, increasing self-awareness, and promoting overall well-being.

Research has proven that mindfulness is not merely just a trend; it's backed by evidence from science. We can enjoy the profuse benefits of mindfulness once we embrace it and make it an intrinsic element of our day-to-day activities.

The Impact of Mindfulness on the Brain

Furthermore, neuroscientists found that practising mindfulness can significantly alter brain structure and function.

Mindfulness increases the thickness of the prefrontal cortex, which controls focus and decision-making skills. This leads to better self-command over one's thoughts and actions. In contrast, mindfulness shrinks the amygdala volume involved with fear or stress responses. Minimising the size of this part through meditation diminishes reactivity in response to something stressful.

Additionally, there is increased grey matter content after practising mindfulness which is responsible for cognitive functions like thinking and memory processes being enhanced thus improving focus among others.

"It reshapes your brain," says Dr. Emily Williams who is among those scientists working on neuroscience studies about mindfulness."

Meanwhile, mindfulness also raises activity in the insula which is linked to self-awareness and empathy within the brain. By doing so, individuals are enabled to empathise with others' emotions as well as understand them.

This underlines how affecting mind-body relationship can be when mindful practice is applied thus bringing about mental health improvements in addition to emotional control alteration.

Engaging actively in these methods can lead to a balanced life through the optimization of mental capabilities.

Mindfulness and Physical Health

Apart from the mind, mindfulness practice also has positive impacts on physical health. It is an all-round approach to well-being. The incorporation of mindfulness in our daily routines will see us reaping numerous benefits that enhance a healthier and happier life.

Reduced Inflammation and a Boosted Immune System

According to research, practising mindfulness can reduce inflammation in the body. Chronic inflammation has been linked with diseases such as heart disease, diabetes, and some cancers. Thus, regular mindfulness practice helps to decrease inflammation while supporting a healthy immune system.

Lowered Blood Pressure

Additionally, there have been studies showing that practising mindfulness reduces blood pressure in individuals. This issue is one of the major concerns for people's health which could result in serious cardiovascular problems. Incorporating mindfulness techniques into our everyday lives will help lower high blood pressure reducing the risk of cardiac ailment.

Improved Sleep Quality

Many people have difficulty sleeping, with either chronic insomnia or poor quality of sleep. Mindfulness practices can calm the mind and facilitate relaxation that leads to better sleep quality. Practising mindfulness before bed, or incorporating mindful breathing exercises into our routine before we sleep, could thus result in excellent sleep and the next day waking up feeling refreshed.

In summary, mindfulness is a natural and effective way of improving our physical health. By minimising inflammation, boosting immune system functioning, reducing blood pressure, and improving quality of sleep, mindfulness sets the groundwork for wellness in the body and happiness in life.

Unpacking how mindfulness works

Mindfulness practice involves several processes that contribute to its overall advantages. Through grasping these mechanisms of action, we are able to appreciate how mindfulness is beneficial to our general well-being.

The Parasympathetic Nervous System: Promoting Relaxation and Reducing Stress

Another mechanism through which mindfulness works is by activating the parasympathetic nervous system. This part of our autonomic nervous system promotes rest and digestion or relaxing and balancing our bodies when we are under stress. Once we engage in mindfulness exercises that activate this section of the parasympathetic nervous system, it becomes easier to be calmer and more relaxed.

Enhanced Attention and Awareness: Cultivating Present-Moment Focus

Attention as well as awareness within us get sharpened by practising mindfulness too hence giving a deeper focus on what is happening at a given time. As one pays much attention to oneself, thoughts, feelings, sensations arise without making any judgement about them.

Activation of the Default Mode Network: Quieting the Mind's Chatter

By doing so, it activates the default mode network (DMN) among other brain regions that become active while one's mind wanders to self-referential thoughts. It cultivates stillness within this area thereby reducing internal dialogue and enabling us to be more present.

Improved Enteroception: Tuning into Bodily Sensations

Our ability to sense what is happening inside our bodies is known as enteroception. Mindfulness practices enhance our interoceptive awareness and allow us to notice more physical signs such as the pounding of our hearts, breathing, and muscles twitching. Practising mindfulness helps individuals connect with their bodies and respect their body's demands.

These mechanisms work together for a balanced relationship between mind and body that promotes mindfulness for wellness, reduces stress, and encourages self-awareness. As we better understand these mechanisms, we can begin to invoke mindfulness in our lives every day.

Learning Mindfulness through Breathing Exercises

Breathing exercises are a simple and effective way to begin practising mindfulness. When these exercises are done without judgement, focusing on the breath sensation, they bring one's awareness to the present moment and create stillness or calmness.

One common method is the "4–7–8" breathing exercise. This technique requires taking a deep breath in through the nose for 4 seconds, holding it for 7 seconds, and then slowly exhaling out of the mouth for 8 seconds. It promotes a profound relaxation response in your body.

 "Mindful breathing is an amazing way of ensuring that you keep your feet on this moment while also reducing stress. Every breath can help you come back to the present moment, thus giving you peace within."

Depending on how often you do it, mindful breathing for a few minutes daily may have a significant effect on your well-being. It also helps reduce anxiety levels, increases concentration, and enhances overall mental health.

It could be in the morning as an inspiring start to your day; at work breaks to relax; or before sleep so as to cool down and get ready for bed; mindfulness breathing can be easily incorporated into your regular schedules.

Benefits of Mindfulness Breathing:

Stress reduction: Mindful breathing activates the body's relaxation response, which helps lower the level of stress while leaving one more calm than before.

Improved focus and concentration: Through attending to our breath we develop our ability to stay present or focused at any given time.

Emotional well-being: Practising mindful breathing can help us control emotions better and enhance overall emotional health status.

Better sleep quality: Participating in mindful breathing prior to sleeping induces complete relaxation in both mind and body hence improving the quality of sleep.

Remember not to judge when doing mindful breathing correctly because doing so is key. Watch your breath and enjoy what is happening now around you completely. Prerequisite training can enable this to happen, making it a more powerful tool for maintaining mindfulness and thus being centred and grounded in life.

Body Awareness and Mindfulness

By integrating body awareness exercises into your mindfulness practice, you can enhance the mind-body connection. This means you can observe the sensation of your body without evaluating it; thus, one becomes more aware and lives in the present moment.

The Body Scan Technique

The body scan technique is a powerful method for developing body awareness. It involves systematically focusing on all areas in the body from toe to head, noting any feelings or tension spots. Through this exercise, we become more aware of our own bodies' subtle messages, which allows us to have a better grasp of our physical wellness as well as promoting relaxation.

"This scan helps us in listening to our bodies in a non-judgmental way, noting any discomfort or tightness and having compassion with our physical sensations."

Mindful Walking

Mindful walking is another way to learn about your body. Focus on the sensations moving through your body as you walk instead of thinking or being distracted by anything. Take note of how it feels when your feet touch the ground, the motion of your body, and the pace at which you breathe in and out. This will aid in bringing your mind back into the present moment thereby making you fully experience that instant.

"Practising mindful walking may make us enjoy simple movements and realise more beauty around us. It makes us be present within ourselves and improves our mind-body connection."

By incorporating practices like body scan and mindful walking into your mindfulness routine, it serves to further deepen personal presence and awareness for one's own physical self. These practices can increase the effectiveness of mindfulness techniques as a whole and contribute to better well-being.

Cultivating Mindfulness through Meditation

Meditation is a powerful technique that enables people to cultivate mindfulness. When you set aside some time for meditation sessions, you will begin noticing every small thing within yourself without being affected by negative ideas and emotions. Focused attention meditation and open monitoring meditation are two common types of meditation which can help individuals develop their sense of mindfulness.

Focused Attention Meditation: Enhancing Awareness

In focused attention meditation, concentrate on a particular object or physical feeling, such as breath. Find a comfortable sitting position then pay attention to the feelings that arise when air goes in or out of your nose while breathing or enters into your belly. If you notice something distracting you from watching breath, kindly bring attention back to breathing only. This helps strengthen the ability to stay in the moment as well as sharpening focus.

Open Monitoring Meditation: Observing Thoughts and Sensations

Open monitoring meditation involves attending to thoughts without judgement, feeling emotion, or sensation in one's own flesh. You should sit comfortably with eyes closed focusing purely on the stream of consciousness coming across your head observing them as they come up and subside. This encourages non-reactivity and acceptance of thoughts and emotions, promoting a more mindful state.

"Meditation is not about forcing the mind to be quiet; it's about finding the quiet that is already there." - Deepak Chopra

Both forms of meditation have different benefits and can be practised exclusively or in combination. Incorporating meditation into your daily routine can deepen your mindfulness practice and support your overall well-being.

Applying Mindfulness in Daily Life

Remember, although formal mindfulness practices are important, we must also bring mindfulness into our everyday lives. Mindfulness is not only something done in dedicated meditation sessions; it is a way of life that applies to all aspects of living.

The challenge of practising mindfulness on a daily basis is to fully live in the present moment. Instead of being lost in thoughts about what has happened before or becoming anxious about the future, we should ground ourselves in the present so that we can experience every moment fully.

Another way to practise this form of consciousness throughout our daily lives is through engaging mindfully. By doing this, we bring our full attention to the things around us whether they are thoughts, emotions or actions.

"When we engage mindfully with the present moment, we tap into a deep sense of aliveness and connect more fully with our experiences."

In order to bring mindfulness to our daily lives, it can be applied in various ways. This includes, but is not limited to, preparation and eating food, talking with family or simply doing household chores.

Everyday life awareness and being present help make mindfulness an integral part of the daily living process. This consequently enables us to value each moment and appreciate its beauty in turn resulting in overall well-being improvement and feeling of peace and satisfaction.

Chapter 10

The Value of Reflection for Insight and Personal Growth

Reflection is an extremely essential tool for personal development and self-improvement. It enables individuals to see the things they have done wrong and learn from them, leading to positive changes. This chapter will delve into the importance of reflection with particular reference to two effective methods, i.e., daily habits and journaling. These practices enable you to incorporate reflection into your daily routine so that you can unlock your full potential.

This lifelong process is an ongoing path of self-improvement guided by reflection. A deeper understanding of oneself, values, and goals is gained by taking time to look back at past experiences. Reflection helps us identify our patterns, strengths, as well as weaknesses, increasing our awareness towards ourselves.

The simple but effective habit of everyday reflection has the potential to improve our lives greatly. Daily reflecting on one's thoughts, actions, and behaviours enhances self-awareness, decision-making skills, and problem-solving abilities. Reflection daily improves our vision by making us achieve a greater focus on how we go about making progress in pursuit of our goals.

Journaling is a typical and powerful form of reflective practice. It helps us gain more insight into emotions as it gives us a detailed account of what we have gone through. Journaling can be used as a medium for expression where we can freely share our ideas, leading us to know ourselves and grow personally.

To get the most out of journaling as a self-improvement tool, one must develop some helpful habits. Among these strategies are journaling regularly, using prompts or questions that guide reflection, experimenting with various formats for journaling, or maintaining consistency. We require such strategies to make sure that we benefit immensely from journaling as well as guiding us effectively in improving ourselves.

Reflection also plays a crucial role in setting and achieving our goals. By reflecting on past experiences, strengths, and areas for improvement, we can set more meaningful and realistic goals; reflection clarifies our values and priorities while pointing out hindrances and outlining action plans. It is a tool that enables one to become self-empowered in both personal and professional aspects.

Furthermore, gratitude makes reflection more effective for self-improvement. Thus, concerning the positive areas of our lives, expressing gratitude leads to increased happiness and fulfilment. Gratitude practice within the reflection process increases well-being holistically and nurtures self-development.

Reflection is not only beneficial for personal development but also plays a crucial role in professional growth. When we reflect upon our experiences as professionals, we can identify areas for improvement, learn new skills, and improve our performance. Reflection allows us to have knowledge of ourselves, learning from what is happening around us, making us achieve our dreams.

In the end, reflection should be part of our daily lives since it is an ongoing learning process. Reflection promotes continuous personal development, unlocks new insights, and brings about positive changes. Reflection combined with mindfulness becomes a powerful tool to enable individuals to fully participate in this process, leading to deeper insights and understanding.

It is essential to incorporate reflection into our everyday lives so that we can enjoy its fruits. By making it a habit, setting aside dedicated time each day, using prompts or journaling, and integrating reflection into our routines, we ensure regular self-reflection and fuel our self-improvement journey.

Come with us as we look at the value of reflecting and how it can help you grow as an individual, improve your life, and move closer to achieving your goals.

The Necessity of Reflection in Self-Improvement

Reflection is a powerful tool for self-improvement since it aids individuals in gaining deeper knowledge of themselves, their values, and their aspirations. By reflecting on past experiences, individuals are able to identify patterns, strengths, and areas of improvement. This self-awareness is crucial for personal growth.

We open up an opportunity for self-discovery and reflection when we engage ourselves in reflection. It gives us space to pause and see what is running through our minds, emotions, or actions, thereby creating meaning from our experiences and learning from them. We gain insight through this process by identifying our strengths besides those areas where we can make improvements.

Renowned psychologist Dr. Sarah Williams said: "Reflection acts like a mirror that enables us to clearly see ourselves; understand why we do things; take deliberate actions that are in line with our values."

By looking back on what has happened to us before, we may be able to identify repetitive behaviours or patterns that may be holding us back from reaching our full potential. Such self-awareness enables one to lead a more proactive life and take necessary steps towards personal development.

Additionally, reflection helps us create meaningful goals that will direct the course of our lives, hence a sense of purpose. Looking within allows us to clarify our values, which means knowing exactly what matters most in life, as well as aligning what we do with whatever is expected of it by aspiring for something else, thereby living a more fulfilling life.

Dr. Emily Thompson, a well-known life coach and personal development advocate, says: "Reflection is the key that unlocks the door to personal growth and transformation. It empowers us to learn from our past, live more authentically, and create the life we truly desire."

To sum up, reflection is a crucial element in the process of self-improvement and personal growth. This assists us in realising who we are, where we need to improve, set goals that are meaningful, as well as doing things consistent with our dream life. So, by including reflection in our everyday lives, it helps us get a better understanding of ourselves so that we can keep improving ourselves every day.

Advantages of Daily Reflection

When done daily, reflecting on events can be a powerful tool for self-improvement as well as personal growth. By blocking out some time each day for systematic reflection on our thoughts, actions, or happenings, it has opened me up to tremendous opportunities for growth and transforming my entire being.

Increased self-awareness is among the key benefits of daily reflection. More insight into oneself and how he/she functions becomes possible when we contemplate what goes on within our minds or hearts. Such awareness helps one discover his/her strengths, weaknesses, and areas that require improvement leading to personal development.

Furthermore, daily reflection develops decision-making skills amongst learners. While reflecting on previous decisions and their consequences, one could understand how they make their own choices. With heightened consciousness comes an ability to make informed decisions henceforth in order for more thoughtful ones being taken next time around.

Reflection plays a major role in enhancing our problem-solving skills. Whenever we take a step back to scrutinise our challenges, there is every possibility that we will discover similarities, alternative methods, and solutions. In turn, this self-awareness and thinking process allows us to come up with efficient ways of solving problems, thus overcoming any hurdle easily.

Moreover, everyday reflection brings about clarity as well as purpose in life. By reflecting on our goals, values, and dreams we can act based on our true calling. This focus gives us direction, motivation, and satisfaction in our lives both at personal and professional levels.

The Power of Daily Reflection

With daily reflection habits, we are perpetually learning new things that help us grow into better individuals. This means that each day becomes an opportunity for personal development. Hence let's embrace the force of daily reflection to begin a period of profound self-discovery.

"Daily reflection is akin to taking a step back to examine one's life from a different perspective. It educates us about ourselves through the wise use of experiences for improved decision-making."

Role of Journaling in Reflection

Journaling is an important aspect when it comes to self-reflection and personal development. Writing down such thoughts, feelings, or experiences allows one enough time for retrospection, hence creating self-awareness.

Journaling unlocks the door to self-discovery by transposing thoughts into words. Through writing out emotions, we can recognize what sets them off or where else it may be appropriate for attention.

One remarkable thing about keeping journals is that it records growth processes over time. By rereading what has been recorded before, you will note how far you have gone and understand your own progress till now.

Journaling allows thoughts to bloom freely without fear or reproach from anyone else. It enables one to express their inner selves without pretending or minding others' opinions about themselves but rather as a place for meditation and introspection.

When one practises journaling they foster personal development. As a result, it becomes an instrument for self-realisation by helping one make continuous steps in learning and growing. Journaling lets us clarify our intent, goals, and set the stage for change.

John Quincy Adams said, "Reflect upon your present blessings, of which every man has many." Therefore through journaling, we can recognize and be grateful for the good things in our lives and thus enhance our connection to ourselves as well as the world around us. So, take a pen and let journaling transform your life. Allow it to be a part of you when undertaking the process of self-reflection and growth.

Developing Effective Journaling Habits

Journaling is a strong tool that helps individuals improve themselves as well as grow personally. For one to effectively tap into its vast potential, he/she must develop good practices in keeping journals that will enhance reflection. By utilising these strategies, you can maximise the value of journaling as a path of self-discovery/self-improvement along the way.

To develop effective journaling habits, one must dedicate time to the activity every day. This way, you create a pattern and turn journaling into your priority in life. Morning, evening, and any other convenient moments when you may find time to do it are ideal for making this habit part of life improvement.

Journaling requires consistency. This habit lets a person think about what has happened and how they have changed day after day.

Besides frequent writing, the employment of prompts or guided questions is another way that can be used to enrich reflection. Through these prompts, you can enter more deeply into your thoughts, emotions, and experiences which allow for richer and better reflections. Some such questions that will guide your journaling and prompt introspection are, "What have I learned today" or "What am I thankful for?"

Moreover, practising different formats of journaling can add diversity and layer to your journaling practice. Gratitude journals focus on creating positive thinking through recording things you appreciate each day. In contrast, dream journals provide an opportunity to delve into personal aspirations as they disclose desires of our subconscious minds. By trying out various forms of journaling, you can adapt your practice depending on what is important to you.

"Gratitude journals or dream journals could open new horizons for understanding yourself."

Effective journaling habits require consistency in their application. When done daily like this, it helps you review the progress and growth made up till now without fail. Whether they write a few lines or several pages consistently, maintaining the act of showing up at their journals reinforces the habit in them leading to a much more profound self-improvement journey.

For developing these effective habits in journal writing; setting aside dedicated time for it, use of prompts, trying different formats as well as remaining consistent are required to make full use of this tool for self-improvement. Discover the power contained in reflections thereby embarking on a transformative journey towards self-discovery and personal growth.

Reflection and Goal Setting

Reflection is an important aspect of goal setting. When people take the time to reflect on their past experiences, strengths, and areas for improvement, they can set more meaningful and realistic goals. Reflection assists individuals in defining what is important to them by providing clarity on their values and priorities so that they can align their objectives with such things.

By reflecting on their past successes and challenges, individuals can identify barriers that may prevent them from achieving their goals. This self-awareness enables one to come up with actionable plans that are specific to the particular situations thus increasing chances of goal attainment.

"Reflection serves as a powerful tool for self-improvement and success where we learn from our pasts and shape our futures."

Self-improvement is a lifelong journey that requires reflection along the way. It has the ability to help track progress, modify goals or reset actions according to changes in circumstances. It also enhances the ability to celebrate milestones achieved, learn from setbacks experienced, and make necessary adjustments to move forward.

"Reflection drives us towards bettering ourselves by becoming who we truly are."

Goal setting without reflection can lead to misaligned pursuits, unfulfilling achievements, and a lack of personal growth. Incorporating reflection into the goal-setting process enables people to pursue goals that truly resonate with their inner aspirations and provide them with a sense of fulfilment.

Reflection and goal setting are intertwined, thus allowing us to make the right choices that will help us lead meaningful lives.

Practising Gratitude in Reflection

Gratitude is an effective tool that enhances the reflection process as well as supports self-improvement. By deliberately including gratitude in reflections we redirect our attention from life's negatives toward its positive aspects; this goes a long way in making our lives happier, fuller, and more optimistic.

When we practise gratitude while reflecting, we take time to acknowledge and appreciate the blessings and opportunities surrounding us. We get to appreciate our experiences on a deeper level and what they have taught us. This mindset fosters contentment with ourselves making it easier for us to see beyond obstacles or difficulties that perhaps befall us leading to learning from such eventualities.

"Gratitude unlocks the fullness of life. It turns what we have into what we want".

Chapter 11

Empower Your Physical Wellbeing with Macronutrients and Balanced Nutrition

We cannot underscore enough the importance of physical well-being in our quest for good health in everyday life. This is foundational to human health and vitality needed for a long, satisfying life. However, what does "physical well-being" really mean? How can we put this firm foundation in place?

Physical well-being goes beyond just being free from disease or injury; it encompasses living a lifestyle that promotes vigour, strength, and liveliness. This means understanding and implementing exercise schedules, eating balanced diets, as well as ensuring enough rest, among other things. Simply stated, it represents our capacity to perform our day-to-day tasks efficiently with leftover energy for stress management or emergencies.

This section aims to highlight two important building blocks necessary for achieving optimal physical well-being: understanding macronutrients and balancing your diet. These factors largely depend on the kind of food we eat, hence directly affecting how healthy our bodies are.

Macronutrients Overview

Before diving into an elaborate explanation of macronutrients, let's come up with a succinct definition of what they stand for. Macronutrients consist of proteins, fats, and carbohydrates - the three main components required by the body in large quantities. They each have unique yet intertwined responsibilities in growth and functioning, as well as maintaining the body system. In simple words, they act as the main sources of energy facilitating complicated physiological processes.

Proteins help hold cells and tissues together while promoting growth. All parts of our bodies - from hair to enzymes - contain some protein.

Fats serve as efficient fuel, although they are often believed to be responsible for causing weight gain when taken excessively. Moreover, they aid in the nutrient absorption process, hormone production, and homeostasis maintenance.

Carbohydrates are broken down into glucose that runs cellular activities, making them the primary source of energy for the body. From keeping muscles moving to powering digestion processes, carbohydrates form an integral part.

The next sections will provide further insights on macronutrients. But to know these elements, it is necessary to understand not only their individual functions but also how they are interrelated to support the body system in an efficient way.

Basic Guidelines in Nutrition

Having a background on macronutrients, we can now discuss balanced diets. There is so much information about nutrition, including different diets, tips, and advice that can be overwhelming. However, focusing on practical principles makes the path towards long-term physical well-being easier. Consuming nutrient-dense foods such as fruits, vegetables, whole grains, and lean proteins while minimising processed foods, staying hydrated, and embracing variety lays a strong foundation for good nutrition.

Basically, the understanding of nutrition as well as maintaining the appropriate balance based on one's personal requirements is what defines physical wellness. Moving forward involves learning more about these constituents to increase our knowledge base with the addition of whole foods while maintaining a balanced diet that promotes good health.

How to Incorporate More Whole Foods into Your Diet

Let us discuss ways through which we can incorporate more whole foods into our diets. What do you mean by 'whole food'? These are minimally processed items without any additional ingredients or artificial additives. They include fruits, vegetables, whole grain cereals, lean meats, nuts, and seeds. Why choose them? Whole foods provide essential nutrients such as proteins, carbohydrates, fats, and fibres in higher quantities with fewer added sugars and unhealthy fats.

Fruits & Vegetables: Increase your intake of fresh fruits and vegetables that are loaded with key vitamins, fibre, minerals, and antioxidants. Make them part of your salads, snacks, or smoothies, ensuring varied micronutrients within your meal plan.

Choose whole grains such as brown rice, oats, quinoa, and barley for more fibre that helps in digestion and gives a feeling of fullness for weight management.

Lean Meats: Try chicken breasts or turkey instead, which are leaner sources of protein compared to most other meats that contain a lot of saturated fat.

Nuts & Seeds: Achieve this by including almonds, walnuts, chia seeds, and flaxseeds in your diet. They are rich in monounsaturated and polyunsaturated fats, fibre, and protein. You can add them to salads, smoothies, or simply snack on them.

Incorporating whole foods need not be abrupt. Start by slowly replacing processed components from your meal with whole ingredients. This includes choosing whole grain rather than white bread, fresh fruits instead of canned ones, and lean meats rather than processed alternatives; but once again, make sure you have a balanced variety to obtain these nutrients optimally for better results during workouts.

Balancing Nutritional Intake

Having understood macronutrients as well as the significance of whole foods, the next essential step towards good health is striking a balance in nutritional intake. But what does this involve?

A balanced diet means many things and little at the same time. In simple terms, it involves dividing daily calorie intake between macronutrients – carbohydrates, fats, and proteins – following dietary guidelines. However, different food choices within this range differ in nutrient densities.

Dietary Guidelines for Americans: To maintain optimal nutrient levels while managing caloric intake to prevent weight gain or health issues, adults should get 45-65% of total calories from carbohydrates, 20-35% from fats, and 10-35% from proteins. These numbers can be taken as guideposts which have to be adjusted by individual nutrition needs, taking into account such factors as age, level of activity, and health condition.

Nutrient-Dense Foods: Nutrient-dense foods form an important aspect of a balanced diet. These foods contain more essential nutrients than their energy content implies. For example, fruits, vegetables, lean meats, seafood (such as oysters or crabs), nuts (like almonds), and seeds (like flaxseeds). When selecting sources of protein, think about the individual whose consumption also provides other nutrients such as lentils with fibre or salmon that contains omega-3 fatty acids.

Calorie Consideration: Balancing extends beyond macronutrient distribution; it involves managing total caloric intake. When one consumes more calories than required, he/she gains weight which may consequently lead to a number of health problems. There is thus the need to understand energy balance that is calories consumed versus calories expended for purposes of achieving an ideal weight.

Portion Control: Portion management is also a key tenet in balancing nutritional intake because even nutrient-rich diets could contribute to weight gain if taken excessively. This awareness helps regulate calorie consumption while keeping variety and quality intact.

Balancing nutritional intake cannot fit all cases. Balancing nutritional intake is a process that is not static but dynamic, which is affected by lifestyle, physical activities, general health, and personal ambitions. Therefore, the need to make conscious choices daily to bring together a variety of nutrients into the body while appreciating this individuality.

The path towards good health and well-being starts with understanding macronutrients and whole foods. These components are synthesised through a balanced diet that harmoniously integrates different nutritional units as fuel for our bodies. Subsequent sections will discuss practical ways of achieving this equilibrium, thereby helping you in crafting ideal meal plans.

Constructing a Balanced Meal Plan: Practical Tips

Once macronutrients, whole foods, and basics of nutritional balancing have been covered, let's walk through the practical side of things – building a balanced meal plan. A balanced meal plan is both science and art, merging personal needs, food choices, and nutrition theories.

1. **Divide Your Plate:** Just imagine your plate with segments to make it a well-balanced one. Follow the USDA's MyPlate model by filling half of the plate with fruits and vegetables, one quarter with lean proteins (animal or plant-based), and another quarter with whole grains. This helps provide diverse nutrient intake across macronutrients.
2. **Select Whole Foods:** Whenever possible, choose whole foods such as brown rice instead of white rice or fresh fruit rather than canned fruit. These options offer more fibre and essential nutrients that help in preventing chronic diseases.
3. **Diversify Protein Sources:** Do not eat only animal proteins; use plant sources too. For example, if you had chicken for lunch, you might want to consider lentil or chickpea curry for dinner. This ensures a wide range of amino acids essential to health as well as other nutrients.

4. **Incorporate Healthy Fats:** Not all fats are bad for you. Use avocados, olive oil, nuts, and seeds as sources of healthy fats containing monounsaturated and polyunsaturated fats that are beneficial for heart health.
5. **Add Variety & Color:** Eat different types and colours of food to consume assorted vitamins, minerals, and antioxidants in your diet. Carrots and sweet potatoes contain lots of vitamin A while spinach and kale are rich in iron and calcium respectively.

Let's illustrate a sample balanced meal plan adhering to these principles:

Sample Balanced Meal Plan:

Breakfast: Overnight oats made from rolled oats + almond milk + chia seeds (whole grains + healthy fats), topped with blueberries + nuts (fruits & protein).

Mid-Morning Snack: An apple + a few almonds (fruit + healthy fats).

Lunch: Grilled chicken salad with colourful veggies such as bell peppers, cherry tomatoes, and cucumber dressed in olive oil (protein + vegetables + healthy fats).

Dinner: Steamed brown rice served with stir-fried tofu and mixed veggies sautéed in minimal oil (whole grain + plant-based protein + veggies).

Note that this is illustrative, and actual meal plans should reflect personal preferences, dietary restrictions, and caloric needs.

Conclusion: General Thoughts on Interlacing Macronutrients and Balanced Nutrition

To sum up, physical health is a subtle issue based on consuming nutritious foods carefully. Awareness of macronutrients, adherence to balanced diet patterns, and understanding of whole foods collectively contribute to maintaining this equilibrium, ensuring our bodies function optimally.

Good physical well-being is not instant. It involves a series of small conscious moves made daily towards a healthier life – such as choosing brown rice instead of white rice; eating fresh fruits rather than sugary snacks; engaging in enjoyable exercises; establishing an individualised sleep routine.

The field of nutrition may appear complicated due to various advice and fads but amidst all these intricacies there are timeless nutritional principles – the importance of macronutrients, nutrient-dense whole foods, and balanced diets for keeping optimal body weight as well as total well-being.

Physical Well-being and Sports Performance

To perform better on the field requires more than just being fit; nutrition is also important. Simple sugars fuel high-intensity exercises, fats are used for endurance activities, and proteins help muscles recover after training. Research reported by betterhealth.vic shows that athletes who have balanced diets perform better than those with imbalanced diets.

Diverse Diets and Long-term Illnesses

Apart from physical performance maintenance, our diet significantly determines our susceptibility to chronic diseases. Some research done by diabetesjournals.org shows that a diet rich in processed foods and saturated fats may increase the risk of type 2 diabetes whereas one comprising whole foods and equal macronutrient distribution may lower the risk of this disease. Nutrition is crucially related to chronic illnesses; hence it serves as an essential aspect of human life.

Quality of Life in General Including Sleep

Well-balanced eating habits improve people's lives beyond physical benefits. All macronutrients including proteins and carbohydrates keep fatigue away, lift up moods, and improve concentration. Moreover, sleep patterns are influenced by nutrition. According to a study conducted by sleepfoundation.org, individuals who consumed meals with high amounts of sugar were more prone to having awakenings during the night while those who had higher fibre intake spent more time in deep sleep.

In conclusion, understanding macronutrients and adopting a balanced approach to nutrition is an effective basis for physical wellness. Nonetheless, accomplishing this objective is progressive; there is no definite timeline for acquiring knowledge on healthy eating but rather it involves making informed choices every day.

Remember, as you strive for optimal health, that knowledge is power. Knowing what nourishes our bodies will make us choose wisely, thereby contributing to the vibrancy of our unique body systems. Keep learning, exploring, and tuning into your body's signals – every step towards better health is undoubtedly worthwhile!

Chapter 12

The Mental and Physical Benefits of Different Exercise Types: Establishing a Daily Exercise Routine

Welcome to our complete guide on the mental and physical benefits of different exercises. This chapter will set you on the right path if you want to establish an everyday exercise routine.

Good overall health is maintained by regular exercise, both mentally and physically. In this chapter, we will look at different types of exercises along with their unique benefits. If you want to improve your cardiovascular health, build muscle strength, or decrease stress levels, then there is a type of exercise that can help you achieve that.

Through setting up a daily exercise program, you get to enjoy these exercises and make your life better. Not sure where to start? Do not worry, we have got your back. Let's jump in!

Understanding the Importance of Daily Exercise

Do you often find it difficult to squeeze in some time for workouts in your schedule? It's understandable considering... Between work, family, and everything else, who has time for everyday workouts? However, before you completely put off the idea, think about this: daily exercise is very important for good physical and mental fitness.

Routine exercises have numerous advantages like elevation of moods and improved mental abilities as well as making muscles strong and bones. Incorporating exercise into your routine can help lower your risks for chronic diseases such as heart disease, obesity, or diabetes, among others, leading to a longer lifespan.

It doesn't have to take much time either. Even just 30 minutes per day spent in moderate exercising, such as speed walking or biking, can do miracles for your health. Therefore, always ensure that physical activity is included in your daily timetable regardless of whether it means taking that walk during lunch hours or having a quick workout at home before bed.

The Physical Benefits of Daily Exercise

Physical health and well-being are highly promoted by exercising regularly. It's not just about maintaining weight but also ensuring that your cardiovascular system, muscles, and bones are healthy, and energy levels are consistent throughout the day. Engaging in daily exercise can improve overall body fitness leading to the following physical benefits:

Improved cardiovascular health: Daily exercise can improve blood circulation and lower risks of heart diseases like high blood pressure, stroke, or heart attack.

Stronger muscles and bones: Regular exercise helps to strengthen your muscles and bones and prevent age-related muscle loss or osteoporosis.

Boosted energy: Exercise increases the production of endorphins that improve your energy levels and reduce fatigue.

Enhanced physical fitness: Daily exercise can boost your physical performance, coordination, and balance making you more agile as well as increasing stamina.

In conclusion, you'll experience multiple physical benefits including a healthier lifestyle involving increased energy if you incorporate a daily workout routine into your life.

The Mental Benefits of Daily Exercise

Apart from just physical advantages, everyday exercising can influence your brain positively. Routine physical activities help to reduce stress levels, make one feel better overall, and promote good-quality sleep. Furthermore, daily exercises have the effect of raising cognitive abilities like focused attention with better memory.

Also, exercise studies have revealed that persons who participate in physical activities often are less likely to suffer from mental disorders such as depression and anxiety. Endorphins released during exercises also provide an all-natural mood boost and contribute to greater happiness levels.

If you include daily exercise in your routine, you can improve not only your physical health but also enjoy the multiple mental advantages that come with regular physical activity.

Various Forms of Exercise

Exercise does not fit everyone. Different types of exercises yield distinct benefits for the body and mind. Let's take a look at the four major categories of exercises:

Aerobic exercises: These are cardio workouts such as running, cycling, swimming, and others that will make your heart rate rise and enable you to burn calories.

Strength training: These involve weightlifting, resistance band workouts, and bodyweight exercises which enable you to build muscles thus increasing bone density.

Flexibility exercises: Such as stretching, yoga, and Pilates help increase joint mobility or improve muscle flexibility.

Mind-body practices: Physical movements plus mindfulness techniques are employed by yoga, Pilates, and other forms of exercise to enhance mental clarity while relieving stress.

Each exercise has its own unique benefits; however, combining these different types of exercise into your routine can help you create a positive well-rounded way of life. You may combine different ones based on your goals and preferences so as to customise your workout regime.

Advantages of Aerobic Exercises

Are you considering enhancing your cardiovascular strength and stamina? Activities like running, cycling, or swimming serve this purpose well. They raise one's heart rate, increase oxygen flow in the body system leading to better lung capacity among other things strengthening the heart muscles themselves.

Apart from being good for cardiovascular fitness, aerobic exercises can also help you lose weight because they burn a lot of calories; they can also add muscle endurance as well as boost overall stamina. Including them in everyday activities can ensure increased energy levels plus enhanced general fitness.

Aerobic exercises are a great choice whether you are starting out in fitness or simply want to switch up your current routine. These exercises can be adapted to suit any fitness level, meaning that they are suitable for everyone.

Benefits of Strength Training

Strength training is an ideal choice if you want to increase bone density and muscle strength. It entails engaging in resistance and weight-bearing movements that challenge specific muscle groups, thus enhancing physical fitness.

Furthermore, strength training helps in building muscle mass, which is crucial for maintaining healthy metabolism rates and burning calories even when at rest. This will be beneficial for weight maintenance or loss purposes.

Moreover, consistent strength training can improve bone density, reducing the chances of fractures and osteoporosis particularly in elderly people. In fact, studies have found that a 15% increase in bone density occurred after just six months of strength training alone.

Loss of muscle mass as we age known as sarcopenia is common among the elderly population. Strength training mitigates this risk by helping to build muscles thereby protecting against age-related muscle wasting. Besides, it can also enhance functional abilities such as mobility and balance.

Your regular exercise practice can be strengthened through incorporating strength training, which has many physical benefits and can enhance your health and wellness.

The Importance of Flexibility Exercises

Flexibility exercises are often overlooked when people think about exercising. However, they are an important component of any good exercise regime. Including stretching, yoga, or Pilates in your daily workouts can bring many advantages to your body and mind.

What flexibility exercises primarily aim at is enhancing joint mobility as well as muscle flexibility. With these exercises, you will achieve better posture, improve athletic performance and have a wider range of motion. Moreover, the tension in your muscles might reduce if you do flexibility exercises making you feel more relaxed and at ease.

Stretching is a popular form of flexibility exercise which helps in elongation and relaxation of tight muscles; it also increases blood flow thereby minimising chances of other injuries during workouts. Yoga and Pilates combine elements of stretching with mindfulness breathing to improve overall health both mentally and physically.

By practising flexibility exercises, you can achieve many benefits for your overall well-being. Flexibility exercises help you target specific goals such as improved joint mobility; muscle flexibility; posture or athletic performance. Why not therefore try including some stretches; yoga or Pilates into your daily workout routine?

Yoga and Pilates: The Mind-Body Connection

If you want a fitness regime that combines physical activity with self-awareness, go for yoga or Pilates. Both practices promote mental focus while decreasing stress levels that eventually lead to general well-being.

Yoga entails poses focusing on flexibility, balance, and core strength among others. Enabling body awareness as well as improving posture is one way practising yoga promotes

relaxation reduces anxiety and stress levels too. Regular yoga practice also offers various physical benefits including increased flexibility as well as cardiovascular health.

Pilates primarily targets core strength plus stability aspects. Controlled precise movements including breathing techniques form part of Pilates kind of movement that are aimed at improving muscle tone, balance and coordination. Pilates can also be used to relieve backache, improve posture and release stress.

Practising yoga or Pilates also includes breathing exercises and mindfulness techniques that promote improved clarity and focus mentally. Overall well-being will be improved if you consistently practise yoga or Pilates and this is how you create a stronger mind-body connection.

Adapting Exercise Routines to Suit Your Goals and Preferences

There's no one-size-fits-all approach to exercising. What should guide your daily exercise routine is your goals as well as preferences. If you want to lose weight through exercise, focus on cardio workouts that help burn calories. On the other hand, if your aim is muscle building, incorporate strength training activities into your routine. To enhance flexibility, dedicate some time to stretching or yoga.

It is important to enjoy the exercises you do in order to remain motivated and sustain them consistently. Try out different exercises until you find the ones that suit your preferences and schedule. If you are a morning person, try hitting the gym in the morning; otherwise, set aside an hour during the evening for workouts.

Remember that your workout routine must change as your goals change or as lifestyle changes occur. Continuously re-evaluating and adjusting it will keep you on track and motivate you towards long-term success.

Getting into Daily Exercise

Starting a daily exercise plan may appear as an intimidating thing to do, but it is a significant process towards being fit and healthy. To succeed, start slowly and tailor the program to your personal objectives and preferences.

Start by setting achievable goals. It is better to begin on a small scale and then increase the toughness of your workouts progressively. Try working out at the same time every day so that it becomes part of your daily routine.

Also, when you start, it is important to choose activities that you enjoy doing. Find something like walking, riding a bike or joining the group fitness class that you would love doing each day.

Lastly, make exercise a part of your regular routine. Instead of taking an elevator climb stairs; go for a walk during lunch break or stretch while watching TV. These minor changes will be able to result in major improvements.

Remember that starting with regular exercise daily is a journey, not a race. It takes time to celebrate each stage passed through it.

Overcoming Common Barriers to Daily Exercise

There are several barriers that hinder one from starting and sustaining a daily exercise routine. One of the most significant barriers is lack of time which can make committing to any workout plan difficult. On top of this, motivation can wane when results take longer than expected.

To overcome these barriers, it's essential for one to remain consistent with their workout routines. Begin slowly but gradually increase the intensity level and duration as well as different types of exercises that one does for them to be motivated more by exercising together with friends or family members.

When you have limited time, consider breaking up your fitness regime into smaller parts spread across the day. Alternatively, if you do not have access to gym facilities, try some body weight exercises at home or buy simple equipment such as resistance bands or dumbbells.

Make sure to warm up before exercising then cool down afterwards if you want to avoid injury in training sessions. If pain comes up see a medical practitioner to recommend different exercises for you.

Remember that only by being regular and making exercise a habit it is possible to achieve permanent results. Don't be disheartened by the setbacks or obstacles and always challenge yourself towards one's goals of being physically fit. Through dedication and persistence, one can overcome all barriers to exercising and attain healthy living.

Making Long-Term Changes for a Healthy Lifestyle

Implementing a daily exercise regimen is the initial stage in leading a healthier life, but it also takes long term changes to maintain a sound body and mind. This requires committing to regular physical activities even on days when you're not motivated or energised.

To make exercise a habit, it should be incorporated into your day-to-day routine. It could mean taking the staircase instead of an elevator, walking during lunch hour, or squatting while brushing your teeth. By incorporating exercise into your day-to-day routine, it becomes easier for you to maintain it over the long haul.

Achievable goals should be set, and your exercise routine must be changed based on how you are progressing. At the point of becoming hardier and more conversant with your program, you can begin to increase the intensity or duration of your workouts on a gradual basis. This will help stave off monotony and ensure that improvements in mental and physical health continue.

Remember too that a balanced lifestyle also means more than just exercise. A nutritious meal, enough sleep, and stress reduction are all key aspects of healthy living. By making little adjustments to your daily life that can be sustained over time, you can experience lasting changes in overall health.

Take things one step at a time and do not be too hard on yourself if there are some setbacks along the way. The key is being consistent, so stick with it and mark your progress. Incorporating regular exercise into your daily routine coupled with leading a healthy lifestyle will guarantee continuous mental and physical benefits for many years.

Chapter 13

Optimising Sleep Habits
and Managing Stress for Restful Sleep

Welcome to this informative chapter on optimising your sleep habits and managing stress to achieve restful sleep. In today's fast-paced world, getting the sleep your body needs can be challenging. Nevertheless, you can improve the quality of your sleep and enjoy a more rejuvenating rest by putting in place the things discussed in this chapter. The significance of sleep shall be examined, how to understand its various stages, tools that may be used to examine our style of sleeping, creation of a peaceful bedtime schedule, and making the bedroom more comfortable.

Additionally, we will talk about how stress affects sleep as well as tips on how to manage stress in our day-to-day lives. You are going to gain good sleeping habits by using our directives and ensuring you have enough time for it since your life would become more productive and satisfying only then. Let's get started with understanding more about optimising sleep habits and managing stress for restful sleep.

The Importance of Sleep

Sleep is crucial for a sound mind and body. Restful slumber is necessary each night to maintain good health, support brain function, stabilise mood, among others. Lack of quality or insufficient sleep has several negative effects including poor thinking ability, emotional disorders, an increase in weight gain, as well as high chances of being infected with chronic ailments such as heart diseases and diabetes.

If you are struggling with a lack of adequate rest through the night, there are common signs that may indicate you have been deprived of some hours, such as fatigue, among others. Ignoring the importance of getting adequate rest can lead to detrimental consequences on your overall health and well-being over long periods, hence making it a duty that cannot be ignored.

By taking steps to optimise your sleep habits and actively manage stress, you can improve the quality of your sleep and reap the many benefits of restful slumber. This makes prioritising getting enough shuteye one of the biggest things an individual can do to safeguard his or her future welfare and health.

Understanding Sleep Cycles

Did you know that sleep is not a continuous state, but rather a series of cycles? Each cycle comprises different stages, which include light sleep, deep sleep, and REM sleep.

During light sleep, your body remains slightly awake, with your brain waves slowing down. Upon entering deep sleep, your brain waves become even slower while your muscles relax completely. In this stage, the body repairs tissues and regenerates them. It also builds bone and muscle and strengthens the immune system.

REM sleep takes place in cycles throughout the night and is important for the consolidation of cognitive function and memory. During this time frame, the mind is highly active, while the body is passive.

For a balanced sleeping pattern, it is necessary to understand how each stage of our slumbering process contributes to overall sleep quality. Therefore, optimising your own sleeping schedules could make you wake up feeling refreshed and rejuvenated.

Assessing Your Sleep Habits

Do you wake up feeling well-rested and ready to tackle the day, or do you drag yourself out of bed feeling groggy and unproductive? Current patterns regarding sleeping, including routine environment lifestyle factors, need to be evaluated as they are essential in optimising restfulness.

First, evaluate your sleep routine. Do you fall asleep and wake up at the same time every day, or is your schedule erratic? Then examine your sleep environment. Is it silent, darkened, and cool or too lighted and noisy?

Furthermore, lifestyle aspects such as exercise, dieting, and stress levels greatly affect the quality of sleep. Does your daily routine incorporate exercises, or are you living an inactive life? Are you consuming foods that promote sleep or rather caffeine and alcohol before bedtime?

Evaluating one's sleeping patterns will enable him/her to point out areas that need improvement to have optimised sleep, hence a peaceful night's rest as well as an efficient day.

Constructing a Sleep Timeline

To enhance your sleep quality, it is important to establish a regular bedtime routine. This ritual informs your body that now is the time for relaxation and winding down. Start by picking a relaxing activity like taking a warm bath or reading a good book. You can also practise relaxation methods like deep breathing or meditation.

Moreover, it's best to avoid activities such as playing with electronic devices or engaging in stressful work just before bed. Instead, include quiet activities like sipping a hot cup of chamomile tea, practising yoga, or listening to soothing music.

Just remember that when preparing for bed in the evening, it is essential to follow calming routines that soothe both the mind and body. Identify what works best for you so that every night you adhere strictly to it without fail. In due course, these activities will become associated with going to sleep, enhancing the quality of restful nights.

Developing a Sleep-worthy Environment

The state of your sleeping place can be very instrumental in determining whether you get enough rest. Begin by making sure that the bedroom setup has been optimised – ensure that the bed is comfortable and supportive while keeping the room clear from dirtiness and clutter, which hinders relaxation.

Additionally, temperature plays a vital part in ensuring an ambient environment for sleeping. Ideally, a bedroom should be cool, between 60-67°F, so that sleep can come easily and last for longer. In case of need, a fan or air conditioner may be used.

Equally important is reducing noise levels to have a conducive sleeping environment. Use earplugs to block all noisy sounds if necessary or find a white noise maker.

The other aspect that can affect your sleep quality is the amount of light in your bedroom. Invest in blackout curtains or wear eye masks at night to block out as much light as possible.

Enhancing the overall quality of your sleep by modifying your sleep environment slightly.

Better Sleep by Managing Stress

Stress interferes with healthy sleep patterns, causing insomnia and other sleep conditions. Luckily, there are multiple effective stress management techniques that contribute to improved sleep and well-being.

For example, mindfulness, which involves being present and fully aware of one's thoughts and feelings without attaching any value judgments. Mindfulness meditation and deep breathing exercises are great ways to practise mindfulness and reduce stress before bedtime.

Muscle relaxation or imagery is another approach to try. These exercises can help to relieve tension in the body and quiet the mind, thereby promoting better sleep.

Stress management and improved sleep can also be achieved through changes in lifestyle. Engage in physical exercise regularly, eat right, and enjoy outdoor activities to decrease stress levels. Moreover, identifying and sorting out stressful situations in your life, such as work or relationship-related issues, can reduce stress levels and improve the quality of night's rest.

With these stress-reduction methods as part of your daily routine, you will manage stress and enhance sleep for healthier well-being.

Exercise versus Sleep

Physical activity not only positively impacts your overall health but also greatly affects your sleep quality. It has been proven that people who exercise regularly have an easier time falling asleep, spend more time in deep sleep stages, and wake up less often during the night.

Your exercise timing may also determine how well you sleep. While some find it disrupts their sleep if they exercise just before bedtime, others think it makes them relax before going to bed. Experiment with different times of day so that you can discover what suits you best. However, avoid doing rigorous exercises late into the night as it increases heart rate, making it hard to fall asleep.

If you are struggling with finding time or motivation to include physical activity into your daily schedule, start small and increase gradually. Even a few minutes of physical activity a day can

make a difference in terms of your sleep quality. Some activities beginners could take up include walking around the block; yoga classes or weight lifting just to mention a few.

Diet versus Sleep

The type of meals you consume has a great impact on your ability to get adequate rest at night. While there are certain ones that promote sounder sleeping patterns such as cherries, almonds, fatty fish like salmon or trout, milk as well as leafy green vegetables among others; others should be avoided when one is retiring, for instance, beverages that have high caffeine content or alcohol.

If you simply pay more attention to what you eat and make minor adjustments in your eating habits, then the quality of your sleep will improve, and you may feel refreshed when waking up.

Maintaining a Regular Sleep Routine

A vital factor that influences how well one sleeps is the consistency of a person's sleep pattern. It is important to establish and sustain regular bedtimes and wake-up times. This helps regulate your body's internal clock and ensures that you get the optimal amount of sleep that your body needs to function at its best.

To form a fixed sleep schedule, choose a bedtime which allows for enough sleep (preferably 7-9 hours per night) and stick to it every day, including weekends. Have a reminder set at least half an hour before bedtime so that you unwind, relax, as well as condition your mind and body for sleep.

Additionally, pick a time for waking up which will enable you to have adequate sleep. Try to wake up at the same time every day, including weekends. This helps regulate your body's internal clock and ensures that you get enough sleep to function at your best throughout the day.

By having consistent sleep patterns, you can teach your body when it is time to sleep and when it is time to wake up, thereby leading to better sleep quality overall and feeling more rested during the day.

Role of Technology in Sleep

Technology has become an essential part of our lives, but its use can affect our sleep quality. Most electronic devices give off blue light, which suppresses melatonin hormone that regulates sleep cycles. This may contribute to problems of initiating or staying asleep. Also, using electronic gadgets shortly before bed can increase screen time, resulting in poor-quality sleep.

To reduce technology's impact on your sleep, try decreasing exposure to screens late into the night. Don't use any devices with screens for about 30 minutes before going to bed, and instead choose dimmer lighting rather than bright ones. Some devices even have screen filters that decrease blue light emissions and, therefore, improve the quality of your night's rest by doing so. Besides, apply the "Do Not Disturb" settings feature on your phone so as not to be woken up at night.

Through such small changes, one can still gain from technological advancements without compromising their levels of good rest.

Strategies for Managing Insomnia

You are not alone if you are dealing with insomnia or other sleeping problems. However, there are several ways of mitigating these conditions and improving the quality of your sleep. Start with relaxation techniques like deep breathing exercises, progressive muscle relaxation, or meditation.

Cognitive-behavioural therapy is another technique that can help you identify and change negative thought patterns that contribute to insomnia. Additionally, creating a calming environment for sleeping as well as maintaining consistent sleep patterns could also be beneficial in this case.

If all else fails, don't hesitate to seek professional help. A sleep specialist can perform a thorough evaluation and recommend the most appropriate treatment options specific to your needs. With commitment and the right points of focus, you can handle insomnia and achieve a well-deserved peaceful sleep.

Getting Professional Help for Sleep Disorders

When struggling with chronic sleep problems, it is advisable to consider professional help such as visiting sleep clinics or consulting with sleep specialists. Sleep specialists are medical doctors who are experts in sleep medicine and can diagnose and treat various sleeping disorders including insomnia, sleep apnea, and restless leg syndrome.

Sleep clinics are medical establishments where patients suffering from sleeping disorders undergo diagnosis and treatment. They may provide services like sleep studies, consultancy with specialists on sleep matters as well as cognitive-behavioural therapy treatment.

For those unsure whether they need professional assistance or not, they should make an appointment with their primary care physician who will then refer them to any suitable expert if required. If you have been experiencing continuous difficulty in sleeping without receiving any form of help that is available, it may result in negative consequences on your general health and life quality.

Natural Remedies for Sleep

Are you having trouble getting a good night's rest without resorting to using medication? You may want to try some natural remedies at bedtime.

Valerian root, chamomile, and other herbal supplements have long served as calming agents and enhancers of sleep. You can buy these supplements in various forms including capsules or tea. Before commencing on any new supplement ensure that you consult a healthcare professional.

Also, natural solutions to insomnia include deep breathing, progressive muscle relaxation techniques. These techniques can help minimise tension and stress levels to enable your body to relax so you can fall asleep.

There are also natural alternatives such as aromatherapy that enhances sleep quality. Essential oils like lavender and cedarwood have calming effects that help in relaxing the mind and body. Add a few drops of your favourite essential oil into a diffuser or apply them directly on your pillow before going to bed.

Using natural remedies for sleep may be one safe way you could attempt restful sleep. Experiment with different remedies to find what works best for you, and always consult with a healthcare professional before trying new supplements or practices.

Lifestyle Adjustments for Better Sleep

If you are having trouble sleeping, small changes in your life can make a huge difference. These changes may be able to enhance the quality of sleep by altering your daily routine and habits.

One main change is improving your hygiene for sleep, which involves having a relaxed bedtime schedule and maintaining comfortable conditions for sleep, such as maintaining a dark room temperature in the bedroom.

Stress also greatly affects sleep patterns. One can manage stress through yoga, meditation, or deep breathing exercises leading to the best kind of restful sleeping pattern.

For instance, reducing caffeine intake as well as establishing regular times for sleeping are some of the lifestyle adjustments that significantly improve the quality of your sleep.

Therefore, try making some lifestyle adjustments tonight that would support your efforts towards resting well at night when faced with insomnia again next time.

Maintaining Healthy Sleep Habits for the Long Term

Now that you have implemented various strategies to optimise your sleep habits and manage stress, it's essential to maintain these changes for the long term. By doing so, you can continue to reap the benefits of restful and rejuvenating sleep.

In addition, lasting optimization of sleep involves setting sleep goals. How many hours do you need to sleep each night? Create a reasonable schedule that will allow you to achieve the recommended quota of rest every night. On weekends too, always wake up at the same time as on weekdays and observe a regular sleep schedule.

Furthermore, make sure you prioritise self-care in your day-to-day activities. This could be engaging in calming activities, practising stress management strategies, or avoiding screens before bed. A commitment to good quality slumber can help maintain healthy habits of sleeping in the long term.

Finally, review and adjust your sleeping patterns regularly as may be necessary. Age, change in lifestyle, and stress are some of the issues that could affect your usual pattern for slumbering. To keep optimum quality and overall health through monitoring and adjusting one's sleeping habits continually.

Remember, healthy sleep habits are essential for overall well-being. By setting sleep goals, prioritising self-care, and regularly evaluating your sleep habits, you can maintain healthy sleep patterns for the long term and achieve restful and rejuvenating sleep each and every night.

Chapter 14

Identify Stressors and
Reactions: A Guide to Managing Stress

This comprehensive chapter will enlighten you on how to manage stress. Stress has different forms, and it affects both the mind and body. We are aware that managing stress is difficult, but we are here to help. In this guide, readers will find information on how to identify their stresses and reactions, as well as learn tried-and-tested approaches to controlling them. By applying these tips, you can achieve stress relief for a healthier life. Let's explore this stress management guide.

Defining Stress

Stress is normal in response to challenging or threatening situations, but if not properly controlled, it may have severe implications for your mental and physical health. There are different types of stress, such as acute, episodic, acute, and chronic. It is crucial to distinguish the kind of pressure you experience for an efficient mode of management.

Acute stress lasts for several minutes up to days (Blonna 2013). This type of pressure occurs when an individual has to deal with a particular situation within a short period, like an exam or job interview (Blonna 2013). Episodic acute stress happens when persons continually come across numerous stressful circumstances (Blonna 2013). This form of pressure leads one into anxiety states, among other effects (Blonna 2013). Lastly, chronic stress refers to long-term responses towards continued pressures in life, such as financial problems or difficult working conditions (Blonna 2013).

If one thinks about it clearly, almost all body systems are affected by too much stress. Physical signs of this state include headaches, muscle tension, and fatigue, while emotional symptoms encompass anxiety, depression, and irritability (Rice & Bevans 2010). Furthermore, chronic strain may heighten risks of serious ailments like heart diseases, obesity, or diabetes, among others (Rice & Bevans 2010).

Once you know what stress means, what types it comes in, and how it affects the body, you can start taking proactive measures to manage stress and live a better life.

Knowing what stresses you

Stress is an unavoidable element of human existence, but not every stressor is equal. Being able to identify the specific sources of stress will enable you to manage your condition well. Some common examples include financial concerns, health problems, work deadlines, conflicts in relationships, and drastic changes in life. Personal events leading to stress come from within yourself, for example, negative self-talks or unrealistic expectations, whereas job-related ones result from heavy workloads, difficult colleagues or bosses, and job security fears. This section will help you recognize these general sources of pressure on you.

Analysing Stress Responses

Different people have different physical and emotional responses to stressors depending on their personalities and situations (Harrington 2010). When stressed, one may experience accelerated heartbeats, hyperventilation, muscle tightness, migraines, and stomach upsets, among others (Harrington 2010). Stress causes both anxiety emotions and rage states like irritability or mood swings which hinder mental focus (Harrington 2010).

To cope with stress effectively and efficiently, one should first know how the individual responds to stress physically. Through this way, the person can easily develop ways of dealing with them and hence reduce their effect on his/her well-being. In this part, we shall focus on some of these techniques that will enable you to know your individual pattern of reacting to stressful situations thereby enabling you to take responsibility for yourself when it comes to managing your level of anxiety, thus staying calm always (Harrington 2010).

Sometimes it is problematic to identify all the factors responsible for your tension levels. There can be hidden stressors in the subconscious mind, which are beyond one's normal awareness. Addressing these subconscious stressors is very important as they can be as impactful as the conscious stresses that you know of and help manage your stress.

Self-reflection and introspection are crucial in unearthing hidden stressors. Reflect on your thoughts, feelings, and experiences by producing a journal, while keeping an eye out for repetitive patterns or themes. Another way of discovering hidden subconscious stressors is with the help of a therapist or counsellor.

Underlying causes of stress may vary widely from person to person but common culprits such as unresolved traumas, negative core beliefs, or unmet needs. By focusing on these root causes, you can make plans that will enable you to cope with stress proactively and achieve a life that is more balanced and fulfilling.

Developing Self-Reflection and Awareness for Stress Management

One must reflect upon themselves so that they can effectively manage their tension. When you practise mindfulness and self-awareness, you become aware of your stress triggers, responses, and develop better control over your emotional well-being.

You could also build self-reflection by spending some minutes every day checking up on yourself. You just need to sit quietly somewhere and try to concentrate on your breath while observing all the thoughts as well as emotions without being judgmental about them. This technique helps you recognize those things or situations that lead to stress in your life.

Mindfulness meditation also helps in creating self-consciousness, thereby improving moments of relaxation hence reducing anxiety. In this method, we are required to live at the present moment through observing our thoughts and emotions non-judgmentally. As a result of practising mindfulness in daily life, one may gain some control over his/her feelings/emotions due to stressful conditions.

Nonetheless developing self-reflection takes time as well as effort. Nonetheless, you can gain a deeper sense of self and effective stress management through the incorporation of these techniques into your daily routine.

Setting Priorities and Managing Time

In terms of managing stress, poor time management can be a major contributing factor. Boosting productivity and reducing the stress caused by overwhelming workloads can be achieved through prioritising your tasks and using efficient time management techniques.

One way to manage time is by identifying what really matters. Select the most important urgent tasks; they are the ones that you have to begin with. This will assist in staying on track, without feeling overwhelmed by an endless list of activities for the day.

Another alternative is using time management methods such as the Pomodoro technique, which entails short breaks that come after work intervals, or else using time blocks where you assign specific chunks of time for given tasks to enhance productivity.

In this regard, it should be known that effective time management does not only entail doing more things, but also taking breaks, having enough sleep and sustaining a good work-life balance. In prioritising your tasks and managing your time well, you can do more with less stress.

Developing Healthy Ways to Cope

It is essential to cultivate healthy coping mechanisms that could deal with your stress in a sustainable way. While there are many methods of stress reduction, selecting those that fulfil the specific needs and preferences will give you the highest chances of success. Consider these coping mechanisms:

Exercise

Physical activities reduce stress excellently since they release endorphins, boosting moods and calming down individuals. For instance, walking for exercise in the park or having a high-impact workout at the gym could significantly affect your stress levels.

Relaxation Techniques

Relaxation techniques like deep breathing exercises, meditation, and yoga can help you reach a serene state of mind. Find yourself a quiet place where you can take some time to focus on your breathing and clear your mind or join a yoga class with others who have similar feelings towards relieving themselves from stress.

Seek Support from Loved Ones

During times of stress, it can be helpful to have friends and family members available as a source of help. Share your emotions with persons you believe are reliable and get them involved when facing tough situations. The main idea is that they will be there for you.

You can effectively manage stress by incorporating healthy coping mechanisms into your daily routine and achieve greater inner peace.

Creating a Supportive Environment

Stress can have an enormous impact on every aspect of life; people either add to or mitigate this pressure. Social support and good relationships can reduce stress levels while improving one's well-being. This section will guide you on how to create a supportive network and develop positive relationships that enhance stress management.

Begin by identifying positive relationships in your life such as supportive friends or caring relatives. You may also opt to join social groups or volunteer in causes that are dear to your heart thereby broadening your social circle. Constructing relationships based on trustworthiness and respect promotes community spirit while supplying emotional assistance during trying times.

Also, it's essential for those around you to understand what you need. For example, talking about your stressors and feelings will enable your loved ones to better support you in the future. Moreover, do not forget to consult experts or even join group counselling sessions for more assistance.

Overall, creating a supportive environment involves prioritising relationships that contribute to your well-being, communicating effectively, and seeking out additional support when necessary. By surrounding yourself with positivity, you can reduce stress levels and improve your overall quality of life.

Setting Boundaries and Saying No

Are you a person who often finds herself overburdened by an excess of things to do and consequently suffers from chronic stress? In order to prioritise self-care and reduce stress, you need to learn how to set healthy boundaries and say no at the right time. Being assertive may seem strange initially, but it is vital for both your physical and mental health. Identify your limitations first, then communicate them clearly to others. Say no in a polite but firm manner on a few occasions as well as always be ready for compromise. There are many advantages that come with setting boundaries and adopting an assertive attitude: one is that it helps in gaining control over life hence reducing stress levels.

Problem-Solving and Positive Thinking

When stressed out, it can be difficult to maintain a positive attitude. Nevertheless, learning problem-solving techniques and cultivating optimistic thoughts can assist you in dealing with stress more effectively. You can cope with stressors more effectively through using problem-solving strategies which address each aspect step by step. This will help you feel less overwhelmed or out of control.

Moreover, by ways of thinking positively as well as maintaining hopeful expectations, individuals are able to develop resistance against pressure. By practising appreciation or looking at situations from different viewpoints, one can change their thoughts and emotions such that they become less stressful.

By having problem-solving techniques combined with positivity and optimism; we arm ourselves with power tools for stress management.

Seeking Professional Help

Coping with stress can be hard, especially if every day feels like no progress is being made. The services of therapists or counsellors could be sought for further assistance when necessary. Such professionals can guide you on how to go about dealing with your stressors as well as the reactions they induce in a supportive environment. They also have various specific tools customised for your situation which will assist you in managing your own personal type of stress.

In case one is not sure whether therapy or counselling will suit their needs, one can try talking to a primary care physician. They may also help you decide whether it is necessary to look for professional assistance or not. Besides, they can link you up with an experienced therapist or counsellor located near you.

Remember, there's no shame in seeking professional help. It takes courage to work on one's mental well-being, which is the reason why such people opt for professional therapy as a way of managing their stress.

Stress Management in Daily Life

Dealing with stress is not an event; rather, it demands everyday attention. It is imperative to include stress management techniques in your daily living for the sake of your mind and body. The following are some practical tips:

Practice Mindfulness

Set aside time in your day for mindfulness exercises such as deep breathing, meditation, or yoga. Even just a few minutes can make a big difference in your stress levels and overall well-being.

Exercise Regularly

Daily exercise helps reduce both physical and mental stress. Find a workout routine that you enjoy and do it every day.

Get Enough Sleep

Stress levels rise dramatically when one does not get enough sleep at night. Sleep about seven to eight hours each night so that you can be fresh during the day. Create a regular pattern of sleeping to enhance your sleep quality.

Spend Time with Loved Ones

Managing stress is vital; therefore, fostering positive relationships is essential. Take time out with loved ones, be it for a meal or stroll. This goes a long way in reducing stress levels to improve your overall well-being.

Set Realistic Goals

Setting goals that are realistic can aid in reducing stress that comes about because of workload pressure. Divide large tasks into smaller achievable objectives. In this way, you will feel like you are making progress and avoid getting burnt out.

Engage in Hobbies

For instance, reading, drawing, or playing any musical instrument can significantly bring down the levels of stress in someone's life, thus giving them a sense of having peace at heart.

By including stress relief practices as part of your daily routine, you can create a healthier and more balanced lifestyle for yourself by reducing how much stress affects you and improving your general health condition.

Celebrating Progress and Maintaining Self-Care

Congratulations on taking the first step towards managing your stress! In fact, celebrating progress is an important step that helps maintain motivation for achieving continuous success. Here, take time to recognize all your achievements regardless of their size and appreciate how well you have been able to manage your stressful situations.

To keep up this progress, it is essential to continue with regular self-care routines. You should dedicate some time each day for activities that make you happy, such as reading, having a bath, or spending time with loved ones.

The ongoing process of stress management also requires one to track their progress over time for effective stress management. Use journals or download tracking apps that help monitor one's level of tension so that patterns are identified and self-care strategies adjusted accordingly when necessary; remember though that self-care and managing stress need regular work too so don't let down the gains made thus far but be sensitive to what works best for you always.

Chapter 15

Physiological Effect of Breathwork and Incorporating Breath Focused Exercises Daily

Welcome to our exploration of the profound impact of breathwork on your everyday life. Discover how simple breathing exercises can bring about significant benefits for both your body and mind. These techniques, though easy, wield remarkable power in regulating stress, enhancing mood and energy, and fostering a sense of balance. By incorporating breathwork into your daily routine, you can experience a multitude of positive effects.

Let's delve into the ways breathwork transforms your health. It goes beyond the simple act of inhaling and exhaling, offering holistic improvements. We'll explore its positive impact on the respiratory system, athletic performance, emotional well-being, and mental health. Additionally, we'll provide practical advice on seamlessly integrating breathwork into your daily life.

How Breathwork Affects Your Health

Breathwork is more than a routine; it's a method to elevate your health. By making it a part of your daily practice, you can increase lung capacity, improve oxygenation, and optimise your overall respiratory health. These techniques trigger a relaxation response, leading to reduced anxiety and stress levels, fostering a profound sense of relaxation. Moreover, breathwork enhances physical performance during exercise, contributing to increased energy levels, focus, and vitality.

The Physiology of Breathwork

Understanding how breath affects your body is crucial. Breath-focused exercises induce physiological changes, influencing heart rate, blood pressure, and stress response. Practising breathwork, such as pranayama, calms the nervous system and decreases the production of stress hormones, promoting mental and physical well-being. Specific breathing techniques improve lung capacity, increase oxygenation, and optimise respiratory health, creating a more balanced approach to overall well-being.

Respiratory System and Breathwork

The respiratory system plays a central role in breathwork. Specific exercises optimise lung capacity, enhance oxygenation, and refine general breathing patterns. Deep, full inhalations, reaching the lower parts of the lungs, facilitate efficient gas exchange, improving oxygen supply to cells and promoting overall well-being.

Breathwork's Effect on the Nervous System

Breathwork extends beyond physical benefits, impacting the nervous system. Breathing habits influence body and mind states significantly. Specific techniques regulate the autonomic nervous system, controlling involuntary functions like heart rate and digestion. Slowing down your breath signals safety to the brain, reducing stress levels and anxiety. Regular practice can reshape the brain's structure, fostering emotional regulation and resilience.

Breathing and Mental Well-being

Breathwork deeply influences emotional well-being. Regular incorporation of breath-focused exercises stabilises emotions, enhances cognitive abilities, and contributes to better mental health. These practices, by inducing a relaxation response, alleviate symptoms of anxiety, depression, and stress. By making mindful breathing a part of your daily routine, you can experience a positive shift in mental and emotional stability.

Breathwork For Exercise Performance

In the realm of exercise, correct breathing patterns significantly impact performance. Incorporating breathwork into workouts improves training duration, outcomes, and overall physical performance. Focused breathing techniques help manage heart rate and oxygen intake, minimising muscle fatigue. Pre-workout routines integrating breathing exercises prepare the body, enhance efficiency, and provide mental focus, leading to better overall exercise sessions.

Integrate Breath-centred Exercises into Your Daily Routine

Your daily routines provide windows of opportunity to incorporate breath-focused exercises. Elevate mindfulness, reduce stress, and foster relaxation by dedicating a few minutes each day to focus on your breathing. Whether during a quiet moment, a walk, or a workout, mindful breathing enhances overall well-being. Explore guided meditations or breathing apps for convenient and tailored exercises to fit your needs.

How to Reduce Stress with Breathing Techniques

Mastering relaxation through breath is a powerful stress-reduction strategy. Techniques like deep breathing, 4-7-8 breathing, and alternate nostril breathing activate the relaxation response, lowering heart rate and reducing blood pressure. Integrating these techniques into your daily routine can significantly decrease stress levels, promoting a sense of calm and overall well-being.

Unlocking Energy and Vitality Through Breathwork

When feeling fatigued, breathwork exercises offer a natural energy boost. Specific breath-focused exercises enhance oxygen delivery to cells, keeping you alert throughout the day. Breathwork aligns with your goals, fostering mental alertness, inner peace, and improved focus, even amidst challenges or distractions. By incorporating breath-focused practices into your daily routine, you can experience heightened energy, quicker recovery, and more satisfying exercise sessions.

Emotional Health and Self-healing with Breathwork

Emotional health is pivotal for overall well-being. Breathwork serves as a potent tool for releasing emotional blocks, promoting self-awareness, and initiating healing. Controlled breathing, focusing on the present moment, aids in easing a restless heart and calming a racing mind. Regular practice enhances emotional well-being, fostering self-awareness, and initiating a journey towards self-healing.

Integrating Breathwork into Your Mindfulness Practice

Blend breathwork seamlessly into mindfulness practices to amplify their effectiveness. Select a quiet, comfortable space, close your eyes, and focus on your breath. Explore different breathing methods during meditation to deepen your practice and enhance mindfulness. During meditation, observe how your breath connects with your body, thoughts, and feelings, fostering presence and inner sensations.

Conclusion: Choosing Breathwork for Total Health

You now comprehend the profound impact of breathwork on your body and mind. Take the step to incorporate mindful breathing into your daily life for better physical health, mental clarity, and a balanced life. Breathwork serves as a stress buster, relaxer, and energy booster. By practising various breathing techniques, you initiate your body's natural healing process, contributing to complete wellness. Begin by being mindful of your breath, especially during waking moments or stressful periods. With consistent practice, you'll gain insight into the effects of breath on your body and mind, realising that mastering breathing is a continuous journey towards optimal health. Breathe deeply, sit right, and embrace the broad impact of proper breathing on your overall well-being.

Chapter 16

Maximise Productivity with Effective Time Management: Evaluating Routines, Setting Goals, and Harnessing Proven Strategies

****

Welcome- to our time management spot. We-'re looking at ways to adjust your daily habits to up your game. Time we'll-arrange matters. It helps comple-te tasks and it paves the path to succe-ss. Often, what sets apart successful folks from ones struggling with deadlines and goals is good time use-.

With this topic, we'll chat about pinpointing wasted time, se-tting SMART targets, and ranking tasks. Plus, let's uncover mode-rn tools and strategies to smooth out your workload and boost output. Our target? Supporting your succe-ss in life, while balancing job and personal life-.

Stay with us to reveal methods for sharpe-ning your time use skills. That helps you be-come more efficie-nt each day. Open up to expe-rt tips on tweaking your work schedule and managing your daily tasks.

Time- Use: The Base for Pe-rsonal Growth

Good time use leads to pe-rsonal growth and success. In our fast-paced world, eve-ry tick-tock matters. Using time well aids se-lf-improvement by adding value and giving us the- chance to make eve-ry moment count.

Organising your time well is ke-y for managing work tasks and personal life. Moreove-r, it makes room for self-enhance-ment, learning new skills, or e-ngaging in important self-care activities. A sound time- plan forms the ideal structure for e-ffective resource- allocation.

Good time manage-ment is key for caree-r success. It's important for workers who want to provide quick, impactful solutions for vital busine-ss issues. At work, time is the gre-atest resource. The- better you can control it, the highe-r your worth. Plus, handling time well leads to job advance-ment.

In short, personal growth nee-ds strong time management. Build your strate-gies, review how you use- your time, and implement he-lpful changes to improve yourself. This le-ads to a balanced work-life, peak pe-rformance, and more productivity. Your journey to pe-rsonal growth starts with disciplined time planning and goals.

Evaluating Your Usual Activities: Finding Time- Bandits

Reviewing your usual activities is crucial for be-tter time manageme-nt. Watch for activities that eat up a lot of your time but yie-ld little benefit. The-se activities, or 'time bandits,' may be- too much social media scrolling or frequently che-cking emails.

Spotting your unique "time wasters" needs self-aware-ness and deep-thinking skills. Doe-s this duty support my goals or just distract me? Keep track of what you do e-ach day by assessing your daily schedule.

While- it's tough to ditch low-value tasks requiring less time-, doing so significantly improves time use. Once- you spot these activities, take- steps to prevent the-m in the future. Limit your social media use-, set browsing times, schedule- email checks, prioritise tasks base-d on importance, amongst others (Bryson & Farrar, 2012). These- changes will save precious mome-nts, boost focus, and improve productivity.

Time Manage-ment and SMART Goals

Time manageme-nt thrives on effective- goal setting. However, goals are-n't identical. That's why SMART goals matter for bette-r productivity.

The SMART acronym means Specific, Measurable, Achievable, Re levant, and Time-bound.

Specific goals ide-ntify the why and what of tasks. Measurable one-s set up clear progress marke-rs. Achievable goals match your resource-s. Relevant targets align with your large-r aim or vision. Time-bound goals have set de-adlines.

SMART goal setting helps filte-r priority tasks and the time nee-ded to complete the-m. Continuously reevaluate these aims, especially if situations change-.

SMART goals enhance time manage-ment capacity, streamlining the goal-achie-vement journey.

The- Eisenhower Matrix: Sorting Tasks

Oftentime-s, tasks can pile up like a mountain. This is where- prioritisation comes in, using something like the- Eisenhower matrix.

This matrix distributes tasks into four cate-gories based on urgency and importance-: Urgent and Important; Important but not Urgent; Urgent but not Important; Ne-ither Urgent nor Important.

If an unexpe-cted issue arises, focus on urge-nt/important tasks. Also, remember to prioritise the important/not urgent tasks. Delete the urgent/not important to-dos, and ignore- the ones in the non-urge-nt and non-important areas.

This tool can help you side step the needle and urgent chores. Take a bit of time- to sort duties based on urgency and importance-, then put this tool to good use.

Beating De-lay: Action Plans

Delay can hinder good time control, but e-ffective tactics can help win. To dodge- feeling overloade-d and stay driven, break down complex chores into smaller bits. Give yourself de-adlines and own up to your tasks.

Crush self-doubt and wrong ideas that fue-l delays. Spot these imaginary roadblocks that stymie- needed action and turn the-m into positive tweaks.

Boost output by setting a daily sche-dule of enjoyable tasks, including a pe-rky morning routine. Make sure to ge-t enough sleep, re-gular exercise, and he-althy food to boost focus and dedication.

These te-chniques assist you in beating delays, e-nhancing productivity, and managing time well.

Improving Focus and Immersion: Consciousne-ss and Intense Effort

Do you grapple to ke-ep focus, especially with boring or comple-x tasks? Boosted concentration aids in making good use of time-. This can be improved by staying conscious or dee-ply interacting with your work.

In consciousness, you stay in the now without any diversions or negative thoughts. Intense-drive, on the other hand, re-quires hard work over a longer pe-riod. Developing both these-skills increases focus, resulting in be-tter output.

Make time- every day for mindfulness. Try meditation for focus exercises. This he-lps you concentrate bette-r. At work, try to limit distractions. This helps you focus more.

Schedule- some quiet time for big tasks. Conce-ntrate on one thing at a time. For hard jobs, use- a timer. Try to go longer each time-. It becomes easie-r with practice.

With these me-thods, you'll see improveme-nts. You'll be able to focus and get more- done. Manage your time we-ll. Stay organised. Learn how to use tools and syste-ms to be more productive.

The- "Getting Things Done" method he-lps. It helps you decide what to do first. You'll focus on urge-nt and important tasks.

There are handy online- tools, too. Try Trello, Asana, or Todoist . They help you ke-ep track of your work. Categorise tasks by how important the-y are, their due date-, and who will do them.

Rescue Time- and Toggl are good for tracking how you spend time. Use- them to find out where you ne-ed to get bette-r. Use what you learn to decide- how to use time best.

You can perfe-ct time management by adopting the- right tools and systems for better workflow.

Powe-r of Delegation and Outsourcing

To enhance- your time management, you ne-ed to learn about dele-gating and outsourcing jobs. By assigning less important jobs to qualified people- or employing specialised se-rvices, you save time and boost quality.

Whe-n you delegate, pair tasks with pe-ople who have the right e-xperience and skills. Provide- easy, clear instructions about what to do, what you expe-ct, and when it's due. Maintain open communication for proje-ct success.

Reducing risks means lower workload. Lean on expertise- from other companies so you're not ove-rloaded and can focus on strategic goals. This way, you get to use- other people's te-chnologies and processes without he-avy investment.

Dele-gation and outsourcing control workload well. By trusting others' expe-rtise, you have more time- for crucial tasks. This increases productivity, leading to e-fficient time manageme-nt.

Fighting Distractions: How to Deal with Interruptions

Distractions can make e-ffective time manage-ment difficult. Use appropriate me-thods to manage interruptions.

Avoid reacting imme-diately to each email or me-ssage. Set specific time-s for these tasks. Limit contacts with colleague-s, friends, and family to only need hours.

Use te-ch tools like browser add-ons or smartphone apps to block non-work-re-lated sites at certain time-s.

These methods can manage- distractions, letting you focus on the job. They he-lp work more productively.

Building a Productive Workspace-: Tips

Your workspace affects your time manage-ment. Keep your are-a tidy and free from disruptions. This way, your focus remains intact. No clutte-r r. No disturbances.

Decorate your space- with positive items like photos or house plants. Make sure you've got good lighting and comfortable- seating.

Improve your work output by deve-loping beneficial habits. Plan your daily tasks, fix your priorities, take- brief breaks to rest and re-fresh.

Use convenie-nt tech tools such as apps for timing or software for project manage-ment.

Overall, a pleasant workspace- enhances time-efficiency habits.

Managing Time and Grouping Tasks: Steps to Improve- Efficiency

Struggling to concentrate? Fre-quently switching from one task to another? Try time- blocking and task batching. They can boost efficiency.

Time- blocking is reserving exclusive- time periods for tasks, free- of interruptions. This is important for controlling emails, attending gathe-rings, and handling multiple projects.

Task batching means grouping similar tasks within a time- frame, reducing task-switching. It saves time-. Allocate time batches for various jobs. Like- setting apart time for emails, or for phone- calls.

Try different routines or task groups to find a suitable- schedule. Being more- efficient helps in achie-ving goals and improving productivity.

Overcoming Time- Management Obstacles: Effe-ctive Strategies

Se-veral barriers hinder good time- management. Poor focus leads to me-diocre outcomes, while procrastination slows progre-ss. Luckily, there are succe-ssful ways to deal with these proble-ms.

Knowing why meeting deadline-s is tough aids in identifying obstacles. Create- a tailor-made plan to confront these spe-cific roadblocks.

Rank tasks according to their relevance- and establish doable targets. Utilise SMART goals to break the workload into digestible- parts.

Organise your workplace in a manner that aids in controlling time- by reducing distractions. Plan the space to maximise efficiency.

Stay disciplined and mindful to ove-rcome time manageme-nt difficulties. Acquire new abilitie-s that can improve your concentration and time manage-ment.

Evaluate and Enhance Your Time- Management Technique-s

Good time management is a constant proce-ss. Regular reviews and adjustme-nts are necessary. It is, the-refore, important to regularly e-valuate time manageme-nt strategies to validate the-ir effectivene-ss in achieving goals.

Examine existing habits, spot time--wasting pitfalls, and evaluate productivity concerning goal attainment nt. Experiment with various work efficie-ncy tactics or try some organisation tools.

Discover the most suitable- methods for you through experime-ntation. Always aim to upgrade your time manageme-nt abilities.

Consistently revie-w and optimally use your time to hit your goals effe-ctively.

Signing Off

Well-done- on completing this guide to managing time! Che-cking your routines regularly can advance pe-rsonal development. Applying te-sted tactics can heighten your output.

Remember, sound time manage-ment needs ongoing adjustment. Create SMART goals, sort appropriately, and avoid postponements. Re--gain control over your day and operate e-fficiently.

Periodically assess your strate-gies for managing time for increase-d productivity and triumphant living.

We value your time, our hope- is this guide has provided useful sugge-stions to better control your timetable-.

Chapter 17

The Costs of Multitasking
and Strategies for Single Tasking

****

If you believe you are a multitasker, think again. Multitasking can look like an efficient way to handle multiple tasks at once but it has hidden costs which might have negative impacts on your productivity and well-being.

Studies have consistently demonstrated that multitasking decreases output, increases errors, and is a big source of stress. The attempt to engage in more than one activity simultaneously leads to inefficiency and greater chances of making mistakes. For instance, according to the findings of the recent research work, multitasking could result in reduced productivity by 40 percent.

On the contrary, single-tasking, or focusing on one task at a time, has been proven to enhance concentration and boost productivity. If you pay full attention to a single task, you will be able to work faster and more efficiently.

This chapter will discuss why multitasking is disadvantageous as well as the benefits of performing tasks sequentially and how this can be achieved by focusing on one task at a time. These measures can help avoid switching between jobs and increase overall achievement.

What is Multitasking?

Multitasking refers to an act of doing many different activities or tasks at the same time. This practice is common in today's fast-moving world where people try coping with numerous responsibilities within limited periods. Examples of this behaviour include talking on the phone while cooking or taking notes during meetings while participating actively in discussions.

The attraction behind multitasking is that we tend to feel that we can do so much more within such little time. However evidence indicates that it could actually be harmful for our health and may hinder productivity. This results from doing several things at once thereby causing our minds to keep swaying between different job demands thus affecting mental aspects negatively including mental health.

"Multitasking is like constantly changing gears in a car—it can be exhausting and take its toll on our cognitive abilities. When we attempt to concentrate on several tasks at once, our attention gets divided so that ultimately our concentration is reduced and errors tend to be more likely."

Despite the drawbacks of multitasking, it also comes with its own fair share of benefits. By doing many things at the same time, people are able to save lots of time. For example, working out while listening to educational videos can be very productive. Also, in appropriate circumstances multitasking might improve productivity by enabling individuals to switch quickly between tasks accomplishing more in a shorter span.

Shortcomings of Multi-Tasking

However, there are as many cons as pros for multi-tasking. One of the major disadvantages is reduced efficiency in total. This results from trying to do too much all at once since one cannot focus completely on a number of activities leading to mistakes and low productivity (it is known that multitasking may slash productivity by about 40%).

Another problem with multitasking is that it increases stress levels and decreases productivity. Concurrently focusing on several issues can create high stress levels thereby interfering with their individual effectiveness leading to substandard performance.

Additionally, multitasking leads to more errors being made. The mind is strained when it is divided among different activities making chances of errors or omissions higher which can be dangerous in fields like healthcare or finance where accuracy and precision are extremely important.

In conclusion, what initially appears as an efficient way of handling multiple tasks turns out to have significant downsides. It reduces the amount of work done, causes more mistakes and subjects people involved into additional pressure. Thus understanding the demerits associated with multitasking is essential in improving one's concentration and efficiency by embracing methods that support single-tasking.

Breaking the Trend of Multitasking

There are several ways through which one can stop multitasking and learn how to focus better and thus improve productivity.

One strategy involves ordering tasks according to priority and completing them one at a time before moving on to the next task. Clear goals set with defined time limits for each task help maintain concentration and discourage performing several duties at a go.

"Through this, one can concentrate all his energy in accomplishing a particular task to the best of his ability."

Moreover, getting rid of interruptions is important when you want to curb multitasking. This might include turning off phone notifications, muting unimportant group chats or closing irrelevant computer tabs.

"It helps to eliminate all distractions around that makes it possible for me to focus more on a single task."

It is hard to break the habit of multitasking and it involves starting small and making gradual progress. Single-tasking is a skill that requires commitment and practice until one achieves increased productivity and longer attention spans.

Time Management Techniques

Breaking the habit of multitasking requires proper time management skills for increased productivity. Time-tested techniques ensure concentration improvement and effective use of time.

The Pomodoro Technique

The Pomodoro Technique is a well-known time management method that focuses on brief periods of intense work interrupted by short breaks. This technique allows one's concentration to be maintained without leading him or her into the trap of multitasking. Set an alarm for 25 minutes (a "pomodoro") which is customary duration and dedicate this session solely to one activity. Take a short break about five minutes long just after every pomodoro before starting another one while spending between fifteen to thirty minutes resting upon completion of four pomodoros. Dividing work into smaller units has been found to enhance focus as well as improve productivity.

Time Blocking

Another efficient approach to time management is time blocking, whereby certain blocks of time are assigned to different activities or tasks. Using a structured timetable that has dedicated time slots for each activity ensures that only one task is done at any given moment. Identify important assignments and allocate specific periods of time that will block out interruptions during which you can focus on the task at hand.

Time management skills like Pomodoro Technique and Time Blocking help fight against multitasking tendencies; they enable one to stay focused and concentrated on each separate assignment.

Mindfulness and Meditation

To improve focus on critical tasks while avoiding multitasking, people should practise mindfulness and meditation. By making these practices part of their everyday routines, individuals train their minds to be present in every task they undertake.

"Awareness is very vital if you are interested in getting the most out of your life by being fully awake in the now."

Mindfulness fosters intense concentration through focusing one's attention on the present moment, avoiding distractions and internal chatter associated with multitasking.

Breathing Exercises

Incorporating mindfulness into everyday life includes simple breathing exercises. Close your eyes for a few minutes, take a deep breath in, and slowly exhale. Focus on feeling air pass into your body as it goes out in order to control your mind, alleviate anxiety, tension, and improve concentration.

Guided Meditations

"Guided meditation assists the brain in being still and uncluttered therefore becoming calm."

Guided meditation sessions often consist of audio recordings directing individuals through relaxations or visualisations that can greatly enhance long-term attention span without any interruptions.

The Power of a Mindful Pause

"If you take a mindful pause it will help you focus again and refresh your mental energy."

Adding mindful pauses between tasks allows for integrating mindfulness into daily life. When moving from one task to another take a momentary break, breathe deeply several times letting go of thoughts about previous activities and concentrate on the upcoming task only. These short breaks help to improve focus and productivity.

By including mindfulness and meditation in their everyday lives, people can overcome multitasking habits and concentrate more on single-tasking. They not only enhance attention but also promote overall wellness by reducing stress levels, leading to a clear mind when working on an assignment.

Setting Realistic Expectations

The desire to accomplish multiple tasks within a limited time frame often leads to multitasking. This may cause overloading and decrease productivity.

"To prevent multitasking, you should set reasonable expectations about what you can achieve within a specific period."

Instead of creating long lists of tasks, identify some few urgent ones requiring your undivided focus. On their part, this reduces anxiety hence better results are achieved if those responsible focus on high-priority assignments.

"Better results can be achieved through concentrating on only a few high priority tasks while ignoring all else; ultimately reducing stress."

If overwhelmed, one is allowed to avoid additional duties or negotiate changes in deadlines. Communicate job scopes and necessary arrangements with colleagues or superiors for effective delivery. Realistic expectations as well as avoidance of burnout bring about more focused approaches that result in increased output and better overall outcomes.

Creating a Distraction-Free Environment

Distractions must be eliminated for a productive and focused work environment. Single-tasking ability is improved, and productivity increases when a distraction free environment is set up. Ways of eliminating distractions include:

Disable Notifications

"Notifications can cause big disruptions and take your focus away." Keep your phone off or put it in silent mode during working hours. It helps to avoid constant disruption from messages, emails or social media.

Shut Down Unwanted Tabs and Apps "Multiple open tabs and apps can blur thoughts and reduce concentration."

To avoid both visual and mental intrusions, close any unnecessary tabs or applications running on your computer. This will ensure that your focus remains only the tools relevant to the current task.

Choose a Quiet Place

"Silence in an office helps one stay concentrated."

If it is feasible, find a quiet place where you will not be disturbed while working. This might be an office within home premises, library room or secluded section within a coffee shop. Reducing noise levels and interruptions creates conducive conditions for deep work.

Set Clear Boundaries

"One needs clear communication with colleagues as well as family members to minimise interruptions."

Inform colleagues, family members about dedicated work time. Make it known when you cannot be reached because of your job's demands. This reduces interruptions thereby maintaining workflow by putting clear boundaries.

"A distraction free environment promotes clarity, focus and productivity."

Creating an environment that fosters single tasking while mitigating distractions improves concentration as well as productivity. Switching off notifications; closing unwanted tabs; finding solitude; or setting limits are some of the actions which contribute towards establishing an atmosphere enabling people to do things one after another.

Practising Self-Care

Taking care of oneself is important in maintaining focus and productivity. Self-care activities also make it possible for people to better engage in single-tasking. By prioritising self-care we allow ourselves to recharge so we may approach tasks with renewed focus and clarity.

Sleeping well is a crucial part of self-care. It improves cognitive function, concentration, and refreshes both body and mind. Developing a regular sleep pattern and creating an environment conducive to sleep are vital for quality rest.

Regular exercise is another way of taking care of oneself that helps in managing stress and improving mental clarity. Participating in enjoyable physical activities, whether it's walking, yoga or going to the gym, leads to the release of endorphins which improve mood and boost energy levels.

Stress management techniques are important. Mindfulness meditation, deep breathing exercises and journaling are all effective stress reduction methods that increase focus too. Taking regular breaks during the day helps to prevent burnout and improve productivity.

"Self-care is not selfish. You cannot serve from an empty vessel."

The integration of self-care activities into daily life effectively manages stress thus creating an environment suitable for single-tasking. One should be reminded on how self-care is not luxury but necessity for wellbeing as well as professional success.

Building Resilience and Flexibility

Resilience and flexibility underpinning ability to single-task are important in overcoming challenges that come with this practice. Accept that you will sometimes fail but do not let failure discourage you. Instead, view failures as learning experiences that guide you on what to avoid next time or how else you can improve yourself if faced with similar situations again Consequently, having a growth mindset which always focuses more on learning than anything else inclusive of adaptability is key.

Looking for Support and Accountability

Beginning the process of single-tasking can be tough, but having a social network that supports your efforts will make it easier. Let colleagues, friends or family members who appreciate enhanced attention during tasks know what you are trying to achieve. These supports will keep you motivated.

"This is also significant because someone who holds you responsible for your actions and encourages you will be essential." "Having someone cheering you up or monitoring your progress makes it easier to stay dedicated to your single-tasking goals".

It is extremely motivating to have someone who understands where you are coming from and can provide encouragement during difficult times or setbacks. Additionally, the use of productivity tools can assist in this regard: for instance, Toggl, a time tracking app helps in staying organised by focusing on one task at a time while Todoist is similar task management software used for this purpose. These tools help assess work progress thus cultivating self-control as well as maintaining attention on single-tasking objectives.

Chapter 18

A Decluttering Guide to Transform
Your Physical and Digital Spaces

Let's dive into a comprehensive section about decluttering. It offers advice for managing both your tangible and online spaces. We live in a fast-paced world where we accumulate things that can hinder productivity and focus. By organising and eliminating clutter, you can create a space that's conducive to thinking.

This segment guides you on tidying up your physical space and reducing online distractions. Our specialist tips and methods for tidying up real-life mess or simplifying your online presence will enable you to regain control and experience peace and productivity.

We'll share practical suggestions, motivational accounts, and priceless wisdom from decluttering experts as we navigate this declutter journey. Our manual consists of helpful details from organising personal items to managing digital files, enabling you to live a clutter-free life.

Get ready. This process involves discarding unnecessary items from your homes, computers, and phones before beginning an organised lifestyle.

The Power of Decluttering Your Physical Space

Keeping mentally sound can be tough when our living areas are overstuffed. A disordered environment creates huge stress. By discarding physical clutter, we pave the way for a quieter and more orderly lifestyle.

Peaceful Spaces Made Easy

The chaos of stuff spread everywhere can ruin our calm. Searching for items amongst cluttered mess can be irksome, resulting in feelings of inefficiency. Decluttering can make our surroundings clear and serene.

Increasing Productivity

A messy room can distract us, reducing our ability to focus. This affects our productivity. But a tidy space highlights concentration, helping us work without interruption.

Steps to Declutter

Decluttering can seem tough, but the right techniques make it simple and satisfying. Begin with dividing the room into smaller sectors, focusing on one at a time. Sort each item – keep, donate, or discard. Their utility or sentimental worth can be your deciding factor.

While decluttering, keep in mind that not all things need to go. The true goal is to create a space that brings joy first.

Why You Should Declutter

Decluttering does more than tidy up your home. It cleans your mind, too. When you clear away clutter, your stress can go down. A clean and organised place is a peaceful place.

How to Tidy Your Digital World

In today's world, we're overloaded with digital content. Email floods in. Random documents and files scatter across our devices. This mess can distract us. But don't worry! There are ways to tidy up your digital space.

1. Start with a Digital Cleanse: Like a physical cleanse, a digital one can be equally refreshing. Review your digital devices. Delete unneeded apps. Remove old photos and files. This will declutter your virtual space, giving you a fresh start.
2. Sort and Arrange: Keeping your digital space neat means sorting and arranging files. Make folders and subfolders for your different needs. Use helpful names. This way, you can find any file quickly.
3. Smarten Your Digital Process: Examine your digital routine. Find places where you can make tasks simpler or automate them. Use tools like project management software or email filters. These can help you manage your time and resources better. "A tidy digital world sparks imagination and concentration, leading to more efficiency and peace." - Tech Guru.
4. Mute Notifications: Nonstop alerts cause digital disturbance. By adjusting notifications only important warnings get through while reducing interruptions, this keeps you focused on the task at hand.
5. Regular Digital Clean-Ups: Digital mess builds up over time, just like physical mess. Schedule regular clean-ups where you examine your files, emails, bookmarks and decide to remove them or organise them properly. This ensures a tidy and systematic digital space.

By using these tips, you'll deal with information overload efficiently and reclaim your digital space. In a busy world, a tidy digital space is soothing and boosts efficiency.

Organizing Physical and Digital Stuff

Whether it's for your home or your online space, being organised is the secret to a clean environment. It helps find what you need quickly and prevents wasting time, improving efficiency. This part will cover different ways of making an organisation system that suits you, via categorization, labelling, and various storage solutions.

An organised space is similar to a smooth running mechanism - everything in its place, enabling you to move effortlessly through your belongings and digital files.

Sorting physical items is a must. First, assess what you have. Then, decide on logical groups. For instance, divide clothes by season, books by types, and kitchen stuff by use. This makes your system neat and swift.

Once you finish arranging, remember to mark. Use simple words or phrases to label boxes, shelves, or folders. This way, you can find things quickly without digging around. Handwritten tags or printed ones work well, as long as they're visible.

But, sorting the physical world isn't enough. Your digital zone needs it too!

Begin by cleaning up your digital files. Take out any redundant documents, create logical file groups, and set up folders that work for you. Like in your physical space, order in a digital one is key too.

When your digital items are tidy, label them. Use a naming system that helps you identify each file's content. Remember the power of tags or metadata for easy searching. Clear labels make it a breeze to find what you need when you need it.

Keeping stuff in order, both things you can touch and things on your computer, is super important. Think about getting boxes, shelves, and cabinets for your things that you can see and touch. Group the similar items together in baskets or partitions so you won't mix them up.

When it comes to stuff on your computer, think about using the cloud or an external hard drive. This way, you free up space on your devices. Quick tip: there's software and apps that let you sync your files across devices. Having your files stored safely and backed up makes you worry less.

Keeping things tidy, labelling them, and using smart storing methods help you stay organised. This will make your space, both physical and digital, less messy and more useful.

Next Level Your Digital Life: Email and Social Media

Our lives now revolve around tech more than ever before thanks to rapid advancements. We use our digital devices, especially email and social media, a lot every day. The downside? Constant notifications, emails, and social media updates can be too much and make you feel stressed. To take back control of your digital life, you need to manage your emails better, take breaks from social media, and limit how much you use digital stuff.

Handling Your Emails

Emails play a big role in our online chats. But when not managed right, they can eat up our time and focus. Using good email tactics can aid in keeping your inbox clean and boost your work rate. Some of these are:

Keep a check on your inbox only at certain times in the day. No need to be constantly peeking. Cancel subscriptions to unwanted or excess newsletters or marketing emails that fill your inbox. Build folders or labels to sort and rank emails for easy check back. Use tools and rules to directly sort incoming emails into the right folders."

Doing this helps you stay on top of your emails and stops crucial messages from getting lost among the hundreds.

Taking a Break from Social Media

Social media changed the way we talk, band together and share info. However, overuse of these sites can hamper our work and raise stress. That's where a planned break from social media can help get back your time and calm your mind. Here are some helpful tips:

Fix daily or weekly limits for your social media time. Use apps that set limits on social media apps or track your use. Turn off non-vital notifications so you aren't urged to look at your accounts constantly. Set 'phone-free' times, particularly in the morning and before bedtime. Social media tends to grab all your free time. Using it with a time limit stops this."

These tips make sure you manage your time and digital engagement better. Taking a break from social media and managing your emails helps keep you focused and keeps digital overwhelm at bay.

Securing Your Digital World

In a world loaded with tech, securing your digital space is crucial. You have personal details, documents, and maybe even some financial info stored online. Protecting it should be high on your list. Whether it's your computer, smartphone, or online accounts, these steps help boost your digital safety:

Using Strong Passwords: Strong passwords are key to secure your accounts. They should be hard for others to guess. Using a mix of letters, numbers, and symbols is a good practice. Also, don't use the same password for different accounts.

Activating Two-Factor Authentication (2FA): This adds a second step to your logins. Alongside your password, you need a code that's sent to your phone. Even if someone guesses your password, they won't get in without this code.

Updating Regularly: Always update your software and apps. Developers release updates with improved safety features. So, keeping everything up-to-date helps prevent hackers from taking advantage of any security flaws.

Being Careful with Emails: Be wary of suspicious emails. Don't click on links or download attachments from unknown sources. Scammers often use email to try and get your personal info.

Backing Up Regularly: Regular backups ensure you don't lose your data if your device crashes or gets stolen. Cloud services or external hard drives are good options for backup.

Using a Reliable Antivirus Program: A strong antivirus program protects your device from viruses, malware, and other online threats. Keep it updated for the best defence.

Being Smart with Social Media: Be mindful of what you share on social media. Adjust your privacy settings to control who sees your information. Avoid sharing sensitive details like your home address or phone number.

Practising Safe Online Shopping: When shopping online, use secure websites. Look for "https://" in the URL and a padlock icon. Avoid saving your card details on websites, and regularly check your bank statements for any unauthorised transactions.

Being careful and taking these safety measures keeps your digital world secure. Just like you lock your front door to keep your home safe, you should lock your digital doors too.

Journey to Minimalism

Minimalism is about having less to create room for more. It's a lifestyle that promotes intentionality, ensuring everything in your life serves a purpose. Decluttering is a crucial step towards minimalism. By simplifying, you free yourself from excess and focus on what truly matters.

Start Small

Begin your journey to minimalism by decluttering one area at a time. It can be a room, a closet, or even a single drawer. By starting small, you avoid feeling overwhelmed. The key is progress, not perfection.

Ask the Right Questions

When deciding what to keep or discard, ask yourself if the item brings you joy or serves a practical purpose. If the answer is no, it might be time to let it go. Minimalism is about surrounding yourself with things that add value to your life.

Embrace the Digital

In a digital age, many physical items can be replaced by their digital counterparts. Consider digitising documents, photos, and other items to reduce physical clutter. Digital minimalism involves decluttering your digital space as well.

Quality Over Quantity

Focus on quality over quantity. Invest in items that are durable, versatile, and truly bring you joy. This applies to both physical possessions and digital content. A curated collection of meaningful items is more valuable than a cluttered abundance.

Mindful Consumption

Practise mindful consumption by being intentional about what you bring into your life. Before making a purchase, consider whether the item aligns with your values and adds genuine value. Avoid impulsive buying and focus on mindful choices.

Capsule Wardrobe

Consider creating a capsule wardrobe, a collection of essential and versatile clothing items that can be mixed and matched. This reduces the need for a large and varied wardrobe, simplifying your daily choices.

Digital Detox

Schedule regular digital detox periods where you disconnect from electronic devices. Use this time to engage in activities that bring you joy, foster connections, and promote mental well-being.

Declutter Your Schedule

Minimalism extends beyond physical possessions. Evaluate your commitments, activities, and relationships. Simplify your schedule by focusing on what truly matters and brings fulfilment.

Gratitude Practice

Embrace gratitude as a core element of minimalism. Appreciate the value of what you have rather than focusing on what you lack. A gratitude practice fosters contentment and reduces the desire for excess.

Mindful Decluttering

Decluttering is not a one-time task; it's a continuous process. Adopt a mindful approach by regularly reassessing your surroundings and letting go of anything that no longer aligns with your values or goals.

Minimalism is a personal journey, and there is no one-size-fits-all approach. Find what works for you and aligns with your vision of a purposeful and intentional life.

In Conclusion

Embarking on a decluttering journey for both your physical and digital spaces is a transformative and empowering experience. It goes beyond creating tidy environments; it's about fostering mental clarity, improving focus, and reclaiming control over your surroundings.

As you navigate the process, remember that decluttering is not a destination but a continuous journey. Embrace the principles of minimalism, be intentional in your choices, and cultivate a lifestyle that aligns with your values and brings you joy.

By decluttering and organising your physical and digital realms, you create spaces that nurture creativity, enhance productivity, and promote overall well-being. Take the first step, and enjoy the transformative effects of a clutter-free life.

Chapter 19

Unlocking Efficiency and Productivity: Automation and Delegation in the Modern Workplace

****

Welcome to the nineteenth chapter. In this chapter, we shall explore the power of automation through technology and how your team members' strengths can be leveraged through delegation. With effective automation and delegation, one is able to unlock efficient workflows that will drive productivity to new heights.

Automation is transforming our work in ways never imagined before by helping us streamline repetitive and time-consuming tasks. We can use technology to automate these tasks hence freeing up valuable time and resources for more meaningful or strategic work. Automation enables efficiency as it relates to entering data, generating reports and offering customer support services among others.

However, automation does not mean people are replaced; it involves using technology to magnify human potential. This is where delegation comes in. Through making good use of their employees' strengths, managers can allocate duties ensuring that each person does what he/she does best. This increases motivation levels as well as engagement while creating a sense of satisfaction.

So come with us as we explore the methods of finding such tasks that can be automated using technology and how one can tap into the full potentiality of his/her team through delegation in this interesting journey together. Let's embrace automation and delegation so as to develop effective workflows, enhance productivity, and achieve success.

Why Delegate Based on Strengths?

Delegating tasks based on employee strengths is a powerful approach that yields numerous benefits. By leveraging individual skills and abilities that each member possesses, you may improve motivation levels in employees leading to increased engagement and satisfaction at work places. Leveraging the strengths of your employees not only improves their performance but also creates an affirmative workplace environment.

"Employees feel a sense of accomplishment and fulfilment when they are given tasks that align with their strengths," says Sarah Anderson, HR Manager at Acme Corporation . "Such motivates them towards overachieving with higher level engagements and satisfactions."

Delegating based on strength also helps reduce the risk of employee burnout. When employees are working on tasks that align with their strengths, they feel energised and satisfied, which helps to prevent burnout and frustration.

Delegating based on strengths also shows trust in your employees. By valuing their unique skills and abilities, you demonstrate faith in their potential for growth and success. Such builds trust, loyalty and commitment among your team members.

How to Identify Employee Strengths?

The process of delegating tasks based on one's strengths starts by identifying the strengths of the employees. Managers can enhance the performance of an individual employee as well as the output of a group by understanding and leveraging the unique talents and capabilities present within the organisation's team. Several methods are used in identifying employee strengths:

Surveys, Interviews, and Feedback Sessions

Conducting surveys, interviews, and feedback sessions can provide valuable insights into the strengths, preferences, and goals of your employees. Focusing on specific inquiries will help you to understand better their areas of knowledge and exceptional abilities.

Assessments like StrengthsFinder, DISC, or Myers-Briggs

Including assessments such as DISC, StrengthsFinder or Myers-Briggs can provide more insights into personality traits, skills and behavioural tendencies. These kinds of tests will help you to spot certain strengths, which are not very obvious.

Observation and Feedback from Others

When identifying strengths in your employees, it is important to observe their performance and get feedback from their colleagues, superiors and clients. When you see how they undertake their duties and relate to others, you are able to have a wider opinion concerning their ability and specialty.

"Talking to others who work closely with that employee can bring different perspectives and insights into his/her strengths that may enhance your own observations."

You can develop a comprehensive understanding of your employees' strengths by using any combination of these methods. You will be able to distribute roles according to their individual capabilities thus helping them achieve their maximum potential.

How do I Delegate Based on Strengths?

Effective delegation by strength requires an understanding of the skills and areas of expertise possessed by your workers. This ensures that the performance of the team is optimised through leveraging on the team members' strong points. Some strategies for successful delegation based on strengths include:

Task prioritisation based on urgency, importance, strategic value

Before delegating tasks, consider if they are urgent or important in relation to your team's objectives. Additionally, identify the organisational value brought by each particular activity. By doing so you will allocate your tasks better ensuring high priority undertakings go to people with relevant abilities.

Assign tasks according to employee's strength

For optimal efficiency, assign tasks that coincide with employees' skill sets, interests or goals. Take note of what they know about a particular area because they might possess applicable experience in it. By assigning tasks that match employees' strong points you are also making good use out of them hence increasing job satisfaction.

Provide clear expectations.

Successful delegation requires clarity and brevity in communication. Clear objectives, deadlines and desired outcomes should be spelt out when assigning tasks. Avoid ambiguity by providing detailed instructions and background information. Make it clear why the task is important and how it contributes to the team's overall goals.

Support and regular feedback.

Support your employees by offering guidance, resources, and regular feedback. Be available to answer questions, provide clarification, and address any challenges or concerns that may arise. Such support will help them deliver their delegated duties more effectively hence building their confidence levels.

"By delegating tasks based on strengths, you empower your employees to excel in their areas of expertise while fostering a collaborative and engaged work environment."

Give regular feedback for continuous improvement. Provide constructive feedback as well as acknowledge their achievements to motivate them and recognize their efforts. Follow up with them regularly for progress checkups; support if necessary; and celebrate successful completion of assignments. This feedback loop creates a positive feedback culture and helps your employees grow and develop themselves.

By delegating tasks based on strengths, you empower your employees to excel in their areas of expertise while fostering a collaborative and engaged work environment. This approach not only leads to increased productivity but also enhances employee satisfaction leading to success of your team and organisation in general.

How Do I Empower Employees To Use Their Strengths?

Empowering your personnel to use their best skills fully requires you to provide them with freedom. Allow them to make choices, find solutions and innovate in their own area of work. When employees are given the chance to exercise their judgement and use their unique strengths, they become more involved and committed.

Offering them openings for learning, growth, and development of their strong points through various challenges and projects is important. Encourage them to undertake tasks that are in line with what they can do and like doing; this way they could surpass the barriers set by the current skill level. The feeling of gaining confidence from personal or professional development will enhance one's self-esteem.

Further than this, rewarding their achievements increased a sense of purpose and self-revelation. They value the inputs made by staff members when recognition is done in a manner that shows how much effort they have put in; hence such people will tend to utilise their strong sides until when it comes to success where it has a positive influence on the entire team. Praise should be publically done or even free things.

In this regard, empowering your employees brings out their potential thus creating a constructive working environment which respects individual strengths. Autonomy, learning opportunities and recognition play an important role in enabling employees to exploit their capabilities effectively thereby enhancing corporate or personal performance.

How to Balance Strengths and Weaknesses?

However important it may be to delegate duties based on individuals' strong points, weaknesses must also be taken care of. Recognizing employee weaknesses is not only crucial but also a basic step towards improvement. If you find out what causes weakness it will enable you to provide constructive criticisms as well as coaching on how they can overcome the challenges faced.

Constructive feedback is essential in guiding employees towards improvement. By specifically giving possible solutions which can be applied by an employee, you help them realise what their shortcomings really are without personally attacking them. Building upon strengths as well as pointing out areas for improvement creates a positive environment.

Coaching is another powerful tool for enhancing employee performance. You can be able to guide other people through their weak points and focus on their positives if you are a manager or team leader. It is during this process that employees get to learn more about themselves, gain extra skills and become open-minded.

"Coaching is unlocking a person's potential to maximise their own performance. It is helping them to learn rather than teaching them." - Timothy Gallwey

For a team to be good at balancing strengths and weaknesses, teamwork must be encouraged. Foster collaboration among workers by building supportive environments in which their weaknesses are complemented by the strengths of others. The total quality of outputs will go up where each one's strength is put to use.

Striking a Balance for Long-Term Success

Balancing between concentrating on one's strong areas while addressing the weak points should always be considered for long-term achievements. By doing so, individuals will have an opportunity to perform excellently in their respective fields as they simultaneously improve in other areas that demand their attention. This is the best approach that can ensure good overall performance amongst groups coupled with personal growth.

Recognize and address weakness through constructive feedbacks and coaching makes the employee grow into his full potential For instance, if the individual's strength comes out during a group assignment, it makes sense why that person should belong into this team because he/she has something different to teach fellows; thus he can prosper with others as well as accomplish extraordinary results together.

Finally, to balance strengths and weaknesses is a holistic approach that includes employee development, constructive criticism, mentoring and team work. However, by developing individuals while maximising upon collective strengths, one can create a winning team that will be successful and have great results.

The Benefits of Delegating Based on Strengths

Delegating tasks based on strengths has various advantages. It also improves overall team performance, increases job satisfaction among employees as well as promotes individual growth. By matching jobs with employees' strengths you increase productivity while maintaining a positive working atmosphere.

"When employees are given tasks that align with their strengths, they feel more confident and motivated to excel. This leads to higher job satisfaction and increased productivity."

Leveraging the collective strength of your team members promotes collaboration and drives success. In this way, you build an environment where teamwork thrives on the ability of every individual.

"The collaboration and synergy that arises from leveraging strengths lead to enhanced problem-solving, increased creativity, and improved overall performance."

When employees are empowered to work in areas where they excel, they feel a sense of fulfilment and accomplishment. For instance, when such persons are tasked with duties suitably aligned to their natural abilities they gain a great sense of fulfilment.

"Employees who are assigned tasks that align with their strengths experience higher levels of job satisfaction, leading to increased loyalty, reduced turnover, and a positive work culture."

Furthermore, delegating based on strength enhances individual growth and development. Individuals can perfect their skills and further gain knowledge in areas which match their talents.

"When employees are given the opportunity to work on tasks that align with their strengths, they gain valuable experience, develop new skills, and grow both personally and professionally."

The benefits of delegating based on strengths cannot be overemphasised. It helps in improving team performance & productivity alongside increasing employee job satisfaction through encouraging collaboration as well as fostering personal growth. With this kind of delegation technique organisations may build a vibrant environment such that their staffs achieve at their maximum.

The Role of Technology in Automation and Delegation

In terms of automation and delegation, technology plays a critical role in enhancing productivity and efficiency. By the use of the automation tools as well as task management software, organisations are able to enhance processes, utilise resources effectively as well as enable team members.

Automation tools revolutionise processes by automating repetitive, time-consuming tasks. This not only saves time for employees but also allows them to focus on more strategic and value added work. The result is that technology facilitates rote activities, thereby freeing up human potential for the more creative and intellectually challenging ones.

Task management software is another essential technology that facilitates effective delegation. Through the use of these tools' managers can efficiently track and assign tasks ensuring fair distribution of duties with set deadlines. These instruments help teams maintain a transparent process while working together on multiple projects.

"Implementing technology that improves productivity, efficiency, and collaboration makes automation and delegation smoother."

Technology solutions that are correct implement help to streamline workflow and also promote inter-team cooperation. When equipped with appropriate tools, communication becomes seamless, knowledge sharing becomes part of the culture and cross-functional projects can easily be managed. The technology becomes responsible for joining people, departments, and teams together thereby creating an integrated and effective workspace.

Chapter 20

The Pomodoro Time Management Technique and Implementing Pomodoro and Variations

****

Hello, and le-t's dive into the Pomodoro Technique- for Time Management! Se-eking better productivity and gre-at time management? You're- in the right place! This section breaks down the- Pomodoro Technique, an effe-ctive approach by Francesco Cirillo in the 1980s. It's all about splitting work into se-ctions for better focus and productivity.

Understanding the- Pomodoro Technique and Its Functioning

We'll clarify just what constitute-s the Pomodoro Technique and how it functions. We-'ll explore the scie-ntific explanation behind this time pe-rception strategy and its bene-fits. We'll suggest easy ste-ps to integrate these- methods into your everyday routine-.

Whether a pupil, professional, or busine-ssperson, the Pomodoro technique- could transform your time management. Re-ady to take control of your time? Let's e-xplore what the Pomodoro technique- offers us!

The Pomodoro Technique- is a proven time manageme-nt solution by Francesco Cirillo, aiming for optimal focus and efficiency at work. Some- view this method as cramming or exhaustive- work, but it promotes divided attention, e-ncouraging bouts of 25-minute focused work periods.

The- term "Pomodoro" is inspired by a tomato-shaped kitche-n timer that Cirillo used during this technique-'s initial conception. Segmenting work into manage-able pieces he-lps people focus bette-r and avoid burnout.

During each "Pomodoro," a person works on one single task without any interruptions. Once the 25-minute interval is over, there is a short break of about 5 minutes to rest. After four Pomodoros in a row, it is allowed to take a long break that lasts between 15 and 20 minutes before proceeding with another series.

This method allows people to work efficiently by making the most of their short-term attention spans and providing them with regular opportunities for rest.

With these intervals punctuated by dedicated breaks, the Pomodoro Technique helps people fight procrastination, manage time better as well as improve productivity. This notion also encourages individuals to establish definite targets for each Pomodoro session hence making it possible to plan your work properly.

In summary, The Pomodoro Technique is a simple but powerful approach to time management that can be applied in various aspects of life such as work, study or personal tasks which aims at helping people maximise their time and be productive.

Benefits of the Pomodoro Technique

The Pomodoro Technique is a time management approach with many benefits for those who crave improved productivity and focus. By using this technique you will be able to arrange your schedule appropriately and get more things done while maintaining some balance with your family life.

Among other purposes of this strategy is creating room for mental relaxation during breaks. Typically, you work in focused intervals as short as 25 minutes then take a short break. During these brakes you can recharge yourself so that you do not get too tired mentally which would improve your overall productivity.

The Pomodoro Te-chnique boosts productivity and focus. It breaks up your work into manageable- parts which keeps work engaging. This tactic combats task ove-rload by speeding up completion time-s.

"I'm a fan of the Pomodoro Technique. It give-s me a bird's eye vie-w of my tasks. It maintains my discipline and keeps distractions at bay."

Plus, the Pomodoro Technique improve-s time-estimation skills. Consistent practice- helps you measure task duration. This gre-atly aids efficient time allocation and e-ffective schedule-planning.

"The Pomodoro Technique e-nhanced my time manageme-nt skills. I now estimate job timing bette-r, which helps me plan and organise work."

This technique also fostered a keen sense- of time's value. Break inte-rvals reveal the spe-ed of 25 minutes. This realisation fostered urgency and focus, boosting productivity and goal attainment.

Additionally, the Pomodoro Te-chnique limits disruptions by curbing potential distractions during work sessions. By cultivating a distraction-fre-e work environment, you can stay focuse-d and not waste time on unrelate-d activities.

"The Pomodoro te-chnique has been transformative-. It's improved my focus, reducing distractions and enhancing productivity." - Sarah Thompson, Fre-elance Writer

This te-chnique can help people- avoid burnout. By incorporating regular breaks, you maintain your health and avoid e-xhaustion. Essentially, it's about balancing work and personal life.

Using the- Pomodoro Technique could improve your daily pe-rformance. It structures your time e-ffectively. It ensure-s you maintain focus and reduces time take-n to finish tasks.

Pomodoro Technique

To start using the Pomodoro Technique, simply set a 25-minute timer and focus on a single task. It's important to avoid distractions and create a productive- environment. A single-task focus e-nhances productivity, unlike multitasking.

When the- timer rings, take a 5-minute bre-ak. Use this time to stretch, drink wate-r or relax, helping reduce- mental fatigue. These- breaks are crucial to avoid burnout while pre-paring for remaining work hours.

Repeat this cycle of focused work and short breaks four times. When you have finished four cycles or pomodoros, it is good to go on longer (15-20 minutes) break activities such as walking around the block, meditating or eating some fruit.

Use this structured time management approach to effectively utilise the Pomodoro Technique. This approach involves working in concentrated bursts with regular pauses so that you keep your productivity levels up while also ensuring general well-being.

The different forms of using the pomodoro technique

A flexible and customizable approach to time management is provided by the Pomodoro Technique that allows a person to adapt it to his/her own preferences and requirements. People can increase productivity and work more effectively if they try out various variations.

There are several different ways to customise the Pomodoro Technique, such as adjusting the length of work intervals and break times. Some individuals may find that shorter work intervals of 15 or 20 minutes work better for them, while others may prefer longer intervals of 30 or 45 minutes. Similarly, break times can be shortened or lengthened to better suit individual requirements.

"My focus increased so much when I broke my work into twenty-minute chunks with five-minute breaks in between. It was involved without being overwhelming."-Sarah, Graphic Designer

Incorporating longer breaks after shorter intervals is another variation. Instead of taking a longer break only after four consecutive intervals, individuals can opt to take a short break after every work interval and a longer break every two or three intervals. This can provide more frequent moments of rest and rejuvenation.

James, a software- developer, share-s, "Every 25 minutes I took a mini-break, ste-pping away from my desk, then returning energised."

People- often alter the Pomodoro Technique using specific tools or software for time- tracking. Apps and timers for tracking work and break periods are- plentiful, ideal

for kee-ping focus sharp. They can send notifications, provide visual aids, or track progre-ss to keep distractions at bay.

Adapting the Me-thod for Specific Occupations or Tasks

Moulding your Pomodoro Technique to fit spe-cific tasks can solve problems. Authors might use long work pe-riods while customer service- reps could find quick tasks easier.

Customising the- Technique to Suit Your Style

The- Pomodoro Technique can be adapte-d to your work styles, making it super handy. By trying out differe-nt strategies, the pe-rfect balance can be struck, le-ading to better productivity and focus.

Adjusting work and break inte-rvals, or even adopting longer bre-aks, integrating time trackers, modifying the- method for specific tasks, are all ways of making the- Pomodoro Technique your own. What comes out is ofte-n your best work.

The Science behind Pomodoro Technique

It is not just any time-management strategy, but a scientifically factored brain productivity/focus hack: The Pomodoro Technique. This method capitalises on our mind's natural ability to focus for short periods followed by restful breaks.

According to research, breaking down work into intervals with regular breaks in between enhances focus, motivation and overall productivity. Integrating the Pomodoro Technique into your schedule optimises your work for better results because you benefit from its science base.

When you work for short durations of time and then take small breaks, you give your brain a chance to replenish its energy. This refuelling prevents mental exhaustion and enables you to perform at higher levels the whole day. It also helps to fight the law of diminishing returns that may arise from long periods of continuous work.

"The Pomodoro Technique is like a power nap for your brain, allowing you to recharge and refocus so you can tackle your tasks with renewed clarity and energy."

Knowing the science behind the Pomodoro Technique will optimise your brain's performance and as such match your working habits. Including regular break periods in your activities can protect against burnout, manage time better and improve overall well-being.

Tips on How to Maximise the Pomodoro Technique

For optimum utilisation of Pomodoro Technique and highest productivity gains, consider these useful tips and time management hacks:

1. Have Pre-cise Goals for Each Session

Begin e-ach pomodoro session with a distinct, set goal. This create-s focus and drive throughout.

2. Minimise Distractions and Stop Doing Many Things at Once

Shut down notifications and unre-lated tabs or apps to reduce inte-rruptions. Concentrate on one thing pe-r pomodoro session as multitasking decrease-s productivity.

3. Take Breaks That Truly Revitalise You

Use your downtime to restore- your energy, both in body and mind. Engage in calming activitie-s like stretching or breathing e-xercises. Sideline- things that drain your energy, like scrolling through social ne-tworks.

4. Choose Tasks Based on Their Importance- and Time-Sensitivity

Prioritise your tasks for e-ach Pomodoro session by their importance and due- date. By early focus on these- tasks, you can progress efficiently in your main dutie-s.

5. Use Time Manageme-nt Programs and Applications

Several programs and apps like Toggl or Fore-st, with timers and analytics, can assist you in acing the Pomodoro Technique-. These tools hone your time- management skills.

6. Play Around with Differing Approache-s

The Pomodoro Te-chnique offers flexibility. You could change- work duration or break frequency to suit your ne-eds. Finding your own work-flow is the goal.

Adopt these- tips into your Pomodoro routine. They'll help maximise the technique's be-nefits. This will lead to increase-d productivity and task efficiency.

Challenge-s in Applying the Pomodoro Technique

De-spite its potential in producing efficie-ncy and time management, use-rs sometimes struggle. Challe-nges include difficulty focusing, being inte-rrupted or distracted, or adhering to the- strict Pomodoro timing.

Focusing for the full work segment can be- tough, especially with numerous distractions or a wande-ring mind. One way to combat this is making your workspace as distraction-free- as possible. A silent environme-nt, no notifications, and clear boundaries will help. Mindfulne-ss is also key. Focus on the task. Remind yourse-lf that staying in the present mome-nt, fully engaged, is important.

Getting use-d to the Pomodoro Technique's strict timing can be- hard, mainly if you're used to working straight through. It's a change that ne-eds self-control and practice. You could start e-xtending work time bit by bit to ease- into the method. Thus, one can boost focus while- keeping the Pomodoro structure-.

Keeping concentration isn't e-asy. Strict time rules nee-d discipline and flexibility. A proper workspace- and gradually lengthening work time can he-lp overcome these- challenges. In the e-nd, you can get more from the Pomodoro Technique.

On the other hand, twe-aking the Pomodoro Technique for your ne-eds can solve some trouble-s. Some feel adjusting the- timing of work intervals and breaks suits their workflow be-tter. Experimenting with diffe-rent options can lead to bette-r focus and more productivity.

Despite hurdle-s like focus issues, interruptions, and strict timing, you can use- the Pomodoro Technique to its full e-xtent. With discipline, the right workspace-, mindfulness exercise-s, and other personal tweaks, one- can become more e-fficient and manage time be-tter.

Certainly! Here's the text with a line space added between each paragraph:

Hello, and let's dive into the Pomodoro Technique for Time Management! Seeking better productivity and great time management? You're in the right spot! This section breaks down the Pomodoro Technique, an effective approach by Francesco Cirillo in the 1980s. It's all about splitting work into sections for better focus and productivity.

Understanding the Pomodoro Technique and Its Functioning

We'll clarify just what constitutes the Pomodoro Technique and how it functions. We'll explore the scientific explanation behind this time perception strategy and its benefits. We'll suggest easy steps to integrate these methods into your everyday routine.

Whether a pupil, professional, or businessperson, the Pomodoro technique could transform your time management. Ready to take control of your time? Let's explore what the Pomodoro technique offers us!

The Pomodoro Technique is a proven time management solution by Francesco Cirillo, aiming for optimal focus and efficiency at work. Some view this method as cramming or exhaustive work, but it promotes divided attention, encouraging bouts of 25-minute focused work periods.

The term "Pomodoro" is inspired by a tomato-shaped kitchen timer that Cirillo used during this technique's initial conception. Segmenting work into manageable pieces helps people focus better and avoid burnout.

During each "Pomodoro," a person works on one single task without any interruptions. Once the 25-minute interval is over, there is a short break of about 5 minutes to rest. After four Pomodoros in a row, it is allowed to take a long break that lasts between 15 and 20 minutes before proceeding with another series.

This method allows people to work efficiently by making the most of their short-term attention spans and providing them with regular opportunities for rest.

With these intervals punctuated by dedicated breaks, the Pomodoro Technique helps people fight procrastination, manage time better as well as improve productivity. This notion also encourages individuals to establish definite targets for each Pomodoro session hence making it possible to plan your work properly.

In summary, The Pomodoro Technique is a simple but powerful approach to time management that can be applied in various aspects of life such as work, study or personal tasks which aims at helping people maximise their time and be productive.

Benefits of the Pomodoro Technique

Pomodoro Technique is a time management approach with many benefits for those who crave improved productivity and focus. By using this technique you will be able to arrange your schedule appropriately and get more things done while maintaining some balance with your family life.

Among other purposes of this strategy is creating room for mental relaxation during breaks. Typically, you work in focused intervals as short as 25 minutes then take a short break. During these brakes you can recharge yourself so that you do not get too tired mentally which would improve your overall productivity.

The Pomodoro Technique boosts productivity and focus. It breaks up your work into manageable parts which keeps work engaging. This tactic combats task overload by speeding up completion times.

"I'm a fan of the Pomodoro Technique. It gives me a bird's eye view of my tasks. It maintains my discipline and keeps distractions at bay."

Plus, the Pomodoro Technique improves time-estimation skills. Consistent practice helps you measure task duration. This greatly aids efficient time allocation and effective schedule planning.

"The Pomodoro Technique enhanced my time management skills. I now estimate job timing better which helps me plan and organise work."

This technique also fosters a keen sense of time's value. Break intervals reveal the speed of 25 minutes. This realisation fosters urgency and focus, boosting productivity and goal attainment.

Additionally, the Pomodoro Technique limits disruptions by curbing potential distractions during work sessions. By cultivating a distraction-free work environment, you can stay focused and not waste time on unrelated activities.

"The Pomodoro technique has been transformative. It's improved my focus, reducing distractions and enhancing productivity." - Sarah Thompson, Freelance Writer

This technique can help people avoid burnout. By incorporating regular breaks, you maintain your health and avoid exhaustion. Essentially, it's about balancing work and personal life.

Using the Pomodoro Technique could improve your daily performance. It structures your time effectively. It ensures you maintain focus and reduces time taken to finish tasks.

Pomodoro Technique

To start using the Pomodoro Technique, simply set a 25-minute timer and focus on a single task. It's important to avoid distractions and create a productive environment. A single-task focus enhances productivity, unlike multitasking.

When the timer rings, take a 5-minute break. Use this time to stretch, drink water or relax, helping reduce mental fatigue. These breaks are crucial to avoid burnout while preparing for remaining work hours.

Repeat this cycle of focused work and short breaks four times. When you have finished four cycles or pomodoros, it is good to go on longer (15-20 minutes) break activities such as walking around the block, meditating or eating some fruit.

Use this structured time management approach to effectively utilise the Pomodoro Technique. This approach involves working in concentrated bursts with regular pauses so that you keep your productivity levels up while also ensuring general well-being.

The different forms of using the pomodoro technique

A flexible and customizable approach to time management is provided by the Pomodoro Technique that allows a person to adapt it to his/her own preferences and requirements. People can increase productivity and work more effectively if they try out various variations.

There are several different ways to customise the Pomodoro Technique, such as adjusting the length of work intervals and break times. Some individuals may find that shorter work intervals of 15 or 20 minutes work better for them, while others may prefer longer intervals of 30 or 45 minutes. Similarly, break times can be shortened or lengthened to better suit individual requirements.

"My focus increased so much when I broke my work into twenty-minute chunks with five-minute breaks in between. It was involved without being overwhelming."-Sarah, Graphic Designer

Incorporating longer breaks after shorter intervals is another variation. Instead of taking a longer break only after four consecutive intervals, individuals can opt to take a short break after every work interval and a longer break every two or three intervals. This can provide more frequent moments of rest and rejuvenation.

James, a software developer, shares, "Every 25 minutes I took a mini-break, stepping away from my desk, then returning energised."

People often alter the Pomodoro Technique using specific tools or software for time tracking. Apps and timers for tracking work and break periods are plentiful, ideal for keeping focus sharp. They can send notifications, provide visual aids, or track progress to keep distractions at bay.

Adapting the Method for Specific Occupations or Tasks

Moulding your Pomodoro Technique to fit specific tasks can solve problems. Authors might use long work periods while customer service reps could find quick tasks easier. Customising the Technique to Suit Your Style

The Pomodoro Technique can be adapted to your work styles, making it super handy. By trying out different strategies, the perfect balance can be struck, leading to better productivity and focus.

Adjusting work and break intervals, or even adopting longer breaks, integrating time trackers, modifying the method for specific tasks, are all ways of making the Pomodoro Technique your own. What comes out is often your best work.

The Science behind Pomodoro Technique

It is not just any time-management strategy, but a scientifically factored brain productivity/focus hack: The Pomodoro Technique. This method capitalises on our mind's natural ability to focus for short periods followed by restful breaks.

According to research works, breaking down work into intervals with regular breaks in between enhances focus, motivation and overall productivity. Integrating the Pomodoro Technique into your schedule optimises your work for better results because you benefit from its science base.

When you work for short durations of time and then take small breaks, you give your brain a chance to replenish its energy. This refuelling prevents mental exhaustion and enables you to perform at higher levels the whole day. It also helps to fight the law of diminishing returns that may arise from long periods of continuous work.

"The Pomodoro Technique is like a power nap for your brain, allowing you to recharge and refocus so you can tackle your tasks with renewed clarity and energy."

Knowing the science behind the Pomodoro Technique will optimise your brain's performance and as such match your working habits. Including regular break periods in your activities can protect against burnout, manage time better and improve overall well-being.

Tips on How to Maximise the Pomodoro Technique

For optimum utilisation of Pomodoro Technique and highest productivity gains, consider these useful tips and time management hacks:

1. Have Precise Goals for Each Session

Begin each pomodoro session with a distinct, set goal. This creates focus and drive throughout.

2. Minimise Distractions and Stop Doing Many Things at Once

Shut down notifications and unrelated tabs or apps to reduce interruptions. Concentrate on one thing per pomodoro session as multitasking decreases productivity.

3. Take Breaks That Truly Revitalise You

Use your downtime to restore your energy, both in body and mind. Engage in calming activities like stretching or breathing exercises. Sideline things that drain your energy, like scrolling through social networks.

4. Choose Tasks Based on Their Importance and Time-Sensitivity

Prioritise your tasks for each Pomodoro session by their importance and due date. By early focus on these tasks, you can progress efficiently in your main duties.

5. Use Time Management Programs and Applications

Several programs and apps like Toggl or Forest, with timers and analytics, can assist you in acing the Pomodoro Technique. These tools hone your time management skills.

6. Play Around with Differing Approaches

The Pomodoro Technique offers flexibility. You could change work duration or break frequency to suit your needs. Finding your own workflow is the goal.

Adopt these tips into your Pomodoro routine. They'll help maximise the technique's benefits. This will lead to increased productivity and task efficiency.

Challenges in Applying the Pomodoro Technique

Despite its potential in producing efficiency and time management, users sometimes struggle. Challenges include difficulty focusing, being interrupted or distracted, or adhering to the strict Pomodoro timing.

Focusing for the full work segment can be tough, especially with numerous distractions or a wandering mind. One way to combat this is making your workspace as distraction-free as possible. A silent environment, no notifications, and clear boundaries will help. Mindfulness is also key. Focus on the task. Remind yourself that staying in the present moment, fully engaged, is important.

Getting used to the Pomodoro Technique's strict timing can be hard, mainly if you're used to working straight through. It's a change that needs self-control and practice. You could start extending work time bit by bit to ease into the method. Thus, one can boost focus while keeping the Pomodoro structure.

Keeping concentration isn't easy. Strict time rules need discipline and flexibility. A proper workspace and gradually lengthening work time can help overcome these challenges. In the end, you can get more from the Pomodoro Technique.

On the other hand, tweaking the Pomodoro Technique for your needs can solve some troubles. Some feel adjusting the timing of work intervals and breaks suits their workflow better. Experimenting with different options can lead to better focus and more productivity.

Despite hurdles like focus issues, interruptions, and strict timing, you can use the Pomodoro Technique to its full extent. With discipline, the right workspace, mindfulness exercises, and other personal tweaks, one can become more efficient and manage time better.

Integration of the Pomodoro Technique into Daily Life

pomodoro technique is not just about studying or working but fits into different facets of life. It is possible to practise Pomodoro Technique on various tasks so that you can gain control over your time for more productivity while maintaining a healthy work-life balance.

You might also find this useful in whatever field you are in including studies, writing assignments or even household chores. These activities should be broken down into sessions where one focuses followed by small short breaks to avoid drifting away from the task at hand.

"Integrating my daily routine has been revolutionary," says a working professional who learned about this method by reading an article online."I even use it for household stuff. Sometimes it keeps me motivated and enables me to complete my duties without being distracted."

Using the Pomodoro Technique for Leisure Activities

One way of making sure that you take advantage of your free hours is through applying this method on leisure activities. By setting aside specific intervals of focused leisure activities such as reading a book, playing a musical instrument or involving yourself in a hobby, you can be fully present and enjoy your free time without any guilt or distractions.

"I enjoy reading but I often find it difficult to allocate enough time for it." Mark, an ardent bookworm and Pomodoro Technique participant says. "I'd rather use the Pomodoro Technique where I read for 25 minutes then take a break. It's very nice because it allows me to unwind and delve into my books even while I'm still working on other things."

By integrating the Pomodoro Technique into your daily life consistently, you can establish a structured approach to time management that is well balanced. This not only

Chapter 21

Unlocking Social Skills: Benefits and Developments of Quality Relationships

****

In this era of digitization where myriad distractions and speed characterise it, cultivating deep and meaningful relationships has become a difficult task for many people, but the rewards are worth it. This is why one should put trust, quality time and social skills into building relationships that will be rewarding in future.

Robert Waldinger, an American psychiatrist, conducted an extensive research at Harvard University that made it clear that our health and happiness depend on the quality of our relationship with others. Social connections do not merely entail having a high number of contacts on your phone or a massive following on social media. They are about having close ties with other people who can take care of you. These often take time to develop and require nurturing through understanding and mutual respect.

Social Connection and Emotional Support really important

Social connection and emotional support are two very critical aspects of human life because they give us a feeling of being loved, valued or even understood by someone else. Lack of this leads to loneliness which is believed to be healthwise equivalent to smoking 15 cigarettes a day as per the study done by researchers from Brigham Young University thereby pointing towards significant impact on mortality rates.

Good social relationships enhance self-esteem, mental well-being as well as physical health. Strong social support enhances resilience against stress according to the American Psychological Association (APA). It also lowers blood pressure while extending life span.

Emotional support is vital in terms of validation, sharing experiences encouraging positive mental health; conversely sometimes acting as a buffer from negative experiences or trauma because it affords individuals an avenue to cope built on understanding and empathy which are some aspects helpful in forming positive relationships.

Therefore, developing such bonds calls for attention to personal tools through which we interact successfully with others. Trust building takes place over time helping us gain confidence with each other by constantly displaying respect, revealing compassion, listening skilfully and expressing ourselves clearly – these helps establish quality linkages.

So let's get down to brass tacks —Let us Developing Quality Relationships

Quality relationships can bring about serenity, guidance and a significant sense of belonging. They often serve as the linchpin for our well-being and contentment with life. However, how can one get there in order to develop a quality relationship? This is not something one achieves but rather a process that demands time, patience, understanding, communication and most importantly trust.

Trust in relationships acts like cement; it holds the whole structure together. It allows us to be ourselves without fear of being judged or misunderstood. Trust is established when individuals are consistently warm, reliable, transparent and responsive to the emotional needs of others. It gives rise to positive dialogues, enables vulnerability and creates strength in relationships. According to Pew Research Centre 88% of adults believe that trust is an important element in any successful relationship.

In order to be able to trust one another, people must create a relationship which generally takes time but in the end, is worth all the effort that you put into it. People can only be authentic when they feel safe around each other, which makes this bond stronger.

Relationships need effective communication for their development. Fostering understanding among the people involved in any deal needs clear and consistent communication. It is necessary to hold conversations where everyone feels listened to because this encourages empathy and respect for different perspectives of others. The Harvard Business Review posits that good communicators are more likely to foster both personal and business relationships.

Additionally, dedicating quality moments forms the backbone of great relationships. Investing time facilitates mutual understanding hence stronger relationships. This goes beyond just being there; it entails actively participating in shared hobbies or interests and thus building memories.

Developing such relationships over time also requires patience. In our digital age of instant gratification we prefer quick results in many instances which doesn't always bode well when it comes to nurturing relationships. Building trust requires patience and understanding as it is a slow process especially during times of conflict or misunderstandings.

As such, the ingredients that make up quality relationships include trust, effective communication, spending time together as well as patience. These elements are intricately connected and they serve as building blocks for strong ties between individuals. Keep in mind that there is no one-size-fits-all guidebook on how to have perfect relationships; it changes with individuals and experiences. Although building relationships is a challenging journey it can be enjoyable with an amazing outcome at the end.

Linking Cognitive Aspects - Relationships and Learning Interdependencies

It is not only our emotions that require relations interaction but also cognitive development too where there social skills play an important role as well.Researchers have found out that reasoning, critical thinking capabilities, language proficiency skills,literacy skills sets have been developed through the processes of creating bonds with others. Importantly, understanding the broader concept of cognitive development requires treating these aspects as interdependent.

First and foremost, let us look at how relationships contribute towards our knowledge of language and literacy. For example, a loving bond between a mother and her child ensures that the child is exposed to a rich vocabulary right from birth which ultimately helps in building a healthy language foundation. Similarly, reading together makes literacy development more enjoyable as children get to engage with books and stories. Emotionally satisfying relationships also promote empathy for others' experiences and perspectives thus increasing our comprehension of narratives as well characters.

Another example is mathematics – how can relationships be connected to it? The impacts of relational interactions are more pronounced in terms of abstract concepts such as pattern recognition, sequencing, cause-effect analysis; all of which are the basic building blocks necessary for mathematical understanding. Involvement in activities such as sorting objects by colour, comparing sizes or counting them together within safe environments support real-life applications of these ideas making it easier to comprehend.

At this juncture cultural competence must be mentioned regarding developing quality relationships within today's global society. With the world now more digitally connected than ever before, cross-cultural interactions have become the norm. Cultural competency enables one to better navigate social interactions across different cultural contexts hence successful relationships in diverse settings. This process is supported by open-mindedness that aids in establishing curiosity about different cultures thereby deepening and broadening our knowledge base.

As we embrace the above observations, it is worth mentioning that social relations are not just about satisfying basic requirements of socialisation and emotional well-being. Their significance to cognitive development stems from their ability to improve on language competence, enhance literacy, sharpen logical reasoning, enable mathematics understanding, and develop cultural competency. Therefore, strong social bonds contribute to all-round individuals who can easily tackle various life situations.

All these factors contributing towards cognitive development when integrated within relationships right from the early stages ensure a complete learning experience. This proves that the journey of building quality relationships and social skills is not only about boosting emotional connections but also involves critical aspects for cognitive growth.

Tech-Powered Social Skills

While discussing relationships and social skills, one should never ignore how technology has impacted the field. Notably, technology has revolutionised our communication patterns. Even though personal interaction remains important, offline platforms for communication have been reduced with digital communication becoming an integral part of our lives as well. Next generation learning technologies provide innumerable opportunities for improving our social skills and creating good relationships.

Today's globally connected world demands extensive reach as well as instant connectivity. This opens up a window to engage effectively with these aspects through technologically rich learning environments. There are wider avenues where thoughts can be shared, dialogues opened, challenges cooperatively addressed or even accomplishments relayed –all in a bid to nurture relationships that are building and making stronger bonds.

According to research done it is evident that technology can assist people effortlessly navigate complex social spaces. For instance in some cases people feel more confident expressing themselves in online communities than physical ones. That way barriers of communications break down leading to more candid exchanges and constructive debates. Similarly online collaboration tools encourage teamwork and cooperation – both of which are essential for building sustainable relationships.

Digital storytelling is another powerful tool in enhancing social development using technology whereby individuals could use digital media like blogs, podcasts etc.to share narratives from their experiences or perspectives thus promoting empathy for diverse experiences. In this way, the narratives that are shared may provide comfort to those who seek validation and support; they create a sense of belonging in the digital community as well as stronger bonds.

Furthermore various educational software and apps have been designed to instil some social skills like empathy (understanding emotions of themselves/others), conflict resolution strategies used during disputes or even assertive yet kind means of communication among children and teenagers.

Nevertheless, what can't be overlooked is a balanced approach between real-life and virtual world interactions. In order to keep the human touch alive, healthy screen times should be ensured while personal contacts are encouraged. It's all about employing technology as an enhancer rather than allowing it to take over our social lives.

Further into the 21st century, technology-rich learning environments will continue presenting new opportunities for building relationships and developing social skills. These are challenges within our personal interactions that we must change in order to adapt and grow, learn and unlearn, hence making our society even more resilient against adversity.

In conclusion, technology today shapes our relationships fundamentally. It is becoming more vital towards enhancing communication skills; promoting understanding and empathy among people from diverse communities; encouraging collaboration among them; and generally improving social competencies. When used wisely it can contribute significantly in building good relationships as well as enhancing socio-emotional growth.

Conclusion – Winding Together Intertwining Serve and Return Interactions in Relationships

Our journeys through understanding why developing quality relationships and improving social skills are important, show that our paths are often marked by a series of reciprocal interactions. This recurring pattern is best described as serve and return interactions, a term rooted in the bases of child development research but applies to adult relationships too. These interactions are crucial for fostering relationships, boosting social-emotional development and shaping cognitive growth.

Serve and return interactions represent one's action 'serving' as a prompt for the other to 'return' an answer. This back-and-forth process creates an ongoing interactive loop that helps build rapport and strengthen connections. For instance, when an infant cooks or smiles (serves), the caregiver responds by reciprocating with a smile or loving words (return). Similarly, if someone opens up about personal thoughts or feelings (serve) in adult relationships, a compassionate listener would either acknowledge them or give empathetic commentaries towards the same (return).

The essence of these interactions not only lies in how they are responded to but also how one responds. Thoughtful reactions build trust and strengthen emotional ties while curt or dismissive responses may break apart these bonds.

Serve and return interactions play a critical role in acquiring social skills. They are stepping stones to being able to understand another person's point of view; empathise with their emotions; engage in constructive conversation; develop self-control and resilience that will lead to holistic social-emotional development. According to research done by Harvard University's Center on the Developing Child, these interactive exchanges provide the building blocks for language acquisition, cognitive learning styles, emotional control, even relationship building abilities later in life.

This insight provides powerful lessons on our journey toward relationship-building and social skills mastery. It reminds us that every interaction counts no matter how insignificant it may appear; they have the potential to change our relationships profoundly. By being mindful of each serve and return, we open up possibilities for deeper and richer connections.

To sum up, serve and return interactions are not just about reciprocal exchanges; they form the core of a successful relationship. They are also important in shaping well-being, cognitive development and a strong social fabric. The point is that for each 'serve' we experience, there is always a 'return' we can make – acknowledgment, empathy, encouragement or love – thus adding to our relationships one by one.

Chapter 22

Active Listening Skills and Clearly Expressing Yourself with Assertive Communication

****

Welcome to part 22 of our guide on communication. Here, we will explore two key techniques for effective chat: listening actively and speaking assertively. Each is valuable in forming connections, at home or work.

Active listening means being fully present and understanding, then responding wisely. It helps us connect, show empathy, and ease communication. Alternatively, with assertive speaking, we express our thoughts, feelings, and needs honestly but politely. It's great for self-worth, good relationships, and conflict solving.

In this part, we'll unpack the meaning of active listening, uncover the benefits of assertiveness, and offer helpful tips. We also address hurdles in communication, suggest ways to handle conflicts, and show how these skills fit in different contexts, from online chats to work meetings and cross-cultural exchanges.

Gaining active listening skills and learning to assertively communicate will make us better communicators, deepen our connections, and support our personal growth. Now, let's dive into the realm of mindful listening and respectful discussion.

Why Active Listening Matters

Good communication is key both in work and personal life. Here, active listening becomes crucial. It's not just about hearing but tuning in completely to the speaker. This way, understanding is achieved by both sides.

By listening actively, trust grows. This makes talking with others better. This kind of listening is a courtesy to the speaker. It further sets a good domain for deep and meaningful talks to happen.

"Active listening isn't limited to words; body language and changes in tone speak volumes too."

Active listening makes for better communication. It helps us understand others' points of view. Plus, it reveals details we may have skipped. It cultivates a sense of belonging, understanding and empathy.

"Active listening is key to strong communication. It helps build strong ties, handle disagreements and encourage teamwork."

Active listening is a habit that needs practice. It calls for full focus during talks and lessening of distractions in the environment. Moreover, it needs the use of clarity-seeking questions. Such questions help extract more meanings from what has been said. Plus, paraphrasing or summarising can help ensure correct understanding."

By being good listeners, we can build better connections, boost our communication, and make our workplaces more pleasant.

Why Assertive Communication Matters

Assertive communication, when used right, is key. It lets people express themselves clearly and with confidence. Their thoughts, feelings, and needs can be shared in a polite, clear way. This form of communication offers lots of benefits and can promote self-growth.

Healthy connections stem from effective communication. Open and honest dialogue is the result of practised assertive communication. This fuels trust and understanding, letting people freely share their thoughts and recognize others' viewpoints. This creates solid bonds.

In addition, assertive communication builds self-assurance. By speaking assertively, individuals feel valued and real. It emboldens them to voice their opinions and set their boundaries in both personal and professional contexts.

Not to forget, objecting respectfully is vital for conflict settlement. It helps avoid unnecessary struggles and find solutions that are fair to everyone. This fosters peace within individuals and groups.

Assertive communication boosts confidence, letting people defend themselves from abuse or intrusion. It fosters self-reliance, empowerment, and self-advocacy.

Good communication skills are tied to assertiveness. It builds healthy relationships, enhances self-esteem, and aids in managing conflicts. Being assertive allows full communication and realisation of personal potential.

Practising Active Listening

Communication isn't just about talking, but also active listening. Achieve better interaction by applying active listening techniques.

A technique is to look directly at the speaker, showing that you're engaged and interested in their message. This body language allows for catching non-verbal cues to understand their feelings better.

Active listening involves nodding and using body gestures correctly. It signifies that you're digesting the information, prompting the speaker to share more of what they think or feel.

Another helpful practice is asking questions to understand the speaker better. This signifies interest and facilitates more insight, saving from unnecessary assumptions.

Paraphrasing refers to restating the words of a speaker into your own words. It proves understanding on your part and confirms your correct interpretation.

Lastly, summarising or restating the speech consolidates information and helps pick out critical points made by the speaker. Thus, it helps in bringing out main ideas and ensuring that both parties understand each other's views.

These active listening techniques need regular practice so as to improve one's communication skills. This will allow you to establish better connections, handle conflicts efficiently and create a collaborative environment in personal as well as professional relationships.

Assertive Communication Strategies

Assertive communication involves applying numerous strategies that encourage openness and honesty while talking. Through these methods, such as effective communication, expressing needs or opinions assertively can become easier, leading to stronger relationships.

Using "I" Statements

One way of being assertive is using 'I' statements when communicating with others. These statements avoid sounding like accusations or confrontations by framing thoughts and emotions in terms of one's own perspective. For example, instead of saying "You never listen to me," you could say "I feel unheard when I do not feel listened to."

Being Specific and Direct

It is important to practise assertive communication in a clear and concise manner. Avoid using vague language and state your thoughts, needs, and expectations directly. This will ensure that what you need or want from the other person is stated clearly so as not to be misconstrued.

Positive Talk

Positive talk makes communication easier. Don't criticise. Choose words that promote understanding and teamwork. This helps to change conflicts into productive talks.

Listen Well

To communicate assertively, you must listen well. Focus on the speaker, make eye contact, and understand their ideas and feelings. Show them you respect and understand them by listening closely.

Using these strategies helps people express themselves more clearly, strengthens bonds, and makes communication more effective.

Breaking Down Communication Barriers

We need to be alert to barriers blocking effective communication, preventing the smooth flow of information and understanding. Different kinds of focus issues create these barriers, including distractions outside, not paying attention, cultural diversity, and emotional disruptions. To overcome them, empathise, understand, and listen actively.

Distractions

In our busy world, numerous activities divert our attention, forming broad barriers to good communication. Persistent phone notifications or surrounding noise during a conversation can divert our attention from the current topic. To overcome this, one must create a conducive environment that supports effective communication, keeping focus on the speaker and keeping external factors at bay.

Not Paying Attention

When people don't pay attention, communication stumbles. They might be there, but not really. Their mind could be elsewhere. This hinders good interaction, especially with folks from different cultures. Looking someone in the eye and responding both verbally and with body language is a solution. This is active listening. It shows that you respect what they have to say, and it makes communication better.

Culture Clashes

Culture can get in the way of chatting well. Different cultures have unique ways of speaking and set rules. This can cause confusion between the people of these cultures. The answer? Cultural sensitivity. Work hard to see different viewpoints. Adapt how you communicate. Be open-minded and unbiased. This boosts understanding between different cultures.

Emotional Walls

Emotions affect how we talk. Negative ones like fear, anger, and worry can fog thinking and judgement. They make effective conversation tricky, even causing fights and breakups. Empathy is the answer. It means understanding how others feel,

stepping into their shoes, and responding suitably. This allows everyone to feel heard, making communication healthier.

In summary, to break these barriers, we must focus on the person we're chatting with, creating a fitting environment, respecting cultural differences, and practising empathy. This makes communication smoother and more efficient.

Handling Conflicts Effectively

Conflict is part of life. Whether at work or home, issues arise. Effective conflict resolution is crucial. Active listening and assertive communication are key here. Understand the issue, listen actively, and communicate assertively.

Understanding the Issue

Firstly, figure out the problem. What's the conflict about? Often, conflicts are not about what started them, but deeper issues. Be open and honest, and listen actively. This gives a deeper understanding of the problem, aiding its resolution.

Active Listening

Next, actively listen. Let the person express themselves fully without interrupting. Make eye contact and use body language to show you're listening. This provides them the comfort of sharing their feelings and thoughts openly.

Assertive Communication

Finally, use assertive communication. Express your thoughts, feelings, and needs clearly. Be honest and direct, but also respectful. This opens a path for a healthy discussion and solution.

Remember, conflicts happen. They are a part of life. However, handling them well promotes growth, understanding, and stronger connections. It's an opportunity for positive change.

Applying Skills in Different Contexts

These communication skills are versatile. They adapt to various settings, like the workplace, online chats, and cross-cultural interactions.

Workplace Communication

In the workplace, active listening and assertive communication are essential. They help build a positive work environment, ease conflict resolution, and enhance teamwork. Managers should promote these skills among employees, fostering a healthy and productive workplace.

Online Chats

Online communication is prevalent in today's world. Here, misunderstandings are common due to the absence of non-verbal cues. Active listening becomes crucial. While typing, ensure clarity. Use emoticons or emojis to convey emotions. Be assertive yet respectful to avoid misinterpretations.

Cross-Cultural Interactions

In a globalised world, cross-cultural communication is frequent. Different cultures have unique communication styles. Active listening is key here. Respect and adapt to diverse communication norms. Use assertive communication wisely, considering cultural sensitivities. This fosters understanding and cooperation across cultures.

Conclusion

Active listening and assertive communication are powerful tools. They enhance our interactions, strengthen relationships, and promote personal growth. By incorporating these skills into our daily lives, we can navigate various communication contexts with confidence and effectiveness.

As we conclude part 22, remember that communication is a continuous learning process. Practise active listening and assertive communication regularly, and watch as your connections flourish and conflicts transform into opportunities for understanding and growth.

Chapter 23

"Understanding Emotional Intelligence: Detecting and Responding to Emotions through Nonverbal Clues"

****

Welcome to part 22 of our book. Here, we will explore two key techniques for effective chat: listening actively and speaking assertively. Each is valuable in forming connections, at home or work.

Active listening means being fully present and understanding, then responding wisely. It helps us connect, show empathy, and ease communication. Alternatively, with assertive speaking, we express our thoughts, feelings, and needs honestly but politely. It's great for self-worth, good relationships, and conflict solving.

In this part, we'll unpack the meaning of active listening, uncover the benefits of assertiveness, and offer helpful tips. We also address hurdles in communication, suggest ways to handle conflicts, and show how these skills fit in different contexts, from online chats to work meetings and cross-cultural exchanges.

Gaining active listening skills and learning to assertively communicate will make us better communicators, deepen our connections, and support our personal growth. Now, let's dive into the realm of mindful listening and respectful discussion.

Why Active Listening Matters

Good communication is key both in work and personal life. Here, active listening becomes crucial. It's not just about hearing but tuning in completely to the speaker. This way, understanding is achieved by both sides.

By listening actively, trust grows. This makes talking with others better. This kind of listening is a courtesy to the speaker. It further sets a good domain for deep and meaningful talks to happen.

"Active listening isn't limited to words; body language and changes in tone speak volumes too."

Active listening makes for better communication. It helps us understand others' points of view. Plus, it reveals details we may have skipped. It cultivates a sense of belonging, understanding and empathy.

"Active listening is key to strong communication. It helps build strong ties, handle disagreements and encourage teamwork."

Active listening is a habit that needs practice. It calls for full focus during talks and lessening of distractions in the environment. Moreover, it needs the use of clarity-seeking questions. Such questions help extract more meanings from what has been said. Plus, paraphrasing or summarising can help ensure correct understanding."

By being good listeners, we can build better connections, boost our communication, and make our workplaces more pleasant.

Why Assertive Communication Matters

Assertive communication, when used right, is key. It lets people express themselves clearly and with confidence. Their thoughts, feelings, and needs can be shared in a polite, clear way. This form of communication offers lots of benefits and can promote self-growth.

Healthy connections stem from effective communication. Open and honest dialogue is the result of practised assertive communication. This fuels trust and understanding, letting people freely share their thoughts and recognize others' viewpoints. This creates solid bonds.

In addition, assertive communication builds self-assurance. By speaking assertively, individuals feel valued and real. It emboldens them to voice their opinions and set their boundaries in both personal and professional contexts.

Not to forget, objecting respectfully is vital for conflict settlement. It helps avoid unnecessary struggles and find solutions that are fair to everyone. This fosters peace within individuals and groups.

Assertive communication boosts confidence, letting people defend themselves from abuse or intrusion. It fosters self-reliance, empowerment, and self-advocacy.

Good communication skills are tied to assertiveness. It builds healthy relationships, enhances self-esteem, and aids in managing conflicts. Being assertive allows full communication and realisation of personal potential.

Practising Active Listening

Communication isn't just about talking, but also active listening. Achieve better interaction by applying active listening techniques.

A technique is to look directly at the speaker, showing that you're engaged and interested in their message. This body language allows for catching non-verbal cues to understand their feelings better.

Active listening involves nodding and using body gestures correctly. It signifies that you're digesting the information, prompting the speaker to share more of what they think or feel.

Another helpful practice is asking questions to understand the speaker better. This signifies interest and facilitates more insight, saving from unnecessary assumptions.

Paraphrasing refers to restating the words of a speaker into your own words. It proves understanding on your part and confirms your correct interpretation.

Lastly, summarising or restating the speech consolidates information and helps pick out critical points made by the speaker. Thus, it helps in bringing out main ideas and ensuring that both parties understand each other's views.

These active listening techniques need regular practice so as to improve one's communication skills. This will allow you to establish better connections, handle conflicts efficiently and create a collaborative environment in personal as well as professional relationships.

Assertive Communication Strategies

Assertive communication involves applying numerous strategies that encourage openness and honesty while talking. Through these methods, such as effective communication, expressing needs or opinions assertively can become easier, leading to stronger relationships.

Using "I" Statements

One way of being assertive is using 'I' statements when communicating with others. These statements avoid sounding like accusations or confrontations by framing thoughts and emotions in terms of one's own perspective. For example, instead of saying "You never listen to me," you could say "I feel unheard when I do not feel listened to."

Being Specific and Direct

It is important to practise assertive communication in a clear and concise manner. Avoid using vague language and state your thoughts, needs, and expectations directly. This will ensure that what you need or want from the other person is stated clearly so as not to be misconstrued.

Positive Talk

Positive talk makes communication easier. Don't criticise. Choose words that promote understanding and teamwork. This helps to change conflicts into productive talks.

Listen Well

To communicate assertively, you must listen well. Focus on the speaker, make eye contact, and understand their ideas and feelings. Show them you respect and understand them by listening closely.

Using these strategies helps people express themselves more clearly, strengthens bonds, and makes communication more effective.

Breaking Down Communication Barriers

We need to be alert to barriers blocking effective communication, preventing the smooth flow of information and understanding. Different kinds of focus issues create these barriers, including distractions outside, not paying attention, cultural diversity, and emotional disruptions. To overcome them, empathise, understand, and listen actively.

Distractions

In our busy world, numerous activities divert our attention, forming broad barriers to good communication. Persistent phone notifications or surrounding noise during a conversation can divert our attention from the current topic. To overcome this, one must create a conducive environment that supports effective communication, keeping focus on the speaker and keeping external factors at bay.

Not Paying Attention

When people don't pay attention, communication stumbles. They might be there, but not really. Their mind could be elsewhere. This hinders good interaction, especially with folks from different cultures. Looking someone in the eye and responding both verbally and with body language is a solution. This is active listening. It shows that you respect what they have to say, and it makes communication better.

Culture Clashes

Culture can get in the way of chatting well. Different cultures have unique ways of speaking and set rules. This can cause confusion between the people of these cultures. The answer? Cultural sensitivity. Work hard to see different viewpoints. Adapt how you communicate. Be open-minded and unbiased. This boosts understanding between different cultures.

Emotional Walls

Emotions affect how we talk. Negative ones like fear, anger, and worry can fog thinking and judgement. They make effective conversation tricky, even causing fights and breakups. Empathy is the answer. It means understanding how others feel, stepping into their shoes, and responding suitably. This allows everyone to feel heard, making communication healthier.

In summary, to break these barriers, we must focus on the person we're chatting with, creating a fitting environment, respecting cultural differences, and practising empathy. This makes communication smoother and more efficient.

Handling Conflicts Effectively

Conflict is part of life. Whether at work or home, issues arise. Effective conflict resolution is crucial. Active listening and assertive communication are key here. Understand the issue, listen actively, and communicate assertively.

Understanding the Issue

Firstly, figure out the problem. What's the conflict about? Often, conflicts are not about what started them, but deeper issues. Be open and honest, and listen actively. This gives a deeper understanding of the problem, aiding its resolution.

Active Listening

Next, actively listen. Let the person express themselves fully without interrupting. Make eye contact and use body language to show you're listening. This provides them the comfort of sharing their feelings and thoughts openly.

Assertive Communication

Finally, use assertive communication. Express your thoughts, feelings, and needs clearly. Be honest and direct, but also respectful. This opens a path for a healthy discussion and solution.

Remember, conflicts happen. They are a part of life. However, handling them well promotes growth, understanding, and stronger connections. It's an opportunity for positive change.

Applying Skills in Different Contexts

These communication skills are versatile. They adapt to various settings, like the workplace, online chats, and cross-cultural interactions.

Workplace Communication

In the workplace, active listening and assertive communication are essential. They help build a positive work environment, ease conflict resolution, and enhance teamwork. Managers should promote these skills among employees, fostering a healthy and productive workplace.

Online Chats

Online communication is prevalent in today's world. Here, misunderstandings are common due to the absence of non-verbal cues. Active listening becomes crucial. While typing, ensure clarity. Use emoticons or emojis to convey emotions. Be assertive yet respectful to avoid misinterpretations.

Cross-Cultural Interactions

In a globalised world, cross-cultural communication is frequent. Different cultures have unique communication styles. Active listening is key here. Respect and adapt to diverse communication norms. Use assertive communication wisely, considering cultural sensitivities. This fosters understanding and cooperation across cultures.

Conclusion

Active listening and assertive communication are powerful tools. They enhance our interactions, strengthen relationships, and promote personal growth. By incorporating these skills into our daily lives, we can navigate various communication contexts with confidence and effectiveness.

As we conclude part 22, remember that communication is a continuous learning process. Practise active listening and assertive communication regularly, and watch as your connections flourish and conflicts transform into opportunities for understanding and growth.

Chapter 24

Identifying Boundaries in Personal and Professional Relationships to Avoid Burnout

****

Growing as a person is ke-y to a happy life. Without clear boundaries, it's tough. Not e-veryone can share the-ir limits well. This can cause them to be- tired, upset, and eve-ntually drained.

Join us as we explore- how setting boundaries boosts healthy re-lationships, supports growth, and improves our overall state of mind. By compre-hending and setting these- limits, we can take bette-r care of ourselves and build de-eper connections.

The- chapter starts by highlighting why setting personal and work-re-lated boundaries are ke-y to shaping our individuality and avoiding 'burning out'. Clear communication of our limits is not just about respecting a re-lationship, but it aids in its growth too.

This chapter covers many types of boundarie-s. We'll learn about the various strate-gies of setting boundaries in re-lationships and work, and how to tackle associated challenge-s. By the time you complete- this chapter, you will know how boundaries can enrich your life-.

Ready to dive into the re-alm of personal growth? Let's discover how boundarie-s affect our relationships.

Boundaries and Pe-rsonal Growth

Setting your limits boosts personal growth. It helps individuals to ide-ntify their core values, ne-eds, and priorities. It boosts self-aware-ness which further leads to se-lf-growth. It signals we value our emotional he-alth, energy, and time. It prove-s we respect ourse-lves and deserve-respect from others as we ll.

Learning how to gain more- respect from others involve-s understanding our own standards and those of others. It's about strong communication skills and advocating for ourse-lves. This approach helps us make smart choice-s, build stronger relationships, and live a happie-r life.

Boundaries play a key role- in personal growth, which is always evolving. As we be-come more self-aware-, we can fine-tune our boundarie-s to better refle-ct our values and goals. Thus, we learn more- about who we are and our place in the- world, enhancing resilience- and satisfaction.

Exploring Different Types of Boundarie-s

Healthy relationships, both personal and profe-ssional, rely on good boundary setting. Differe-nt types of boundaries contribute to pe-rsonal growth. Physical boundaries relate to pe-rsonal space; emotional boundaries cove-r thoughts and feelings; time boundarie-s designate how long a specific activity will last. Unde-rstanding these boundaries can he-lp create practical limits that both protect your we-ll-being and foster growth.

Setting Boundarie-s in Personal Relationships

While pe-rsonal relationships are a vital part of our lives, the-y can also be sources of stress and te-nsion. Setting boundaries in personal re-lationships is a crucial step towards personal deve-lopment and building healthier conne-ctions. When implementing the-m, speak plainly, honestly yet re-spectfully. Below are some- pointers on how to set boundaries with family, frie-nds, or romantic partners:

Discover Your Ne-eds and Limits

Don't enforce limits without knowing what you ne-ed. Reflect on your prioritie-s and stress triggers. This is crucial to discuss your boundaries e-ffectively.

Clarity is Key

Whe-n you set boundaries, be e-xplicit, be clear. Say what actions you cannot tolerate- and spell out the reactions, following boundary violations. To make- your point, say, "I am uncomfortable when…" or "I prefe-r r…".

Persistence is Power

Continuing with your boundaries is essential. It he-lps others understand that you mean busine-ss. Stand your ground.

Respect for All

Respe-ct is a two-way street. It's esse-ntial to uphold others' boundaries too. Hear the-m out, learn their prefe-rences and limits, then adapt.

Care- for Yourself

Managing relationships can be hard, both e-motionally and physically. It tests your resilience-. So, engage in activities that uplift you. He-althy hobbies are a good idea.

Setting rule-s in personal connections can breathe- new life into a person. It builds powe-r and brings about much-needed change. This leads to self-respe-ct and helps foster bonds among people-.

Workplace Boundaries

At work, setting boundarie-s is key to growth and avoiding burnout. Workers struggle balancing work and pe-rsonal life, leading to stress. Barriers at the workplace aid employe-es' focus on self-care and care-er goals.

Work-Life Balance Challenges

Work demands invade pe-rsonal time, causing difficulty unwinding. Striking a work-life balance ne-eds firm personal rules e-nforced by individuals. But it's tricky due to workplace culture-, individual values, and conflicting aspirations.

Workplace Barrier Tactics

Se-tting work boundaries can use strategie-s like task delegation, re-alistic goal setting, and self-care. Discussing the se with colleagues and bosse-s helps maintain boundaries. Excelle-nt communication fosters a supportive work culture.

Boundary Benefits

Creating limits helps us grow. The outcome-? Less stress, sharper focus, and be-tter work productivity. This allows for a satisfying life due to be-ing in control of our personal and professional circumstances. As a re-sult, we perform bette-r at work.

Boundaries and Looking After Yourself

Establishing limits is ke-y to self-care. It's about realising and sharing our boundarie-s, whether that's with ourselve-s or others.

We set spe-cific limits for our time, energy, and fe-elings. This focus on self-care he-lps avoid burnout, leading to a healthier se-lf. Saying no is crucial, allowing yourself to rest and regain e-nergy. This leads to constant happiness without stre-ss.

Yet, setting boundaries isn't e-asy. We're not accustomed to tre-ating ourselves this way. The solution? Start small, re-main consistent, and gradually become stronge-r at setting limits. We can find support from friends, family, or the rapists during this process.

Over time, se-tting healthy boundaries leads to se-lf-respect, personal growth, and a more-fulfilling life.

Effective Boundary Communication

For example, while setting up personal development and healthy relationships one has to talk about those limits effectively. The guidelines followed when expressing your needs and limits assertively include;

Use "I" Statements

Instead of using "you" start your statements with "I" hence avoiding a tone of accusation which can result in the other person becoming defensive. For instance, instead of saying "you always interrupt me," say "I feel hurt and disrespected when I am interrupted."

Be clear and specific

When establishing boundaries don't use indefinite statements. Be clear on what behaviours you consider unacceptable and state openly what will happen if someone trespasses them. For example, don't say "Don't be rude to me." Instead say something like, "It's unacceptable that you shout at me or insult me during our conversation because I will cut off the conversation immediately."

Practise active listening

Therefore make sure you have understood their perspective and feelings and also seek for compromise as well as common ground so that a good relationship can be maintained.

Stand firm

Although people should be allowed to change their restrictions as need arises, they should never let others pressure them into compromising their values or needs but rather stand firm in communicating them forcefully even if it may lead to momentary uneasiness or conflict within the relationship.

By practising effective communication when setting boundaries, we can promote healthy and respectful relationships in both personal and professional settings, resulting in greater personal development and well-being.

Understanding and Re-specting Boundaries of Others

We- don't only set and convey our own limits. It's just as vital to accept othe-rs' borders. Seeing and re-specting these line-s is a sign of empathy, regard, and concern. It he-lps establish good relationships and personal growth. Such mutual re-spect nurtures an open, trusting, and caring e-nvironment, showing the importance of boundarie-s.

To understand their boundaries, we- need to observe- others. Be alert to the-ir words and actions. Furthermore, good listening skills are- needed. The-re should be no assumptions or pressure- on them to share more than the-y're comfortable with. Respe-cting their borders may mean acce-pting they might avoid some activities or talks if the-y feel uneasy.

Hence, respecting othe-rs' boundaries requires unde-rstanding, being mindful, and empathetic in e-qual parts. This practice creates a zone- that fosters personal growth, authenticity, and he-althy relationships.

Scanning and rethinking Boundaries

In your journe-y towards personal growth and nurturing good relationships, communicating your boundaries e-ffectively is esse-ntial. Here are ke-y principles when expre-ssing your needs and boundaries asse-rtively:

Adopt "I" Statements

Re-visiting your boundaries requires se-lf-honesty. Do your current limits still aid you, or do they hinde-r personal growth? Are there- places where firme-r or more flexible boundarie-s could help? Asking yourself such questions can kick-start the- revaluation of your boundaries.

Changing one's limits can be- hard, but it's necessary for ongoing personal growth. It de-monstrates a readiness to e-volve, not remain stuck or rigid. Constantly rese-tting these limits ensure-s individuals stay healthy and can care for others in the-ir lives.

Keep in mind, se-tting limits is an evolving process. It calls for self-aware-ness, communication, and adaptability to the pressure-s of personal growth and changing situations.

Challenges with Se-tting Boundaries

Establishing and upholding boundaries important for personal growth and he-althy relationships can be a hard task. Many folks struggle with cre-ating clear limits, be it in their pe-rsonal or work life.

Main Hindrances to Setting Boundaries

A typical issue is the fear of conflict and re-jection. Some avoid creating limits, so the-y don't stir up conflict. This leads to difficulties expre-ssing their needs or constraints.

Anothe-r hurdle may be guilt, espe-cially when creating boundaries in pe-rsonal relationships. A person might fee-l bad prioritising their wellbeing ove-r others', which makes expre-ssing and holding these limits a challenge-.

Ways to Overcome Resistance

You can overcome these- challenges if you understand that se-tting boundaries is key for personal growth and se-lf-care. Begin with, deve-lop assertive communication methods and conside-r any guilt associated with setting these- constraints as normal.

Talking with loved one-s or a therapist can simplify the task of setting boundarie-s, especially for beginne-rs or those finding it tough. Remembe-r, it's a process - mistakes and adjustments are- part of the journey.

Tackling boundary-relate-d problems head-on can help individuals gain control of the-ir personal and professional lives, le-ading to happiness, growth, and wellness.

Issue-s Caused by Overstepping Boundarie-s and Conflict Resolution

Crossing boundaries can spark conflicts that hinder pe-rsonal growth and harm relationships. However, the-se conflicts can also be valuable opportunitie-s for learning. The secre-t is expressing your concerns whe-n boundaries are crossed cle-arly and actively listening to the othe-r person's point of view. If a compromise se-ems out of reach, consider involving an unbiase-d third party such as a mediator. They can promote productive- conflict resolution and deter future- boundary crossings. Remember, navigating conflicts fosters personal growth and healthier inte-rpersonal relationships.

Getting He-lp and Consulting Professionals

Boundary setting, although crucial to personal growth and he-althy relationships, can be tough to grasp. Here-'s where professionals can be- of great help. Therapy or life- coaching can give people de-eper insights into their ne-eds and limits whilst improving their communication and conflict resolution abilitie-s.

Sometime-s, getting support from a professional can be a positive- step for someone who wishe-s to better understand the-mselves and tackle the-ir problems. Know this - seeking he-lp doesn't signal weakness. Inste-ad, it shows bravery in striving for self-growth and forging healthy boundarie-s in relationships.

Stability and Adaptability

Maintaining a boundary while allowing for adjustments is a fine- tipping point between stability and adaptability. Stability e-ncourages steadiness and ce-rtainty in relationships. Simultaneously, adaptability permits shifts to me-et new demands.

Re-garding personal growth and boundary establishment, I'd re-commend a level of adaptability. But you should maintain ste-adiness in your principles and non-negotiable-s. This means you should anticipate and accept compromise-s but firmly state your non-acceptance for spe-cific situations.

In contrast, occupational boundaries can bend for teamwork and collaboration while- ensuring steadiness in work e-xpectations and personal convictions. Tweaking or re-inforcing borders requires hone-sty from both co-workers and supervisors.

People- may need to tweak the-ir boundary-drawing methods during conversations about personal re-lationships. Still, it's crucial that partners stick to a designated rule- set outlining their relationship, e-ven though these rule-s should remain fluid. It's essential that couple-s regularly review the-ir boundaries due to changes in life- circumstances or personal dynamics.

Finally, well-rounde-d growth needs balance and unde-rstanding of your own limits. Doing so, you build healthier ties without losing yourse-lf in them. You focus on your wellbeing and pe-rsonal growth.

Chapter 25

Networking to Boost your Career & Personal Development

****

Welcome to lesson 25.

We're talking about networking. It's a skill. It can give your career a boost and help you grow as a person.

You use networking to make relationships that help your career. You meet new people. You make professional contacts. You use these for your own growth.

Networking: Important for Growth

Networking helps you grow. It's key for your career. You reach out to others in your field. You learn from them. They give you insights and knowledge. When you have lots of contacts, you have chances for new things. You can improve your skills. You can keep up with the latest in your field. Networking helps you when you have issues in your career.

"Think of networking like a Swiss army knife. It has many purposes. You connect with professionals. You gain knowledge. You can find new opportunities. It's your lifeline in an always-changing world."

When you network, you meet people. They can mentor or support you. They show you the ropes with useful information about your job. Networking makes links. These links let you see different views. They help you think up new ideas which helps personal growth further.

See networking as a skill booster. By talking to experts in your job area, you can learn lots. Remember, you might also pick up new details. This way, you always keep learning. You stay up-to-date with your industry too.

Be on Your Toes

"Networking isn't a one-off event; it's a constant task that demands energy and focus."

To make networking truly work for you, you have to be on your toes. You must be forward-thinking. Take part in seminars, workshops, and conferences to grow your contacts. Be active on LinkedIn and participate in discussions. This increases chances of making meaningful ties and growing personally.

Networking Does Wonders for Your Career

Networking is crucial for moving up in your career. It's abundant in benefits that boost one's job growth. Networking lets you widen your professional circle. This enhances chances of discovering new avenues, promotions, and career growth.

By networking, people can discover secret job opportunities. These jobs might not be posted through normal methods. Those with many contacts stay ahead. They know about industry changes and upcoming job roles, which gives them an edge in their career.

In simple terms, networking gives people a stage. It makes their talents shine. At events or online, like on LinkedIn, they share what they're good at. Their name gets around in the business world; they become people that companies want to keep.

And it's not just about showing off. Networking helps you meet important people, too. Get to know the big shots, the people who can advise you and really boost your career. They help you with problems, with challenges.

When your network is strong, you can use it. All those people you know, they're like your brain trust. They've been there, done that. You can ask them anything, share ideas, maybe even work together.

So, why network? It connects you with people, opens up job avenues you didn't know about, lets you show off your skills, and brings you pretty interesting friendships. Networking can crank up your career and make personal growth take wings.

Building Solid Connections for Self-Improvement

Developing potent links is key for self-growth and career progress. Hard work is required to forge invaluable bonds that can open doors to limitless opportunities. Here's how to establish a robust network:

1. Engage in Industry Gatherings

Business get-togethers like forums, workshops, or network-building events are perfect spots to meet new faces and widen your professional circle. Consistent presence at these gatherings allows you to initiate discussions, exchange contact details, particularly with those having similar interests or professional fields for enhanced offline interaction.

2. Join Professional Bodies

Being a member of professional bodies or work-related organisations can certainly provide networking opportunities and access to useful resources. These communities offer industry experts, they conduct workshops on diverse subjects and regularly display current trends. Actively participating in these groups pushes your network forward, connecting with like-minded individuals.

3. Harness Social Media

Digital platforms such as LinkedIn are essential for networking in today's web-enabled world. Construct a profile showcasing your abilities and past work, then start interacting with other professionals in your industry. Engage in topic-groups, partake in discussions, and share insightful tips. This approach connects you with global professionals, pushing your network past local confines while staying updated on industry happenings.

4. Keep Your Connections Strong

Building a strong network involves more than just making contacts. Stay in touch with the professionals you meet. You can email, call, or meet them, if possible. Show you care about their career progress and lend a hand when you can. A simple act of encouragement can strengthen your professional bonds and prove your worth to them.

"Think of it as planting seeds. If sown thoughtfully, over time, they will sprout and offer many opportunities for personal growth and career success."

Patience and effort are required for network growth, but they pay off in the long run. Participate in industry events, join professional groups, use social media wisely, and nurture your relationships. This will build a solid network to support your overall growth.

Best Networking Methods for Career Progress

Effective networking can be the key to career and personal advancement. Networking is more than exchanging business cards or getting more LinkedIn contacts. It's about creating meaningful interactions that benefit both parties. Here are some methods to maximise benefits from networking.

1. Attend Networking with Genuine Curiosity

Networking isn't a one-way street; it's an opportunity to connect and learn from others. So be truly interested when networking. Show enthusiasm to learn, which will build connections based on shared goals and common interests.

2. Listen Actively

Active listening plays a vital role in networking. So, lend an ear to what others have to say. Engage them with insightful questions and solid discussions relevant to your interests or your career. This way, your attentiveness will leave a lasting impression and foster deeper connections.

3. Provide Help and Support

Remember, networking isn't only about gaining but also sharing. So, if someone in your network requires help, be there for them. This aid can be problem-solving, presenting important resources, or extending needed advice. Helping others makes you reliable and proficient.

"Networking is about fostering relationships and helping others thrive."

4. Stay in Touch and Keep Connected

Don't let the initial meeting be the final interaction, no matter the hierarchy. Try to keep in touch with your contacts regularly. Send personal emails, utilise social media like Facebook, or plan meet-ups or virtual meet-ups. Each person brings unique experiences to enrich discussions. By remaining connected, career relationships thrive over time.

Making connections boosts your job progress and self-improvement. By using these smart tactics, fresh paths unfold, helping you discover more about you and others. Plus, it creates a robust community of seasoned professionals to aid your job advancement.

Using Connections for Job Progress

Networking isn't just forging links. It's about using these links to speed up your job development and drive your career upwards. Think of your network as a pool of mentors, advisors and specialists from your field providing guidance for your journey.

To cash in on your network, consider mentorship. The wisdom and support from such guides can be priceless as you tackle the hurdles and intricacies of your career. Their direction can speed up your learning and improve your performance, pushing you nearer to your job goals

Also, use your network to stay current. Regular interaction with your contacts helps you in grasping the latest industry trends and stay informed on the job market. They can advise you on the capabilities that are presently in demand and the areas where there is the chance of future expansion.

Building a positive reputation within your network is critical. Being recognized as reliable, proficient, and amiable goes a long way in pushing your career. Being approachable makes others turn to you when they're in need. It's a win-win situation.

Remember, your network is a two-way street. The more you put into it, the more you get back. Whether you're just beginning or an experienced professional, networking is vital for continuous career growth. It's a dynamic process that needs patience, effort, and consistency. So, take a step forward, start connecting, and make your career flourish.

Chapter 26

Mastering Financial Acumen: Build and Control Your Budget to Boost Net Worth

***

In today's rapidly changing economic environment, financial acumen is not only an asset but a necessity. Often, people think that financial acumen has got to do with complex stock market trends or investment algorithms. In fact, it is more about handling money matters effectively and the first step towards this would be to keep track of your income statement and balance sheet and then establishing a budget and tracking net worth.

Financial acumen as a skill enables us to comprehend our financial world and make monetary-sensitive decisions. This forms the foundation of all future financial security and prosperity. More than just being able to pay bills on time or never go into debt. It involves grasping the essence of money, how it comes and goes from our lives, and how it can be managed for maximum benefit.

The Essence of Financial Acumen:

Today as opposed to the traditional view of looking at finance management for professionals only or business people alone in contemporary society everyone needs some level of financial acumen. To individuals it helps in managing personal finances effectively; brings out clearly where our money comes from or goes to help come up with ideas for savings or investments. Therefore, having financial acumen means personal well-being.

For organisations having leaders who possess financial sense is important because it results in better choices made when they are required. It means they have the ability to allocate resources properly, make accurate budget projections, limit waste and enhance profitability. And so whether you run a billion dollar corporation or your domestic economy – financial acumen remains vital.

Boosting Your Financial Acumen:

Developing proficiency in finance takes time. Like any other expertise area, mastering personal finance requires time investment, concentration, and a proper plan of work. The starting point should be monitoring income statements regularly. This habit helps you discover valuable information concerning your expenses culture. Consequently one can identify areas of wastefulness as well as possible savings.

Thereafter the next step is using the data obtained during the tracking process to develop a realistic budget. A budget is in essence a financial plan that sets your spending and saving targets. Budgeting well is about being precise yet flexible, so as not to kill off the lifestyle while accounting for future plans.

Moreover, knowing what net worth stands for forms a critical part of your journey towards becoming financially sound. Your net worth is basically assets minus liabilities. Similar to businesses which measure their value over time, personal net worth can be used to check if you are making progress or not.

Managing Finances Essential Components:

Acquiring financial acumen involves getting acquainted with several aspects of personal finance management. Some of the components that one must be aware of include; knowing your net worth, tracking your income statement as well as balance sheet, having a budget, adhering to personal financial principles and executing the budget successfully.

Net Worth

Your financial health can hardly be measured without understanding your net worth. It explicitly states where you stand at any given moment regarding finances. In other words it is the difference between what you own and what you owe.

Income and Expenditure Tracking

To effectively manage your finances, it is necessary for you to have a clear picture of how much money you make and what you spend on. This constitutes keeping track of every dollar received as revenues and paid out as expenses. Although this might be seen as a boring document, it helps you identify where you spend your money, cuts out unnecessary expenses and assists in making the right corrections.

Budgeting:

A well-crafted budget is a roadmap that will lead you through your financial journey. It does not only tell how much income you expect to earn but also how those funds will be used or saved. Budgeting allows us to provide for our needs and wants while ensuring that our expenditures do not exceed our earnings.

Personal Finance Principles:

There are some basic personal finance principles that can help in managing one's finances better. These principles include saving often, staying away from unnecessary loans, investing wisely for long-term growth prospects, appreciating the importance of having insurance among others are all important elements of good personal finance management for maintaining sound financial wellness.

Budget Execution:

Even the most carefully planned budget is useless if it isn't followed. That's why budget implementation is just as important in personal finance management as budget creation. Consistently sticking to a budget prevents us from making costly mistakes and keeps us on track towards achieving our financial objectives. Such practices like regular budget reviews, close watch over costs, and changes when needed are essential to be successful with the actualization of a designed budget.

Now let's consider how we can improve our ability to monitor the flow of our income and expenses after understanding the components involved in managing finances. This step is critical because, without it, effective financial administration cannot happen.

Understanding Your Finances - Tracking Income and Expenses:

Being financially literate starts with being conscious about what makes up your income and expenses. You may think that this is obvious but many people ignore this simple fact which has great power in their journey towards financial freedom. Knowledge of your income and where it goes on a monthly basis establishes the foundation for proper financial management.

Income Analysis: The Starting Point

The first thing to do when you are trying to track your finances is to identify where you get your money from. For most people, this will involve earnings from work – whether they are working full-time, part-time or as freelancers. However, other sources like rental fees, dividend revenues on investments or some profits generated by small businesses should also be included.

When your revenue fluctuates significantly (as in the case of freelancers or business owners), average your monthly income based on previous months. You might need to keep updating this number in case your earnings vary substantially.

The Importance of Expense Management

On the other hand, with regard to outflows, you must begin by noting all of your fixed costs; that is, expenses such as rent/mortgage payments, utilities bills, insurance premiums and car/other loans that require payment each month without fail. Finally track variable ones like groceries, gas/fuel costs, entertainment events as well as any other type of discretionary spending.

A correct expense list should contain not only routine costs but also occasional ones like annual insurance premium or unexpected charges such as medical expenses. In order to have an exact picture of what you spend for at least one-three months and observe a holistic view of it all in general.

To actually gain control of your personal finance, document every dollar you spend. Although initially it may seem boring, this will provide insights into your current financial habits and areas that need to be worked on.

There are several financial management tools or applications that could help one track their expenses more easily. Note how important it is to be consistent with expense recording since it will help you identify patterns and trends in your spending which in turn gives you power to control them.

Reasons Why You Should Use Financial Management Tools

In today's digital business world, there are budgeting and expense tracking apps designed to simplify the process of recording income and expenses. They come with automatic categorizations for transactions, reports for critical information, setting budgets on specific categories as well as providing comprehensive tracking by connecting many accounts.

It is this efficient combination of both data (income and expenditure) that begins the foundation for a workable budget (a topic we shall look at later). Now let us go deeper into coming up with an effective budget based on how we should track our finances.

Aims of Constructing a Pragmatic Budget:

Constructing a financial plan is like developing a roadmap towards achieving monetary objectives. This provides an overview of earnings and expenditures thereby enabling goal-setting in terms of money matters. Nonetheless, a good budget does not necessarily mean putting down figures; it means knowing about one's financial habits and getting ready for tomorrow's needs.

Principles of Making a Budget

For an actualized budget, the first step is understanding what contributes to your income base while you also keep record of every spending category. In other words, the last section explained how to keep track of these two elements. Then draft a rough copy budget once you have all these details in place.

In general, fixed costs (such as rent or mortgage), variable costs (like groceries), savings, discretionary expenses (e.g., entertainment), if relevant debt payments ought to be funded. The main thing is to find a balance between meeting your current needs and planning for future finances.

Income-based Budgeting: A Realistic Approach

Spending should be tied down by income received. Consequently, start your budget process by accounting for all the sources of monthly revenue you have. Allocate this earnings among different spending categories depending on priority – basic living needs first, then savings & investments and finally other expenses.

One common approach to income-based budgeting is the 50/20/30 rule which suggests using half of the income on rent/utility bills/groceries, saving/investment/debt repayments at 20% while using 30% for luxuries such as entertainment/restaurants/beauty salons.

Tactical Budget Requests

Controlled budget requests help set spending boundaries. This means creating expenditure limits in each category based on past actuals and anticipated future trends. Be practical when doing this and consider any potential expenditures.

For example, if $400 has been spent every month for groceries during the last three months, it would be sensible to reserve that much money for meals in your budget. Also keep in mind price increases or special occasions.

Prioritising Costs

In budgeting, not all expenses are of equal importance and are therefore categorised differently. This means that there should be a clear hierarchy of costs in which basics (such as renting/buying houses and essential services) come first while other things like entertainment and dining out appear as the last in the list. As a result, this practice ensures financial stability and supports successful saving goals.

Understanding Cost Accounting Standards

Knowing cost accounting standards can make one's money work harder for oneself besides being an effective manager of money. Nothing more than markers which are able to measure, allocate & disclose costs on financial statements is defined by these patterns. In terms of personal finance – using such laws may help appreciate the nature of costs making it easier to create an effective budget.

Managing Finances, Creating Budgets:

Once you have a budget in place, the next step is to make sure you're adhering to it. When you look at your finances normally one has to ensure that every coin spent is within the limits set out earlier on and at the same time optimise wherever needed. There are many strategies available for controlling and optimising your budget, such as considering contract financing options or taking advantage of cost accounting standards.

Contract Financing

Financing plays an important role in managing budgets both at personal and professional levels. On similar lines with businesses who opt for contract financing choices thus effectively managing their cash flows; individuals need to know how different types of financing can apply in their own situations.

Mechanisms of Contract Financing

Massive corporations use this system pretty often but essentially its general principle can be good for individual expenditure control too. For instance, if you have an upcoming expense like tuition fees or a large purchase which should be paid at a future date, saving a specific amount monthly based on anticipatory calculations can provide financial relief over time.

Optimising Your Budget

A well-managed budget isn't static; it requires adjustments based on changing circumstances and opportunities for optimization. This includes ways such as minimising unnecessary expenditures, identifying areas where savings could be increased or cost-efficient modifications can be introduced without compromising the quality of life.

To illustrate, let's consider your food expenses category - if dining out represents a significant portion here causing an overshoot in spending limits consistently; switching to homemade meals or occasional dining can resolve this without sacrificing much on satisfaction levels. Similarly exploring bulk-buy discounts, off-season deals for recurring purchases can lead to substantial savings over time.

The same approach applies for larger expenses too- taking advantage of early payment discounts on tuition fees, switching to cost-effective insurance plans, refinancing your mortgage for lower interest rates are significant steps towards optimising the budget.

Leveraging Cost Accounting Standards

Organised and efficient management of costs is possible through cost accounting standards. In personal finance management it is also possible to use these principles. By categorising costs into various groups, analysing them over time and pointing out inefficiency – you can easily control your spending.

Getting Acquainted with These Rules Can Also Help Understand Your Indirect Costs Affecting Your Finances Such as Depleting Assets; Maintenance Expenses Or opportunity costs that are never in budgets.

Regular budget review and adjustment is a basic element of taking control of your financial situation. Doing this will ensure that you always stay in touch with the current state of your finances but above all give you room to be able to change or realign as per your targets or situations around you.

Chapter 27

A Shifting from Scarcity to Abundance Mindset with Money – Building True Wealth Over Time

*****

This chapter will explore financial aptitude and how it can remodel your thoughts from scarcity to abundance. Furthermore, this chapter will discuss building real wealth over time and the steps to financial success.

Why Money Mindset Matters

The way you look at money has a lot to do with the success you will achieve in terms of finances. Having an attitude of abundance where you believe in plenty and that there is room for growth can lead to more opportunities and wealth. Conversely, viewing money with a scarcity mentality limits your financial independence.

"Your money mindset shapes your financial reality. If you believe in scarcity, you will attract scarcity. But when you embrace abundance, you open yourself up to endless possibilities for financial growth."

Finally, dear friend, transforming limited beliefs is indispensable in order to move from living in a place of lack to living the life of our dreams. By challenging negative thoughts and turning them into positive ones, we would be able to tap into our potentiality allowing us to draw more riches and good fortune towards us.

The Power of Positive Thinking

Positive thinking plays a key role in forming our money mindset. The more we focus on opportunities, growth and abundance the more they tend to manifest themselves in our lives. Adopting an optimistic outlook opens new windows that we previously ignored.

Breaking Free from Limiting Beliefs

Many individuals possess deep-rooted mindsets concerning money that tend to hinder their attainment of financial objectives. These self-limiting beliefs emanate from various sources including childhood experiences, societal conditioning as well as negative influences among others. Such beliefs need identification then they should be replaced with empowering ones.

For instance if you think that cash is hard earned, remind yourself of how much wealth surrounds you on a daily basis; besides repeating statements about what wealth is or means could help reframe our minds towards abundance by replacing our old paradigms with new ones.

Always remember that changing your own perspective about finances requires time as well as practice. Continually reinforcing positive beliefs, associating with like-minded and encouraging individuals and taking steps in line with your financial goals are the ways to go about it. This kind of mentality creates a path for better financial success and satisfaction.

The Power of Money in Creating Impact

Money has the power to create lasting impact and bring about positive change. It's more than a tool for facilitating financial transactions because it can save lives, provide access to basic needs or support worthy causes.

Understanding money as a resource and adopting a resourceful mindset allows us to achieve financial success and make an impact on our society.

"Money is a means to make a difference. It can amplify our efforts and create positive change on a larger scale."

The availability of finances makes it possible for societies to address societal problems, solve global challenges, and even promote humanity's welfare. Money is what drives us towards medical discoveries, education programs or even campaigns for a sustainable environment.

At the same time, it is important to note that money should also support people and organisations who are trying to make a change in their respective fields. Through giving to charitable organisations, funding social enterprises or sponsoring community-based projects, we can use our financial resources to cause a ripple-effect of positive change.

The Ripple Effect: Money in Action

However, financial resources have the power to ignite a sequence of events far beyond the initial investment:

Money can be used by individuals for higher education and acquire some relevant skills which will improve employment opportunities as well as increased earning potential.

Through improved economic status, individuals can give better lives to their family generations thus eradicating poverty completely from their lineage.

Money can catapult entrepreneurs and visionaries into real-life situations where they launch innovative enterprises and consequently promote economic development and job creation. Philanthropists and impact investors can also help make this world better through financing initiatives aimed at addressing social problems as well as protecting the environment and supporting sustainable development and greater equality among nations.

By realising the potential of money resources and using finance for good, we may create an environment in which our actions multiply the impact they have thus creating a brighter future for all mankind.

Money for Causes

To make any difference in life it is necessary to generate money. However, this is not about striving for wealth because of material things but having finances that enable you to contribute to your favourite initiatives or causes.

By blending your goals with what you want to achieve in terms of assets you will bring huge results that will last forever.

Switching from Scarcity Mindset to Abundance Mindset

Do you always worry about how you are going to get more cash? Do you often think about what you don't possess instead of what you do? It's time for a paradigm shift from scarcity into abundance.

Abundance mindset suggests that there is no limit or end towards monetary growth. It means that one should focus on gratitude, abundance and the feeling of having enough. Changing your thinking about money could change everything and let wealth start flowing right at your doorstep.

Recognizing and Replacing Limiting Beliefs

To begin with shifting from scarcity to abundance mentality, the first step is to identify and reframe your limiting beliefs. The first thing to do is find out which negative thoughts or beliefs never allow you to embrace abundance. Replace them with positive affirmations that provide you with a sense of empowerment as you trust in yourself that you can get rich.

"I have numerous opportunities to build wealth."

"My life is full of financial abundance."

Feeling Grateful

One of the most powerful techniques for changing a scarcity mindset into an abundant one is gratitude. Take a few moments every day to acknowledge what you are grateful for including any financial blessings in your life. By focusing on gratitude, you will transform your view from scarcity to abundance hence more positive experiences and increased wealth will be attracted into your life.

Surrounding Yourself with Positive Influences

The people we associate with play a big role in shaping our way of thinking. Always be around people with an abundant mentality who inspire and motivate you towards achieving financial success in life. They will keep reminding you what an abundant mindset looks like hence helping attract prosperity into your personal space.

Setting Financial Goals

To shift your mind to the abundance mindset, clear financial goals must be identified. This can happen once you have a well-defined picture of how you want to achieve financial success. Make particular and measurable objectives that match your values and passions and outline steps towards their realisation.

Investment in oneself

The importance of self-investment in fostering an outlook of abundance cannot be overemphasised. Examples include attending workshops, courses, or consulting with financial advisors about personal/professional development opportunities. Acquiring skills, knowledge and adopting the right attitudes puts one at a better position to attain financial abundance.

Transforming scarcity mindset to abundance is a process that calls for devotion, sacrifice and practice. Some ways include; recognizing and reframing limiting beliefs, practising gratitude, surrounding yourself with positive people who will impact your life positively, setting deliberate financial goals and investing in oneself. By doing this, you will change your attitude towards money and draw more money into your life.

Narrative vs Financial Outcomes

In our lives, we use stories to explain our money situation. Stories are so powerful that they can inspire us to take control of our own finances as well as guide our investment decisions. Whenever we listen to genuine tales being told we become open to converting ourselves.

This makes narratives relatable in addition it helps complex concepts about money easier to understand through emotional links created by storytelling. A fascinating story crafted by finance experts can simplify their expertise for anyone around the globe.

"Narrative serves as a bridge between the specialised world of finance and individuals' lived experiences – shaping how we see and relate to money, ultimately guiding our financial choices."

We feel motivated when other people talk about similar experiences with ours thus making us engaged in pursuing financial success relentlessly. Relatability makes these stories important because they enable us to overcome difficulties and embrace chances.

Furthermore, storytelling enables people to learn from real-life experiences of others' mistakes or triumphs; allowing them not to make the same mistakes. For instance, hearing accounts of financial failure or success helps to inform our own financial decision-making.

Authentic Narrative's Power

Moreover, it is possible to enhance financial literacy and enable individuals' improved financial decisions by using narrative and storytelling in the context of financial education. When explained through narratives, finance topics become more understandable since individuals can easily relate them to their personal lives.

"Storytelling appeals to our emotional intelligence by making finance education more engaging and relatable. This approach breathes life into various aspects of finance and encourages learners to actively partake in the learning process."

In addition, narratives build self-confidence in people against psychological barriers common with financial decisions. Seeing oneself within successful or resilient stories increases one's belief that they have the capability of growing financially.

Narrative Shaping Financial Outcomes

Financial success demands understanding how stories connect with outcomes. By connecting with stories that resonate with our values and objectives, we can determine how we use our money for better results.

Through the use of authentic storytelling we can challenge limiting beliefs and shift our thinking away from scarcity into abundance. We can overcome self-limiting beliefs and embrace wealth creation and unlimited possibilities through immersing ourselves in stories of financial growth and resilience.

Stories can shape our financial identity, leading us towards financial goals. By inventing narratives that are empowering, and adopting those narratives, we can have a positive influence on our finances.

Ultimately, this understanding enables us to make more conscious choices about our finances by connecting narratives with pecuniary outcomes. We can use story-telling as a means of informing, inspiring and leading us in our journey to financial freedom.

Scarcity Mindset Defined

Scarcity mindset is characterised by belief in limited resources and lack of abundance. This mindset may be determined by various cultural, psychological or economic factors that influence how individuals perceive opportunities for success.

Feelings of scarcity can become deeply ingrained, affecting one's mindset and actions. When people have a scarcity mind-set they focus on scarcity, lack and constraints instead of possibilities or abundance. This perception hampers personal growth; it limits financial success while creating anxiety or fear over money and resource allocation.

A scarcity mindset is influenced by different cultural factors like limited opportunities for education or employment when one grows up believing that resources are scarce in their environment. Moreover, such a mindset may be reinforced by messages from society surrounding competition and scarce resources hence making people believe that there isn't enough for everyone.

Psychological factors also contribute to a scarcity mindset. Biases like loss aversion or confirmation bias make people believe more in perceived scarcities thus cutting out on chances available. Past experiences of poverty or financial hardships also affect one's mentality thereby reinforcing the belief in lack.

"It perceives the world through tunnel vision where all we see is what isn't there." It prevents us from seeing beyond what is not present to the realities around us."

Understanding the effects of a scarcity mindset is crucial in overcoming its limitations and cultivating a mindset of abundance. It means recognizing that the real nature of global inequality lies in cultural and psychological aspects that contribute to scarcity mentality, leading individuals to change their perspective and adopt a more abundant mindset.

Adopting an Abundance Mindset

Shifting from a scarcity mindset to one of abundance requires consistent effort and persistence. This entails questioning our beliefs, being grateful and changing our thoughts around lack and abundance.

By seeing possibilities instead of limitations, people can open up themselves to new opportunities and have a healthy relationship with money. Having an abundance mindset makes someone understand finance as a tool for personal development as well as for societal growth rather than just scarce things that need to be saved.

The growth mindset is best explained by psychologist Carol Dweck who said:

"Rather than thinking 'Oh I'm going to reveal my weaknesses,' you say, 'Wow, here's a chance to grow.'"

Ultimately, adopting a mindset of abundance is a transformative journey that not only affects a person's relationship with money but also influences their overall well-being and happiness.

Debt and Its Impact on Housing and Inequality

In most Western economies, housing debt is a significant contributor to wealth inequality. The repercussions of the 2008 financial crisis as well as the current post-COVID environment have exposed the adverse impacts of undercapitalization and lack of safeguards in financial markets.

"Undercapitalization and inadequate safeguards in financial markets can result in financially unsustainable home mortgages and growing house prices."

These issues have broad ramifications, including homelessness among people at lower socioeconomic levels. Thus, the gap between the rich and the poor is increasing.

"To address wealth inequality requires an understanding of how debt, credit markets, and housing affordability all relate."

Efforts to address wealth inequality should focus not only on income redistribution but also on creating a fair and accessible housing market. By putting in place measures that ensure prudent lending practices, promote affordable and sustainable housing options as well as enhance financial literacy we can contribute to reducing wealth disparity within society. It is important that we do not overlook how important housing debt is when it comes to wealth inequality. However, if we confront these challenges head-on while fostering an equitable housing system, we may work towards a future where safe affordable housing opportunities are available equally for all.

Making a Difference through Impact Investing

In addition to helping you meet your investment goals, impact investing enables you to make positive social change. Through strategic investments in projects or companies that share your values and mission, you can achieve both social impact while generating returns from your investments.

One area where impact investing can significantly matter is narrowing down the gender-wealth gap. Women have historically been limited by barriers to entry into financial resources' access as well as other inequalities. This form of investment could be used to back programs that empower ladies while promoting gender equality as well as providing economic opportunities.

However, it is not only about gender equality when it comes to impact investing. This covers various social and environmental challenges allowing you to actually contribute in clean energy, education, healthcare and poverty alleviation. By driving investments into projects and companies that address these issues directly, it is possible to help build a more sustainable and fairer world.

"It combines finance's power with the aim of making good things better; this makes it a win-win situation for investors themselves and society as a whole."

Understanding how your money can make a difference is crucial in building true wealth and achieving financial freedom. Impact investments generate both financial returns but also bring about positive social impacts thus giving your investments more significance. Therefore, regardless of whether you are an individual investor or institution one must not underestimate the impacts of investing in impacting changes on earth. Aligning your financial goals with your values can enable you to create lasting impact and play a part in shaping tomorrow.

The Role of Money in True Wealth

Money is important in the creation of real wealth. It goes way beyond just being financially available and has a deeper understanding of how valuable it is and how it can help to lead to complete happiness in life and societal well-being as a whole. Real wealth is not so much about having things, but more about the feelings of security, freedom and opportunities that money can bring. It is the ability to follow one's dreams, make an impact on something they believe in, or something meaningful. In a middle-class context, money serves as an essential form of savings. As such, it allows individuals and families to create a foundation for their futures, providing a cushion against difficult times while opening doors for upward mobility.

"True wealth involves more than simply hoarding money; it entails saving money in order to live a satisfyingly directed life."

By changing our idea about the meaning of riches, we can move from an emphasis on mere possession of wealth to understanding money as a tool that promotes welfare or change for better living. This implies considering other factors outside financial accessibility like good health both physically and mentally, relationships, personal development aspects among others plus being part of community services.

Finally, genuine riches have more to do with achieving financial stability while striving for an enriched existence. It encompasses directing our finances towards our values and hopes hence enabling us to live lives that are full of purpose that makes positive impacts on people around us.

The Connection between Money and Research

Money and research are inseparable when it comes to understanding the financial impact of various factors. For example, through data analysis and research, one can gain valuable insights into financial patterns that would promote informed decision-making. In this regard, research is primarily important in understanding certain factors such as: market trend analysis or studying the effects of financial policies such as prices and income in developing financial acumen and driving financial success.

We live in a data-driven world, where information plays a crucial role in gaining a competitive edge. As the financial markets change and become more complex, so does the need for reliance on data analysis and research. So far seen historical trends are of great importance to researchers who can develop strategies to mitigate risks or maximise returns.

"Data analysis and research lay the foundation for informed decision-making in the financial landscape."

For instance, using data analysis helps to identify potential market trends thus allowing investors to make informed investment decisions at an appropriate time. The impact of diverse finance policies can also be studied leading to their possible implications hence enabling policymakers' effective strategic planning. Moreover, research stretches beyond financial markets to incorporate macroeconomic analysis, industry study as well as consumer behaviour study among others. Organisations can only make sound decisions if they understand how these aspects may influence their finances, hence improving their performance levels and giving them a competitive advantage.

The Importance of Research in Financial Acumen

Research is an integral aspect of building up one's financial acumen. This is because it provides one with a solid foundation built on knowledge that enables them to make sound decisions regarding their finances. Should you be an investor, business owner or someone who manages personal funds then seeking for information will enable you to analyse risk along with opportunity of your investments hence making choices based on logical thinking.

"Through research, individuals can gain a deep understanding of the financial landscape, anticipate trends, and ensure their decision-making aligns with their goals and aspirations."

Financial literacy together with research enables an individual to evaluate certain investment opportunities, determine the reliability of financial service providers and also come up with long-term financial blueprints. Thus, people can only adapt their techniques if they are constantly researching and staying updated in relation to the dynamic financial landscape.

In conclusion, it is clear that money and research have a lot in common. In respect to this, data analysis plus research help individuals or organisations in acquiring valuable insights necessary for making informed decisions resulting in success in finance. This will enhance one's financial acumen through embracing research and welcoming new knowledge in order to make sound financial decisions and accomplish their fiscal objectives.

The Importance of Action in Financial Decision-making

Financial acumen is not just about understanding money and financial concepts; it is also about taking action and implementing strategies for financial success. However important knowledge may be; we only start progressing towards our goals when we combine it with action taken. We can find solutions to these challenges by taking action hence making better financial decisions. So, realisation of aspirations depends on the steps we take every day so as to achieve our dreams since actions speak louder than words.

"Success is not the key to happiness. Happiness is the key to success. If you love what you are doing, you will be successful."

When it comes to building true wealth over a long period of time, the most important thing is taking action. Through action we implement our financial plans, increase our investments and create opportunities for ourselves. Our understanding and intentions would remain stagnant without action, our financial potential untapped.

Making Theory Work

Financial decision-making requires more than just theoretical understanding. It requires putting into practice what we know, taking calculated risks and learning from experience. Action helps us to improve our skills, adjust to changing situations and face the world of finance complexity.

"The future belongs to those who believe in the beauty of their dreams."

By doing this, we open doors for new opportunities and possibilities in life. We learn from both our victories and mistakes therefore making better decisions that have better financial outcomes. Every step will take us closer towards achieving financial goals that are realistic as well as developing enduring affluence.

Overcoming Inertia and Fear

Taking actions in financial decision making means overcoming inertia and fear. It is easy to be caught up in analysis paralysis or become afraid of making mistakes. It's through action that we break down these limits that hold us back thereby unlocking our personal finance potential.

"In the end, we only regret the chances we didn't take."

Action challenges us to come out of our comfort zones thus embracing growth opportunities. With more confidence on handling finance risks comes an assurance that you can do anything you want regarding your finances. Action shows us all that indeed we have invited financial success into life.

The Power of An Abundance Mindset in Building Lasting Wealth

Embracing an abundance mindset is essential for lasting wealth creation. Therefore, it becomes imperative to cultivate gratitude and shift perspective from scarcity to abundance as a foundation for financial growth.

A critical step towards adopting an abundance mindset is setting clear financial goals as well. You will be able to concentrate your efforts once you identify what exactly you want financially thus making informed choices which are aligned with your future vision.

"Surround yourself with positive influences. Seek out individuals who have achieved lasting wealth and learn from their experiences. By surrounding yourself with like-minded individuals, you will be motivated, inspired, and exposed to new ideas and opportunities."

Self-improvement is also an important way of embracing abundance mindset. An investment in constant personal and professional development will broaden your knowledge base and open up fresh financial achievement opportunities.

Opportunities for Financial Growth and Long-Term Wealth Accumulation

By cultivating an abundance mindset you open doors to financial growth opportunities and long term wealth accumulation. Instead of focusing on scarcity and limitations, you will develop a mindset that sees potential and abundance in every situation. With this mentality of abundance you will be more likely to take calculated risks, try different ways of generating income or make some strategic investments. This action-based approach increases chance opportunities for financial success as well as sustainable affluence.

Conclusion

Financial acumen unlocks the path from scarcity to abundance and builds lasting wealth over time. By having a deep understanding about money, its possibilities can completely change one's mind set into a successful individual. One must appreciate the need to view money as an instrument for effecting changes and bringing about positive results. If individuals channel their finances in a responsible and strategic manner, they can transform their localities into better places.

Growing true wealth entails understanding, acting, and changing one's way of thinking. Through adopting an attitude of abundance, defining financial objectives precisely, and acting promptly; people can build their pathways to achievement. With devotion and hard work, anyone can possess monetary sagacity, accumulate riches, and have a name that will never be forgotten in the annals of time.

Saving on Recurring Costs and Strategies for Short and Long-Term Goals

****

Here in Chapter 28, we're tackling financial smarts and methods for saving cash. We'll show you how to stash money away, meet your current and eventual targets, and seize your financial destiny. We'll be exploring how to cut ongoing expenses and successful techniques to help you fulfil your immediate and distant financial aspirations.

As the financial realm transforms, creating potent saving methods becomes paramount. By finding out and trimming down ongoing expenses, you can set aside more funds for your financial goals. Whether your aim is to create a rainy-day fund, accumulate enough for your dream holiday, or prepare for your golden years, this chapter will arm you with useful guidance to maximise your savings. From cultivating a savings perspective to making your savings automatic and sourcing expert advice, we'll tackle all vital steps to ensure you win financially.

So, are you set to get the most from your continual cost-saving plans and learn a few tips to fuel the growth of long-term investments? Keep in mind, every step you take builds a more prosperous tomorrow for yourself.

The significance of cutting down on Recurring Expenses

A common strategy people use in trying to save cash is to identify the everyday, recurring expenses. These are typically unnoticed, mundane expenses that can really affect our budget. Potential savings can be unearthed by deeply analysing things like our monthly utility bills, subscriptions or memberships.

"Cutting down regular costs is a smart strategy to better manage home or business budgets.Small changes in everyday expenses can free up cash for investments in personal finance."

Regular Costs

Regular expenses can pile up and eat into hard-earned income. By scrutinising bills, more money can stay in our pockets. This allows us to save, repay debts, or fulfil life goals.

Finding Regular Costs

By examining routine expenses, money-saving areas are unveiled. Cutting down electricity use and conserving water can lower utility bills. Unsubscribing from unused services can also save a lot like ending gym or streaming memberships.

"The impact of recurring costs on our budget can surprise us," says financial planner Lisa Thompson. "By scrutinising our financial duties, we can better decide if there are critical expenses we can drop or shrink."

Forming a Budget and Recording Expenses

A budget is key for limiting spending. By noting monthly expenditures, we understand where our money is going. There's an app known as a budget tracker; this provides detailed spending records. This helps pinpoint areas where we can reduce spending.

"Budgeting steers us towards our financial targets," Michael Anderson, a finance guru, reflects. "By overseeing our outgoings and mindful spending, our choices mirror our beliefs and priorities."

The Merits of Cutting Regular Costs

Beyond some monetary breathing space, trimming regular expenses has multiple benefits. The following are steps we can take to slim down these expenses:

- ✓ Invest in short and long-term goals.
- ✓ Boost our financial robustness and adaptability.
- ✓ Reduces dependency on borrowing or credit for unexpected situations.
- ✓ Instill a feeling of autonomy and self-reliance in one's financial journey.

"Lessening regular costs isn't about pruned expenses. It's about asserting your financial health," underscores Mark Roberts, a finance wizard. "By focusing on saving and mindful spending, we lay a sturdy base for a secure and prosperous path."

Formulating Tactics to Decrease Regular Costs

Among effective penny-pinching tactics, curbing recurring costs stands tallest. By clever spending and frugal choices, overall expenses can be lessened without compromising necessities. Here are some possible methods to economise on regular costs:

Talking About Rates and Discounts

Feel free to discuss rates or discounts with the companies you patronise. It could be your internet service, insurance policy, or gym membership. Sometimes, they have special deals that can help you save money. Understanding what their competition offers can give you an edge in those discussions.

Ending Undesired Memberships or Subscriptions

It's not uncommon to sign up for something and then realise it's not needed. Review your regular spending and pinpoint memberships or subscriptions you could cancel. For example, stop paying for unwanted streaming services, magazine subscriptions, or delivery boxes. The money saved can go towards investments.

Adopting Thrifty Living Habits

Thrifty living means saving money but still having a good lifestyle. This entails smart spending, identifying ways to cut back on unwanted costs, and focusing on financial goals. Think about thrifty tactics like cooking meals at home, searching for good deals, or reducing luxury expenses. These small adjustments can lead to substantial savings over the years.

Cutting Costs While Keeping Needs Met

Although lowering costs is key, it's crucial to maintain your essential needs. Find places where you can save money without sacrificing your quality of life. For instance, switch to energy-saving appliances and LED lights, or buy economical store brands instead of pricier branded goods.

Always remember, saving on regular costs requires continual vigilance. Review your spending frequently, adapting as needed. By fostering these habits and cultivating a frugal mindset, we'll steadily meet our savings targets while enjoying life.

Saving for Near-Term Goals

Effective money management should include setting aside savings for near-term goals, a crucial part of any sound financial plan. These goals could be definitive milestones or unexpected expenses that might crop up. A cushion of savings for emergencies can instil the assurance and fiscal safety you need.

First, an emergency fund is a major reason to prioritise short-term savings. Life can be unpredictable with unexpected costs surfacing anytime. With a specific rainy-day fund, anyone can sidestep the traps of credit cards or debt when such emergencies arise, disrupting your financial plans.

"It's like a safety net warding off surprise events. We can navigate life's hiccups without jeopardising our financial dreams."

Second, stashing cash for short-term aspirations grants you the power to chase your dreams with adequate resources. Planning a dream vacation, purchasing a shiny new vehicle, or seeding your own boutique business could be within your grasp with dedicated savings earmarked for these purposes.

Think about making your money put aside on autopilot to stick to your savings goals. By setting an automatic transfer from your spending to your savings account, saving becomes regular and easy. This takes the guesswork out of saving and keeps you focused on your financial goals.

"If you automate your savings habits, you forget you're saving. The process becomes so easy that you're always adding to your savings."

Remember, saving for near future goals is like investing in your current and future self. When you have a strong savings base, you're financially ready for life's ups and downs without fear.

Saving for the Distant Future

Savings for the long term are key to long-term financial security and goals like retirement. Everyone needs a game plan to save enough for their golden years.

Getting Ready for Retirement:

Saving for the long run means planning your retirement. Retirement brings financial freedom and peace—if you've actively prepared. For instance, folks might open retirement accounts like individual retirement accounts (IRAs) or 401(k)s for their future.

Looking into Ways to Invest:

Putting money aside for the future is important. Smart investing can add to this nest egg. Before you invest, you should do your homework or ask a money pro.

How you act as an investor matters. Staying calm and focusing on your long-term plan can lead to good results. Quick choices might not always pay off.

Keep an Eye on Your Money:

Money plans should be updated now and then. Changes in life, ups and downs in the market, or new goals can all mean it's time to check and possibly change your plan.

Ensuring a Safety Net:

A financial security blanket is a key part of planning. This might involve saving some of your money in easily accessible forms. A mix of savings and investments might help.

Remember, everyone's situation is different. You might want to see a financial pro for a personalised approach to your money. It's never too early—or too late—to plan for your financial future.

Making Savings Automatic

For many people, saving money can be a challenge. It's easy to spend money, but setting some aside for the future often takes discipline. One effective strategy to overcome this challenge is to make savings automatic.

When you automate your savings, you're essentially making a commitment to set aside a certain amount of money at regular intervals without having to think about it. This can be done through your bank, employer, or financial institution. Here are some ways to make savings automatic:

Set Up Automatic Transfers:

Most banks allow you to set up automatic transfers between your checking and savings accounts. You can choose the frequency and amount of the transfer. It's a simple way to ensure that a portion of your income goes directly into savings.

Utilise Payroll Deductions:

If your employer offers direct deposit, you can often split your paycheck between different accounts. Allocate a percentage or a fixed amount to go directly into your savings account. This way, you won't even see the money in your checking account, reducing the temptation to spend it.

Explore Employer-Sponsored Retirement Plans:

Many employers offer retirement savings plans, such as 401(k)s, with automatic contributions. Take advantage of these plans, especially if your employer matches contributions. It's an effective way to save for the long term without having to think about it.

Use Apps and Tools:

There are various apps and financial tools designed to make saving automatic. Some apps analyse your spending habits and automatically transfer small amounts into savings. Look for tools that align with your financial goals and preferences.

Automatic savings not only builds your savings consistently but also takes the effort out of manual transfers. It's a set-and-forget approach that helps you prioritise saving without constantly thinking about it.

Sourcing Expert Advice

While managing your finances and savings, seeking expert advice can be invaluable. Financial professionals, such as financial planners or advisors, can provide guidance tailored to your specific situation and goals.

Here are some key considerations when sourcing expert advice:

Credentials and Qualifications:

Ensure that the financial professional you consult has the necessary credentials and qualifications. Look for certifications like Certified Financial Planner (CFP) or Chartered Financial Analyst (CFA) to ensure that the individual has received proper training.

Experience and Expertise:

Consider the professional's experience and expertise in areas relevant to your financial goals. Some financial advisors specialise in retirement planning, while others focus on investment strategies. Choose someone with expertise that aligns with your needs.

Fee Structure:

Understand the fee structure of the financial professional. Some advisors charge a flat fee, while others work on a commission basis. Be transparent about fees and ensure that you're comfortable with the arrangement.

Communication Style:

Effective communication is crucial in a financial advisory relationship. Choose a professional whose communication style suits your preferences. They should be able to explain complex financial concepts in a way that you understand.

Fiduciary Responsibility:

A fiduciary has a legal obligation to act in the best interests of their clients. It's advisable to work with a financial professional who operates under a fiduciary standard, prioritising your financial well-being.

Reviews and Recommendations:

Seek reviews and recommendations from friends, family, or online sources. Positive testimonials and recommendations can give you confidence in the professional's ability to deliver results.

Regular Check-Ins:

Establish a schedule for regular check-ins with your financial advisor. Regular reviews ensure that your financial plan stays aligned with your goals, and adjustments can be made as needed.

Remember, expert advice is a valuable resource, but ultimately, you are in control of your financial decisions. Use the guidance of financial professionals to inform your choices and make informed decisions that align with your financial aspirations.

Conclusion

In this chapter, we delved into the importance of cutting down recurring expenses, whether they be utility bills, subscriptions, or memberships. Identifying and reducing these ongoing costs can free up funds for your short-term and long-term financial goals.

We emphasised the significance of creating a budget and tracking expenses to gain insights into your spending patterns. By adopting thrifty living habits, negotiating rates, and ending undesired memberships, you can effectively cut down on regular costs without compromising your lifestyle.

Saving for near-term goals and making savings automatic were highlighted as essential components of a robust financial plan. Whether it's building an emergency fund or saving for a dream vacation, automated savings make the process seamless and consistent.

Looking ahead, we explored the importance of saving for the distant future, particularly for retirement. Planning for retirement involves understanding different investment options, staying informed about your money, and ensuring you have a financial safety net.

Lastly, we discussed the benefits of sourcing expert advice when managing your finances. Financial professionals can provide personalised guidance based on your goals and financial situation. It's crucial to choose a qualified advisor, communicate effectively, and regularly review your financial plan.

By implementing these strategies and cultivating sound financial habits, you can navigate the complex landscape of personal finance, meet your financial goals, and build a secure and prosperous future.

Stay tuned for Chapter 29, where we'll explore the realm of investments, covering diverse options and strategies to grow your wealth. Whether you're a novice or an experienced investor, this chapter will equip you with the knowledge to make informed investment decisions.

The Basics of Investing: Understanding Different Investment Vehicles and Managing Risk

****

It also can be overwhelming and thrilling to invest. The first step is to understand the basics before getting started. This chapter will discuss the different investment vehicles and how they can help you manage risk better for long-term success.

When it comes to investing, the opportunities are limitless. Each asset class offers its own benefits and risks; these range from shares, bonds, real estate and alternative investments. Experts suggest that one way to navigate this minefield is diversifying your portfolio – meaning you spread your money across several asset classes so as to balance risk against potential returns.

The other approach which is commonly used by many people is starting with index funds or ETFs (exchange-traded funds) that offer wide market exposure and often have lower fees compared to actively managed funds. These funds follow certain market indices such as S&P 500 thereby allowing investors an opportunity of investing in a diversified portfolio without necessarily having to pick single stocks.

On the other hand, there are individual stocks that can give higher yields in terms of return on investment although they are risky too. You should conduct thorough research and consider your risk tolerance before making any individual stock investments.

Additionally, bonds provide a conservative investment option with fixed interest rates and less risk compared to shares. Other types of investment such as hedge funds or commodities adds another layer of diversification but might be more volatile as well.

In this chapter we will go through the investment risk ladder; this helps us group assets based on their relative risks. By understanding this ladder you can make decisions about what type of investments fit into your overall portfolio strategy.

You can navigate the world of investments with confidence by fully grasping different forms of investment vehicles and ways of managing risks for them to achieve sustainable long-term results for you. So let's get started on our exploration of the amazing world of investments!

Understanding the Investment Risk Ladder

The risk ladder assists investors in creating informed choices when constructing portfolios because it classifies diverse asset classes. Each step on the ladder corresponds to an asset class that has its own risk-reward profile. Let us now examine various asset classes:

Cash

At the very bottom of the risk ladder is cash, which provides stability and guaranteed return of capital. Cash position is considered as a low-risk investment strategy since it carries the highest level of security while interest received from it may be minimal.

Bonds

Bonds are debt instruments issued by corporations or government agencies. They offer fixed interest rates and provide investors with regular interest payments. Thus, bonds are seen as lower risk than stocks and can generate a predictable income stream. Nevertheless, their value can fluctuate due to market conditions.

Mutual Funds

Mutual funds pool money from multiple investors to create a diversified portfolio of stocks, bonds, and other securities. They are managed by professional fund managers who make investment decisions on behalf of the investors. Mutual funds allow you to get a diversified portfolio without having extensive knowledge about the market.

Exchange-Traded Funds (ETFs)

Exchange-traded commodities (ETCs) are much like mutual funds but are quoted on stock markets. They give investors exposure to different underlying indices, sectors or asset classes. ETFs can be traded throughout the trading day at a price based on market supply and demand. Diversification, flexibility and lower expense ratios than mutual funds are other advantages of ETFs.

Shares

Shares represent ownership in a company and offer investors the potential for high returns. Nevertheless, they also encompass greater risks. Stock prices tend to be volatile, while individual entities may face financial difficulties or market declines. Investing in shares requires doing thorough research and following market trends.

Non-Traditional Investments

Non-traditional investments may cover different assets such as real estate, hedge funds, private equity and commodities. These investment products have varying risk levels and investment returns. While they can offer diversification benefits as well as higher returns in some cases, they are generally less regulated and more volatile than traditional asset classes.

Knowing the various asset classes of a portfolio is useful for constructing it properly balanced with enough diversification. By understanding your risk tolerance level vis-à-vis investment objective and time frame you could be able to make rational choices to optimise expected return while managing risk.

Investing Rationally and Simply

When it comes to investing, being rational about it is key; just keep things simple! Many experienced investors realise that when it comes to their risk preferences they need to spread their portfolios across different asset classes; however this is not true for beginners starting out with index funds or exchange traded funds (ETFs).

"Index funds and ETFs are great options for new investors. They allow investors to mimic broad-based indexes such as S&P 500 without actually having to choose stocks."

However, building a diverse portfolio which includes individual stocks, real estate and alternative investments can be an appealing option for those who want to manage their own investments. This will allow investors to potentially optimise returns while controlling the levels of risks.

"Diversification is key to sensible investing," says smith. "By spreading your investments across different asset classes you can help reduce the impact of market fluctuations and minimise the risk of putting too much money into one investment."

When making investment decisions, it's important to consider financial returns for investment and other economic factors. It is important to keep an eye on market uncertainties as well as regulatory barriers that may affect investment decisions since things keep changing hence need to adapt accordingly.

"Successful investing is not about timing the market or following fashions," advises Smith. "It requires a well-thought-out strategy that one sticks with, evaluates continuously and adjusts when necessary."

To enhance chances of successful investments, minimising uncertainties and addressing regulatory obstacles become very vital. By doing so, an investor can be well positioned for long-term growth and have a higher chance of achieving financial planning success.

The Importance of Economic Environment in Investment Decisions

Investment decisions are dependent upon or influenced by the economic environment. Investors should consider a number of factors including state of economy, market conditions and policy changes in order to make informed investment choices.

Favourable situations for investments are created when the economy is growing and strong, coupled with low joblessness. Stocks usually do well in such conditions thus offering possibilities of growth and returns to investors. In the same way, boom economies can cause a favourable effect on real estate markets making it a good choice for investment.

Inflationary environments can also significantly affect investment decisions. When there is inflation commodity prices tend to rise, thereby making them possible lucrative investments. Investors must look out for signs of inflation and consider these when making decisions on investments in commodities.

"Investment decisions may be influenced by factors such as economic uncertainties that come about because of population ageing or climatic changes leading to market volatility and risks."

Additionally, both economic and policy factors can impact alternative investments including private equity, venture capital and hedge funds. For example, altering laws or government policies might have direct effects on these investment classes' performances. Therefore, investors need to monitor policy developments regularly so as to determine their likely effect on alternative investments.

It must be noted that investment decisions cannot be made in isolation from the wider economic context. Economic uncertainties such as population ageing and climate change may contribute to risk and market volatility. These uncertainties affect multiple asset classes; hence they should be considered with care by investors.

"Regulatory reforms and improved corporate balance sheets can boost the prospects for investment."

On the other hand, regulatory reforms and improvements in corporate balance sheets could lead to favourable conditions for investing. Regulatory changes with respect to transparency as well as accountability have a high potential of boosting investor confidence leading to capital influxes. Similarly, companies with sound financial positions have greater appeal to those who seek steady returns on their investments.

The economic environment is an important factor in making investment decisions overall. Investors must understand how economic conditions affect their choices as well as market trends and policy shifts so that they can increase their chances of realising higher returns from their investments.

Global Investment Trends and Strategies

There has been a major shift in the global investment landscape in recent years with emerging market economies (EMEs) playing a larger role in global investment. Meanwhile, investment structures of developed countries have been changing, moving away from heavy investment intensive industrial sectors towards lighter services ones.

One of the notable trends in global investment is the rise of intangible assets and knowledge-based industries. Changes in global specialisation and technological advancements have resulted in increased investments in sectors like software development, research and development or intellectual property. These investments into intangible assets have however become more valuable hence supporting innovation and providing opportunities for investors.

For investors seeking to navigate through the ever-changing investment landscape it is critical to understand global investment trends and strategies. Investors can position themselves for growth by keeping up to date with emerging opportunities in EMEs and adapting their investments to changing structures of investments.

"Investors must stay informed about the potential for investing in emerging market economies. These economies present special prospects due to their fast economic growth, growing consumer markets and untapped resources. However, you should carefully evaluate the risks involved and come up with appropriate strategies on how they can be mitigated."

The Importance of Diversification and Risk Management

Optimising returns and risk management are the main reasons why investors should diversify their investments. By definition, a diversified portfolio means spreading investments across different asset classes, sectors and geographic areas. This reduces the effects of market volatility and improves long-term performance.

I am a financial advisor and I recommend that investors should focus on global investment portfolios with large diversification. This requires allocating investments to various regions, industries and asset classes in order to avoid concentration of risks in one or few areas.

Secondly, managing risks in global investment depends on examining several factors such as political stability, economic indicators and regulatory environment among others. A wide-ranging risk management plan could help them predict possible challenges before-hand and prevent negative effects on their investments.

Strategies for Navigating Emerging Market Economies

Emerging markets offer attractive opportunities for growth and diversification but also pose unique challenges. Nevertheless, navigating through these markets entails having specific strategies tailored for each country's character.

Consequently, partnering with local experts or investment firms who have an understanding of local economies is a way to go. These professionals will help them to identify opportunities that show promise, handle regulatory complexities as well as reduce the risks associated with their investments.

Another way is by concentrating on sectors with potential for high growth that includes technology, consumer goods and infrastructure among others. This is attributable to an increase in demand emanating from an increasing middle class population, urbanisation as well as consumerism in emerging markets. Moreover, it is important to consider long-term prospects of emerging market economies while making investment decisions. Investments made with a long-term perspective enable investors to withstand short-term fluctuations while capitalising on steady growth over time.

"Investing in emerging market economies requires patience and a long-term vision," Sarah Thompson advises who has been dealing with global investors "Thereby adopting strategic approaches complemented by understanding peculiarities of each market enables investors seize an opportunity yet obtain positive returns."

Weak Investment and its Impact on Growth

Weak investment has led to low economic growth and productivity. The reduction of investments during the recession together with slow recovery resulted in a low level of equilibrium growth and lack of job opportunities. This relocation of some weak business investment from developed countries might have affected domestic capital outlays, according to analysts. In addition, advanced economies changed their structure and saw a rising number of intangible and knowledge-based investments at the expense of investments that involve physical assets.Imbalanced global demand is one of the major causes of these weak investment levels witnessed both domestically and internationally. Therefore, this has considerably slowed down investment activities though there are chances for improvement.

"Balanced global demand, reduced uncertainties, and market reforms can potentially drive investment to a higher level of equilibrium," says Adam Smith, an economist.

Nevertheless, actions can be taken to counteract problems resulting from weak investments that hinder economic growth. Governments should encourage investing by granting tax breaks on new capital expenditures or removing regulatory obstacles.

The Importance of Potential Output Growth

Investment is essential in potential output growth which refers to the sustainable level of economic activity that an economy can achieve in the long term. A rise in levels of investment increases potential output growth due to improved productivity rates as well as innovations and advances in technology. This is possible through investment in physical capital, like factories and machinery that can enlarge productivity. In addition, investments in research and development (R&D), education, and training can improve the human capital base of countries leading to higher levels of innovation and skills development.

To ensure future economic growth, it is important for policymakers to understand the importance of potential output growth and develop policies that will encourage investment.

Factors That Influence Investments Decisions

There are many factors that influence investment decisions and shape the investment landscape. Some of these factors shall be explored below.

Investment can be discouraged through weak aggregate demand both domestically and internationally. When there is a lack of demand for goods and services businesses may not invest in new projects or expand their operations because they do not see a market for their products. This affects investors who become cautious hence affecting the total level of investments.

Another key factor influencing investment decisions is the cost of capital that includes interest rates and equity prices. High interest rates or expensive equity prices can discourage investors since they increase borrowing costs or acquisition expenses respectively. Conversely lower interest rates and favourable equity prices reduce the cost of capital which leads to increased investment.

Uncertainties concerning the economy or policy making can impair an environment conducive for investments. Investors may choose to keep their money out because they are unsure about where the economy is headed or whether certain policies will be passed into law in order to avoid jeopardising their returns on investment as uncertainties increase risks for investors making it hard for them to calculate expected returns as well as plan about future implications.

Restrictions imposed on product markets regulations along with infrastructure investments also affect investor decisions. There are sectors or activities whose profitability and feasibility would be impacted by regulatory barriers while others would not.Tackling these regulatory constraints is therefore essential if a supportive environment needs to be created by leaders allowing economic gains.

"The confidence-building measures needed by investors include addressing economic uncertainties; reducing policy uncertainties; and dismantling regulatory barriers that impede the flow of capital, and business growth."

Policy Implications for Higher Investment

Policies aimed at increasing investment are necessary for higher sustainable growth. In addition, macroeconomic policies must address deficient demand, uncertain policies and be supported by structural policies promoting long-term economic growth.

"To enhance the quality and quantity of infrastructure investments, revive public and infrastructure investment, while reducing regulatory barriers."

Public infrastructure investments are considered essential in creating an enabling environment for economic growth. By improving transport connectivity and communication networks as well as provision of public amenities, public investments are able to stimulate business activities and attract private capital thereby contributing to increased potential output growth.

Nevertheless, excessive regulation could hinder investment initiatives. Therefore, there is a need to focus on reducing regulatory barriers that hinder businesses operation and flow of funds into a country in order to create an enabling business climate. Consequently, more businesses will thrive under streamlined regulatory frameworks leading to increased investment.

"Another important factor for increasing potential output growth is addressing the consequences of rising inequality on education apart from low-wage workers."

To attain inclusive growth there is a need to address the needs of low wage earners and cut income inequality. Policies that promote education accessibility and skill development programs for marginalised communities are critical to increasing potential output. Policy makers can lay the foundation for sustainable economic growth by investing in human capital and providing equal opportunities.

An all-embracing policy approach, including macroeconomic policies, structural policies and public infrastructure investment, is needed to foster efficient and sustained growth. Through providing an enabling environment for both public and private investments, policy makers can drive economic growth rates, raise potential outputs and make the future brighter for all.

Amidst Investment Decisions, How Biodiversity is Given a Role

Investors now have biodiversity in their minds when they decide to put their money somewhere considering the impact of investment on the environment and how important it is to preserve biodiversity. This change was driven by increasing awareness of social responsibility among companies and pursuit of sustainable development goals.

Environmental performance plays a significant role for investors who prioritise biodiversity, which would have far-reaching benefits for the company that does it. Investors are able to use this understanding in making choices that help them operate towards securing a longer term future.

'Biodiversity investments can be good for society and business as well. It is not just about saving nature but understanding the fact that there is an economic value derived from biodiversity and this has to be entrenched in our decisions as we invest.'

This will guide the investments based on the consideration of biodiversity because these are responsible principles as investments must take into account environmental aspects holistically. The involvement of biodiversity in business decisions allows businesses to exhibit their commitment towards sustainability while at the same time contributing to preservation of natural systems.

Additionally, investing in initiatives that promote biodiversity can deliver lasting financial benefits. The organisations which take proactive steps towards addressing environmental concerns by incorporating such issues into their operations stand better chances of responding effectively to market changes, regulatory pressures, and stakeholder expectations.

'Sustainable investment strategies focused on biodiversity could enhance competitive advantage, promote innovation and attract investors who care about society.'

Moreover, investors who consider biodiversity frequently identify new opportunities in marketing. As consumers become more environmentally conscious with their purchasing decisions, businesses that embrace sustainability and those that have respect for ecological diversity will see a growth in their market share.

In conclusion, thinking about how biodiversity could influence investment choices is not only a matter of corporate social responsibility but long-term financial performance as well. Companies may support activities promoting sustainability while striving for success themselves.

Investment Strategies: Social Dimensions

considerations are increasingly becoming part of investment strategies. Investors are increasingly recognizing the importance of investing in organisations and projects that address social and environmental challenges. While generating financial returns, impact investing, socially responsible investing, and sustainable investing are some approaches that are aimed at having a positive social impact.

It aims to differentiate itself by driving change in areas such as renewable energy, clean technology, healthcare, education and affordable housing. By allocating investments into such sectors, investors can influence positive transformations aiming to address the severe issues of social and environmental nature.

'Impact investing is an excellent way for your money to be aligned with your values. You could make a meaningful contribution while making money through promoting innovative solutions to societal challenges.'

On the other hand, socially responsible investment (SRI) requires taking into account the social and ethical implications of investment decisions. Similarly, prior to making any investment decisions investors scrutinise companies' corporate governance practices in relation to the environment and society as a whole. In addition they avoid sectors like tobacco, weapons or fossil fuels preferring firms that emphasise sustainability, diversity and good corporate citizenship.

Socially responsible investing allows an investor to back businesses that match his/her ethos thereby impacting positively on society as well. This is one way of being ethical in one's investments while encouraging sustainable practices.'

Sustainable investing involves integrating environmental, social and governance (ESG) criteria into investment decision making. This is about more than just financial returns; it also considers the long-term sustainability of businesses and their impact on society and the environment. Investment in companies which exhibit sustainable practices enables investors to contribute towards a more equitable and sustainable future.

"Sustainable investing provides an opportunity to create long-term value while advancing environmental, social and governance objectives. It means investing in enterprises that are well-suited for the future and are committed to making a positive difference in society."

The integration of social considerations into investment strategies is a fast-changing field. In addition, there is increasing interest in impact investing, socially responsible investment (SRI), and sustainable investing, leading to greater innovation and opportunities in the area. Investors recognize that they can make a difference with their investment choices and are aligning their values with their investments.

This not only creates financial returns but also leaves a lasting mark on society and environment. For example, investors can become essential players if they invest into firms as well as projects aimed at promoting social justice alongside environmental conservation.

Factors Governing Governance Ethical Investment Decisions

Good governance practices are critical for responsible investing. Investors look at corporate governance aspects of companies when evaluating different investment opportunities such as board structure; transparency; executive compensation among others.

"The investable company has a working board of directors who come from diverse backgrounds. Besides, for any investor, one would want to ascertain whether executive compensations are directly linked to long-term growth performance or rather timeliness of informative disclosures given by companies."

Ethical Factors Responsible Investing

Investors consider ethical factors within their decision-making process for instance on human rights or social justice issues. They increasingly realise the importance of supporting ethical businesses that promote social development as well as environmental conservation.

"Values-driven investors," says Sarah Thompson, a sustainable investment specialist, "want their portfolios to reflect this. They seek out companies that are committed to such issues as diversity and inclusion, environmental stewardship and community development."

Ethical Factors Responsible Investing

Meanwhile, ethical factors such as social justice and human rights should also be concerned when making investment decisions. More and more investors understand the necessity of backing organisations abiding by ethical standards and promoting sustainability of the environment.

"Sarah Thompson, a professional in sustainable investment states that "investors want to ensure that their portfolios line up with what they believe in. As a result, they look out for firms which address matters such as diversity and inclusion, environmental protection and community outreach."

Responsible Investing Fiduciary Duty

It is not just about financial returns but also considering the long-term consequences of investment decisions since responsible investing goes beyond financial returns. The principle guiding this approach is fiduciary duty, which requires that investment professionals act in the best interests of their clients.

"We've got to move away from thinking just about profits over the short term," says Michael Smith, an experienced broker who specialises in wealth management. "Investors have to make choices that help us create more equitable and sustainable societies."

Through incorporating governance and ethical factors into their investment choices, responsible investors can support transparent organisations that adhere to sustainability principles. Such aspects may generate sustainable financial returns while at the same time build a better future for society and environment.

Long term growth tailored Investment Strategies

For reaching financial goals it is necessary to customise investment strategies towards long term growth. Consideration must be given to individual risk tolerance levels, time horizons for investments as well specific objectives in order to create an effective investment plan.

This will enable you to develop a plan that meets your specific needs as well as preferences. Asset allocation is a key element in any investment strategy. Spreading investments across different asset classes such as stocks, bonds, real estate and alternatives helps to reduce risk and maximise returns in the long run. This allows you to channel your investments into various sectors and industries thereby reducing the effect of a single investment's performance on your entire portfolio.

"Proper asset allocation is like building a strong foundation for your investment portfolio. In that it helps you balance risk and reward by providing exposure to different investments with the aim of avoiding substantial losses."

Therefore, as market conditions change or goals evolve it is important to consistently monitor one's asset allocation. By taking this approach one can be able to optimise their investments so as to grow over time.

"Flexibility is key when it comes to asset allocation." "By reviewing your holdings periodically and adapting them according to market changes, new opportunities that are in line with long-term financial goals can be captured."

One needs professional advice from a qualified financial advisor as they develop their investment strategy. They should be in position to guide one through the complexities of the markets and potential risks; they should help make informed choices.

Finally, staying up-to-date with market trends and economic indicators will help you develop sound long-term investment strategies besides seeking professional expertise. The trick here is keeping updated on the latest financial news, conducting research and understanding the whole economic macrocosm; these will enable you to make well-informed decisions regarding your investments.

"You know what they say about investing – knowledge is power," Sarah Davis an analyst points out. "The more aware you are about these issues, the better placed you are in making informed decisions incorporating long term objectives."

To sum up, customising long-term growth oriented investment strategies requires careful consideration of risk preferences, time horizon and investment objectives. It takes a lot to diversify your portfolio, regularly monitor and adjust your asset allocation, seek professional advice, and keep informed about market trends and economic factors in order to successfully have a long-term investment plan. This is how you can secure your personal finances and fulfil your financial goals in the long run.

The Future of Investments.

Advancement in technology, need for sustainable investments and ever-changing market trends are some of the determinants shaping the future of investments. These factors have essentially changed investors' approaches towards investing in addition to their decision-making process.

Artificial intelligence (AI) is one significant technological advancement that will affect investment strategies. It has the ability to revolutionise investment analysis as well as result in improved data driven decisions. Investors can now study large volumes of data with algorithms that operate on AI then identify patterns so as to make sound decisions.

"Technology such as artificial intelligence (AI), will transform investment strategies and drive financial innovation."

Another promising technological advancement for future investments is blockchain technology. Blockchain improves transparency, security and efficiency of transactions especially for fund management or real estate among others.

"Blockchain technology will revolutionise the way investment transactions are conducted, bringing transparency and efficiency to the process."

Sustainability considerations are increasingly playing a significant role in making investment decisions. Climate change and sustainable needs are moving investors to companies that give priority to environmental, social and governance (ESG) criteria. In this vein, sustainability-focused investments such as renewable energy and clean technologies have been gathering momentum as more investors recognize their long-term potential and positive impacts.

"Decisions about investment are being influenced by issues like sustainability: climate change, renewable energy."

Future of investment is also defined by market trends. Impact investing is another type of investment that combines financial returns with social or environmental impact metrics; it is gaining popularity in the investment sector. This implies that investing responsibly, an approach which bases on a company's ethical practices and its societal impact, continues to be embraced.. These market trends reflect growing investor awareness and demand for investments that align with personal values leading to positive change.

"Investment landscape has changed because of impact investing today, "impact investing" grows."

To survive in the future of investments, investors will have to keep themselves well-informed and remain flexible enough to adapt fast to new trends and opportunities as they emerge. By embracing technological changes, integrating sustainability concerns into their thinking and aligning their strategies with the prevailing market conditions, investors can avoid being caught off guard by the dynamic nature of the ever-changing investment environment and thus attain their financial objectives.

Conclusion

In summary, understanding different types of investment vehicles as well as managing risk are key elements for successful investment strategies. An investor who wants long term growth in his/her portfolio should consider diversifying his/her investments across various sectors including economic factors while also looking at his/her personal values.

It is important for people to stay updated about the current situation in the markets and consult professionals when needed.

To make good profits from investments there is a need for one to be knowledgeable about how he/she invests which necessitates building a strong foundation on which his/her strategy can be based. As long as appropriate approaches are used, it is possible for investors to manoeuvre through the upcoming opportunities and challenges that will come along with an evolving investment landscape.

Decoding Problems for Money – Tips to Make Extra Cash

****

Welcome to Chapter 30 on extra revenue generation. In this chapter, there are various ways and techniques which aids in the conversion of daily struggles into money making ideas. Be it for a side hustle or an extra source of income, these will help you think differently about your skills and resources.

A lifeline is what supplemental income represents to many people and families in terms of financial stability and the ability to pursue personal interests. Your financial destiny can be shaped by exploring side businesses and other forms of earning additional income; this may translate into infinite possibilities for earning.

Throughout this chapter we will explore various ways to generate supplemental income such as passive income ideas, mlm profitability, dropshipping, print-on-demand , selling digital products, online courses, blogging etc. Every section provides useful insights into different kinds of income streams and how one can use them to meet their money targets.

Therefore, whether you're a stay-at-home mom, student looking for extra dollars or anyone who wants to secure their finances better they should join us as we venture into the field of supplementary funds where great opportunities reside.

Passive Income Ideas to Generate Extra Money

Would you like some extra cash without much hustle? Learn various passive ideas that will help you live a financially stable life without having to work for it. By using these ideas, you can still get more money plus manage any other aspects of your life.

Start a Drop shipping Store

Drop shipping is an excellent option if you want to get involved with e-commerce but avoid inventory management and shipping. You can sell products from suppliers directly to customers without the need to stock inventory when you use drop shipping. This way, one earns money through selling a product without being concerned with its delivery as well as storage.

Create a Print-on-Demand Store

Consider creating a print-on-demand store if you have artistic talent. This process entails designing such products as t-shirts, mugs or phone cases that are only produced and shipped when required. Services like Shopify will help in creating and integrating your store with print-on-demand services.

Sell Digital Products

Do you have specialised knowledge or skills that others would find valuable? Sell digital products such as e-books, online courses, downloadable templates, etc. These things can be purchased repeatedly thereby providing a passive source of income while sharing what you love most in life.

Teach Online Courses

For individuals who enjoy tutoring; making and trading online lesson plans may lead to substantial passive incomes. Udemy and Teachable offer channels through which one can share their expertise with many people worldwide. After completing the course production process on platforms such as these ones, one receives income each time another person registers for the course.

Become a Blogger

If you are passionate about writing and have a specific area of interest, think of starting a blog. That implies, you can make money from your content by use of affiliate marketing, advertising and even sponsored posts. With dedication and quality content, a blog can provide the opportunity to develop an audience who will continue to earn passive income for you.

These are only some passive income ideas you may want to explore further. Try out diverse paths that align with your hobbies as well as skills. These consistent income sources require some initial input, but they will ultimately provide the financial security and liberty you desire.

Drop shipping and Print-on-Demand as Passive Income Streams

Are you searching for ways to get passive income? Drop shipping and print-on-demand are two popular options that can help you achieve your financial goals. With these models, you can create a successful ecommerce business without the need to handle inventory or shipping.

Drop shipping: Through drop shipping, it is possible to establish an online store where suppliers sell directly to customers. When orders are made by customers, the supplier ensures that the products reach them at their locations. It also means that there is no need for one to have stores or inventories managers. It is a low risk business model with little capital required upfront costs making it ideal for beginners.

Print-on-Demand: If you are creative, you can make print-on-demand products which will be sold through various ecommerce platforms. This in turn allows customers to order different customised items including t-shirts, mugs or phone cases among others. In this case goods are only made when an order has been placed by a client which means that production costs will be deducted from revenue when such sales occur. Therefore for people with design skills and an urge to produce new items for clients this is the best way.

With drop shipping and print-on-demand approaches though it is possible to set up passive income streams by using e-commerce power and giving out fulfilment processes. In other words, this is an opportunity to turn your creativity and entrepreneurial desires into money.

Both drop shipping and print-on-demand can be easily set up through platforms like Shopify, which provide all the necessary tools and integrations to start your business. More so, these models give you the flexibility to work from any place and still earn while sleeping.

If you want to create passive income streams, consider drop shipping and print-on-demand. The low investment required, the potential for growth and the scalability factors are what make them attractive choices for anyone who has an interest in starting a company of his own. Begin building your empire of passive income today!

Selling Digital Products and Online Courses for Passive Income

Sell digital products or online courses leveraging on your skills thereby creating passive income streams. As such, with demand for digital resources on a rise, this avenue represents a lucrative option to generate extra cash. No matter if you have a future writer inside you or if you really love design craft, or if you have expertise in any specific field – do not waste it! Turn your knowledge into profit by creating profitable digital assets.

When it comes to digital products, there are infinite options available. This means that one may easily create downloadable items such as ebooks, templates or plugins that cater specific needs and interests of people. Consequently, these are goods that can be sold again and again rendering a constant revenue stream devoid of holding physical inventory. Creating digital products allows you to package your knowledge, skills, and creativity into a format that can be easily shared and monetized.

Online courses also enable you to share your expertise with others and earn passive income. On your preferred subject matter, you can create all-encompassing course materials in video format and sell them for multiple times. This method permits you to target a wide range of people, make a living while sleeping, or have more time because there are no physical boundaries or time constraints.

"Online courses allow you to offer your knowledge and empower others while receiving passive income from the pleasant environment of your home."

The two lucrative industries of selling digital products and online courses are high margin with scalability. Once created, these assets can be marketed, promoted, sold over again thereby generating income for quite a long period of time. Furthermore, the digital nature of these products enhances their easy distribution and accessibility thereby making them attractive to the global audience.

Begin Your Passive Income Journey

Should you have valuable knowledge or skills that you could impact on others, selling digital products as well as online courses offers a great opportunity for earning passive income. In this stream one is able to convert his own expertise into money as well as diversify sources of his income hence getting rid of the pressure related with financial dependency. You should take the very first step towards creating your own empire that will generate passive income.

Blogging and Selling Handmade Goods as Passive Income Strategies

In today's world of technology there are many ways one can achieve passive income for instance blogging and selling handmade goods online. These methods require dedication, creativity and hard work but can bring long-term financial stability.

Monetize Your Passion for Writing Through Blogging

If one has an interest in written content creation and enjoys engaging with others through sharing ideas and experiences then blogging can be an incredible way to earn passive income.. By writing quality posts that engage readers, one can develop loyal followership which he later exploits through monetizing such channels.

"Blogging allows you to express your creativity, share your expertise, and connect with people who share your interests. It's an opportunity to turn your passion for writing into a fulfilling and profitable venture."

One common strategy of monetizing blogs is through affiliate marketing. By including affiliate links to services or products that are linked to the niche addressed in that blog, one can earn commissions on each item sold via the unique referral link. Moreover, passive income may also be generated from sponsored posts and advertisements.

Tap Into the Market of Handmade Goods

Handcrafted items among other physically crafted works could be your ideal option if you have an artistic talent and enjoy making unique things as this will ensure that you generate passive income out of it. With platforms like Faire, Amazon, eBay etc., you have a great number of buyers and also have opportunities to display your art before a large audience.

"Selling handmade goods allows you to showcase your creativity and craftsmanship while earning a passive income. It's a chance to turn your hobby into a profitable business."

There are markets for handmade goods whether it is jewellery, home décor or personalised gifts. By building an online store and promoting your product right you can gain customers without any retail overhead expenses.

Both blogging and selling handmade goods takes time when creating brand awareness as well as building a customer base. In these passive income strategies , consistency, quality, and effective marketing play major roles in achieving desired success results. Therefore with determination, patience and hard work he can convert his hobbies into profit-making enterprises hence deriving benefits from additional income streams.

Stock market investment and online selling for passive income

Investing in the stock market can be a powerful way to generate passive income. This means that you recommend products and services to your audience and, whenever they are bought through your specific affiliate link, you earn commission. If you work with established companies and focus on promoting products that are relevant to your area of expertise, you can make money through your digital presence.

Scalability is one of the key advantages of affiliate marketing. In essence, it implies that as more people join your list and increase their promotional efforts, your earning potential increases as well. If for instance, you run a blog, have a YouTube channel or are active in social media circles, integrating affiliate marketing will not become a problem for you. Just go out there and share your experiences, reviews and recommendations so that people can buy from you.

Another way to earn passive income is by engaging in stock photography. So if photography is something that interests you then consider enlisting some of your high definition pictures on stock photo sites. Mostly, the platforms act as marketplaces where firms, designers among others get visual content needed for creative projects like websites or blogs. You will receive royalties every time someone downloads any of your photos or videos.

The key to succeeding in stock photography is creating compelling visual content that sells. Think about images which can be versatile such as those with scenes at home working spaces, travel pictures or even nature photographs among others. Composition, lighting and aesthetics should be considered; this is to make sure that you have attractive photos different from those made by other photographers.

"Affiliate marketing is one way to earn passive income over time without being involved in the day-to-day operation of the company itself."

Rental Properties and Social Media Influencer: Passive Income Streams

Becoming a social media influencer opens up limitless possibilities where turning your digital presence into an income generating platform is concerned. For example; when you partner with brands and promote what they sell, your income may be in the form of sponsored posts, affiliate marketing, or brand collaborations. This has to do with connecting to your followers while establishing credibility for bringing a partnership that suits your niche and values.

Similarly, merchandising is another way to generate money from your involved fans. This includes physical items like t-shirts carrying your brand name or digital ones such as e-books and online courses which deliver value against your expertise even as you accrue passive income.

Alternatively, rental properties are a tangible means of generating passive income over time. Renting out these properties will guarantee consistent cash flow through rents paid on a regular basis. Moreover, one can also enjoy capital appreciation due to an increase in property value over time which further enhances the potential of passive income streams.

Success in rental property investments involves understanding market dynamics, identifying profitable locations and efficient management of properties. Screening tenants properly and attending to their requests for maintenance will result in positive net operating income (NOI) along with protection of asset value.

"Combining social media influence and rental property investment can give you multiple sources of passive income thus increasing financial security and wealth build up."

Stock Market Investment and Online Selling for Passive Income

If you are in search of passive income, two lucrative options to look at are stock market investment and online selling. These strategies can give you a regular income while allowing you to be your own boss. Let's see how these approaches can help you achieve your financial objectives.

The Power of Stock Market Investment

Investing in the stock market is among the best ways to earn passive income. By purchasing stocks of companies that have a chance for growth, capital appreciation and dividend payments are achieved. The value of your investment may appreciate over time allowing you to sell your stocks at a higher price and make a profit.

However, it is important to conduct thorough research and plan financially before engaging in any stock market investments. You need to keep abreast with market trends, company performance and economic indicators that will guide your investment decisions. It is also worth considering consulting financial advisers or using the online tools that estimate one's risk tolerance as well as help make an informed diversified portfolio that suits an individual's investment goals.

An Online Selling: A Global Marketplace for Passive Income

Another effective method of generating passive income is by online selling. Platforms such as Amazon and eBay create opportunities for reaching out internationally and selling various types of goods. Be it physical items or digital products, this kind of selling allows you to turn what you love doing or are knowledgeable in into an extremely profitable business.

However, when venturing into online selling it is crucial to identify the niche market, find out about demand and price the product appropriately. Likewise, inventory management, shipping logistics, customer service or even marketing strategies will enhance optimization of the online business.

When combining the power of stock market investment with expansive reach offered by online-selling; however, it becomes possible for people to create reliable streams of passive income towards ensuring their future financial stability. Nonetheless, adhering strictly to these strategies requires commitment; continued learning and adaptability on your part regarding how things change over time in the market industry. Start now by examining the choices ahead of you and how effectively they can support long-term financial growth.

Peer-to-Peer Lending and Cashback for Supplementary Income

What are the other ways to increase income? Peer-to-peer lending and cash back programs can be considered as alternatives. These approaches allow you to earn additional money while putting in little effort and having low initial investments.

Peer-to-peer lending involves lending money directly to individuals, bypassing traditional financial institutions. By becoming a lender, you receive interest on loans made by your peers. Borrowers benefit from this form of lending since they usually get lower rates compared to those offered by traditional lenders while lenders make returns on their investment.

Cashback programs are another profitable way of adding extra income. Such systems enable one to earn money as they do their online everyday shopping. By participating in these programs, an individual receives a percentage of the purchases made hence saving on every transaction at the same time. It is like being paid for shopping!

The Advantages of Peer-to-Peer Lending

Why should you consider peer-to-peer lending? One of the benefits is that it can offer better returns compared to other conventional saving accounts or investments. Since interest rates are determined by market forces, one has an opportunity to bargain for a competitive return on one's lending.

Also, there is an alternative source of finance for individuals who do not qualify for traditional loans in the peer-to-peer lending. When you lend directly to borrowers, you are actively involved in helping others achieve their financial goals. It is a win-win situation that facilitates financial inclusion and builds people's capacity.

Exploring Cashback Programs for Extra Income

Who does not enjoy making money while shopping? Cashback programs provide a simple and convenient way of increasing your earnings. You receive cash back as a percentage of the purchase price whenever you buy anything through these programs. It feels like obtaining a discount on every online purchase!

Cashback programs partner with many online stores, allowing customers to earn money while shopping for ordinary items, clothing, electronics, travel and more. The process is simple; join a cash-back program, shop from their portal and get rewarded with cash back. This is an easy means of filling your pockets with some extra cash.

Considerations for Successful Supplementary Income

However P2P lending and Cashback programs may help in boosting income, there are several factors that must be taken into account. In peer-to-peer lending, always remember there are risks involved. Make sure to assess each prospective borrower's creditworthiness carefully as well as your risk tolerance prior to providing financing.

Similarly, when using cash back programs it is important to consider the terms and conditions. For example, some have thresholds before one can withdraw or earn cashbacks from them. Understand the program's rules so as to get everything out of it.

It is possible to create a passive income stream by incorporating P2P lending and cashback programs into your broader financial plan. Diversification of income sources can mean greater security in the foundation of your financial life as well as the advantages brought about by these streams.

Leveraging Skills and Assets for Passive Income Generation

The art of generating passive income involves putting into use personal skills or assets in order to create sustainable means of earning. By understanding your skills and resources, you can find ways to earn passive income and increase your financial security.

Buying and selling websites is one way to generate passive income. This involves purchasing websites with potential, improving them, then selling at a higher price. With your knowledge in website development and online marketing you can take advantage of the growing demand for established online platforms.

Another way to earn passive income is by starting a YouTube channel. Ad revenue, brand partnerships and sponsored content are some of the ways that can be used to monetize the channel provided it delivers the right content and engages the audience. Create valuable content consistently using your passion and expertise hence turning it into a high paying passive income stream.

Another option is investing in Real Estate Investment Trusts (REITs). REITs give individuals an opportunity to own shares in professionally managed portfolios of real estate properties.

Investors make passive income through dividends as well as capital appreciation without being involved in direct property management. This approach allows you to use your assets in order to create a dynamic source of revenue over time.

If you have a talent for design then creating designs available for sale on the internet could be another profitable passive income option. Websites like Redbubble, Etsy or Society6 allow you to exhibit & sell designs on various merchandise such as t-shirts, mugs or home décor products among others. Take advantage of the e-commerce market by utilising your creative abilities thus making money from digital designs passively.

Another way to leverage your assets for passive income is by investing in businesses. You can opt to become a silent partner or angel investor and assist start-ups or existing companies with capital in exchange for a part of the profits earned. This type of investment allows you to earn money without becoming involved in running it.

Just some examples of how you can use your abilities and properties to generate passive income are mentioned above. Multiple revenue streams that operate even if you are not active can be built from your expertise and available resources. Determine the top opportunities that match well with your talents and passions, and begin setting up your passive income portfolio today.

Establishing a Safe Financial Portfolio via Passive Income

Building a safe financial portfolio is important for long-term financial stability. One way to do this is by diversifying your sources of income, integrating some passive earnings streams within them. It provides flexibility, extra earnings as well as possibility for creation of wealth on a long term basis.

This chapter has delved into various passive income ideas that you can consider when trying to achieve your financial goals. These include among others; starting a drop shipping store, selling digital products, investing in the stock market or becoming a social media influencer.

In order for one's different sources of passive income ideas, it should be noted that they must align with an individual's aptitudes and interests. In this way will one not only make more money but also find pleasure in doing so. So why wait? Start looking into these concepts provided on ways to earn passive revenue and take steps toward creating a financially stable future. It's never too late, though, to start producing passive cash flows while ensuring stability in finance; thereby gaining control over your own economic journey right away!

Chapter 31

Embrace Lifelong Learning: Adapting Skills in an Ever-Evolving Digital Environment

****

In today's fast-moving, digitalized world of globalisation, knowledge must grow continually in order to match the pace of rapid technological change. The information age is characterised by exponential growth and continuous change, necessitating a constant addition to our knowledge base. To be candid, only through adopting a lifelong learning attitude will we successfully navigate this sea of knowledge.

Lifelong learning is not just an empty phrase but a lifestyle approach concerned with active acquisition of knowledge for personal and professional reasons. It involves the natural curiosity that opens up new possibilities to humanity while at the same time opens doors to fruitful ideas and their effective solutions in life. This also implies a proactive approach that facilitates adaptability which is an important skill in today's highly dynamic environment.

Adaptability – swiftly adjusting to new conditions - is increasingly being seen as an important learning outcome. Reasoning flexibility and creative problem-solving are fundamental qualities that make people more efficient when dealing with complex situations both inside and outside the education system.

One essential aspect of lifelong learning linked with adaptability relates to learning styles. People have different ways of taking in information. Diagrams and charts work best for visual learners while auditory learners prefer hearing which helps them understand more effectively. There are those who need to do something before they can understand it and there are those who need to know why something has happened before they can learn how it happened. When these differences are recognized the educational process can be modified in such a way as to ensure effective, enjoyable and ultimately successful learning.

Understanding early principles of child development and learning underpins a habit conducive to lifelong learning. When nurtured from inception, children tend to develop an innate love for exploration as well as an adaptable mindset that encourages them to keep on acquiring knowledge throughout various stages of life.

Never before has there been so much change in our surroundings compared to now. We have ourselves, professionals, society among others responsible for keeping up with this change. Through fostering a passion for learning, adaptability, and understanding our distinct learning styles, we can inculcate habits that will not only keep us ahead of the curve but also help us thrive within it.

Role Description of Adaptability

In the era of rapid technological advancements and digital transformations, adaptability is one of the most important skills. This refers not only to technology itself but also to new situations, challenges and opportunities that appear in front of us. In this context, adaptability seen as a sister to lifelong learning becomes an essential skill.

Adaptability implies welcoming change and flexibility in response towards different circumstances. In so doing, adaptable individuals are able to manage uncertainty effectively, function under pressure and demonstrate resilience even in adverse conditions.

This quality is highly relevant for leaders in all sectors. Adaptive leaders who can cope with constantly changing conditions are more likely to respond successfully to sudden shifts taking place within their own spheres. Adaptive leaders are especially necessary during periods of uncertainty such as management changes or business model restructuring processes or adoption of new technologies as they provide stability and coherence during transitions.

A commitment to constant development and transformation is one thing they always share in common. They are visionaries that are full of dynamism and thus encourage experimentation and failure as innovation paths. In this respect, leadership development resources underscore adaptive strategy formulation as a hallmark of successful leadership in the present digital era.

However, adaptability is not only important for leadership roles but also as valuable in educational settings. The world of data offers many opportunities for learning communities, but with them come challenges. Leading transformative educators know how to merge digital tools into teaching approaches while focusing on students' needs.

Technology-centred innovative teaching methods are key to creating inclusive learning environments which cater for diverse learning styles and abilities. Teachers who adopt flexible approaches are more likely to develop a classroom culture that embraces change and promotes critical thinking. Thus, adaptability on the part of teachers contributes to the creation of technology-enriched learning environments that support the education of students for an increasingly digital world.

Moreover, adaptability is closely associated with professional competence attainment. In rapidly changing industries individuals need to be flexible enough and have a great desire to acquire new skills. Doing so enables them to improve their job performance and enjoy what they do even more. It requires continuous development as part of a person's professional routine.

Finally, adaptability is the driving force behind success in personal life endeavours or business settings. Reshaping our leadership skills or modifying educational methods actually requires flexibility in various areas of our existence. By constantly updating our knowledge and developing ourselves further we remain relevant within a dynamic digital sphere.

The embracing of Numerous Learning Styles within Digital Age

In continuous learning processes, understanding individual learning styles is critical when exploring issues on adaptability. Traditional ways of acquiring knowledge have changed due to widespread use of digital platforms in all spheres today including education systems at large scale. As such, it becomes necessary to familiarise oneself with different people's ways of learning so that we can identify where it works best for us.

Learning styles are also referred to as the preferred way of learning, assimilating, and processing information by an individual. Some people are visual learners who understand concepts better when they are illustrated with pictures or other visual aids; some are auditory learners who prefer information which is spoken or written while other students like kinesthetic style where they learn through doing.

Digital tools create opportunities for accommodating diverse learning preferences. For example, visual learners can access YouTube channels and instructional videos; auditory learners can use podcasts and audiobooks. Kinesthetic learners get hands-on learning experience from interactive online quizzes or virtual simulation games.

At the same time, it is important to understand that our brains function best when several senses work together. Consequently, environments rich in technology should make use of multi-modal approaches to teaching that combine text, images, sounds, videos and also interactive materials so as to accommodate a range of learner preferences and therefore ensure effective transfer of knowledge.

Another important consideration relates to modalities for acquiring new skills. In the ever-changing digital world where the needs of the labour market keep changing due to technological advancements made in this area, one has not only to learn but to relearn constantly. This is true for any person – be it students preparing themselves for future employment or working professionals willing to stay up-to-date with their professions.

Digital age has also played a big role. With a lot of readily available resources on the internet, self-directed learning is now more common than ever before. Massive Open Online Courses (MOOCs) provided by leading universities around the world, webinars and online workshops in different areas, and even bite-sized learning apps-for each of these platforms, reskilling and upskilling becomes easier at our own pace and convenience.

However, while technology expands access to know-how and offers numerous alternatives to choose from, effective skill development still requires active engagement, consistency in practice, reflecting on feedback, ability to bounce back from failures and most importantly eagerness to learn. Thus successful learning strategy becomes a blend of digital resources coupled with traditional yet timeless learning principles.

To wrap it up, a personalised approach that recognizes one's learning style along with smart utilisation of digital tools can support an enriching continuous learning journey. Our capacity to adapt ourselves as lifelong learners deepens as we embrace diverse ways of how we could learn in this digital era.

Nurturing Lifelong Curiosity & Ongoing Education

As we navigate through the digital age where continuous learning and adaptability are vital, there is one trait that stands out – lifelong curiosity. This internal drive for more knowledge that goes beyond the surface of everything around us fuels our quest for self-improvement and personal growth. When combined with a commitment to ongoing education, this curiosity can lead us on an enriching path of lifelong learning.

Lifelong curiosity starts in childhood when children ask multiple questions as why is sky blue or how televisions work? Encouraging such curiosity at early stages prepares children who are engaged learners continuing their quest for knowledge even outside organised school settings. It therefore plays a critical role in early child development and learning but this attribute should not stop developing from here; instead it should be nurtured throughout life.

In professional environments, lifelong curiosity translates into an enthusiasm for acquiring new skills and expanding knowledge. The curiousness among professionals drives innovation as they often challenge the status quo and are interested in exploring new ideas or ways of doing things. Such individuals bring fresh perspectives to the workplace which usually lead to innovative solutions and successful problem-solving approaches.

However, transforming this curiosity into fruitful outcomes requires a structure – a framework that encourages exploration while still developing analytical thinking. And this is where ongoing education comes into play.

Ongoing education focuses on constant acquisition of knowledge towards both personal development and professional competence. It may involve returning to formal academia for further degrees or certifications, attending webinars, workshops or conferences, signing up for online courses, or simply reading widely within one's field or beyond.

In today's fast-paced digital world, ongoing education is not just an advantage but a necessity. Advancements in technology and changes in market requirements cause the employment landscape to continually change. Therefore, professionals must keep up with developments and trends in their areas of specialisation. An active commitment towards ongoing education provides effective means for this sustained learning.

In addition, ongoing education also encourages the transfer of knowledge and skills to new situations or domains, a quality that is highly esteemed in modern work situations. For instance, an engineer who has designed a product may need to be conversant with marketing strategies; a manager can benefit from a foundation in coding; on the other hand, before integrating technology tools into his or her methodology, a teacher must know what these tools are.

This means that time and resources spent in continuous training result in increased professional competence, job satisfaction and advancement opportunities. It also equips learners – like students or working professionals – with necessary skills for future careers which do not even exist today if life-long curiosity is combined with it.

To sum up, this combination of life-long curiosity and ongoing education enables us to keep up with the ever changing digital landscape and thrive within it. As we proceed down this path, we develop our ability to learn how to learn again – hence savouring the essence of continued learning.

Putting Theory into Practice: The Real World

In the continuing education journey, there is a necessity to link theoretical knowledge with practical applications. Knowing how theories apply to real-world cases elucidates concepts' importance and ultimately enhances full comprehension.

One field where this translation is paramount is workplace learning. With the rapid pace of technological change in the digital age working professionals must adapt by acquiring new skills regularly. However advanced the concept or strategy behind it might be though, its true value only comes out when successfully put into practice at work places.

Laying down theoretical bases prepares one for implementing new processes or technologies in his/her workplace while practical experiences enable one to understand things that theory doesn't always make clear. For example, managing team dynamics or moving through organisational hierarchies sometimes call for job-based skills more than those gained from formal education settings.

Leader development provides another setting where theory meets practice. Leadership theories explain some basic principles behind effective management styles but they should also be put into context according to individual teams and organisational culture. This means that one must not only know but also translate theories into practical strategies and actions.

In medical practice, theoretical knowledge is essential while the clinical experiences are imperative in enhancing clinical reasoning and decision making. For example, formulation of diagnosis or treatment plans requires a strong background in medical sciences, however, clinical exposure and interaction with other patients are necessary to develop critical thinking skills.

Applying theoretical frameworks to real-life situations also allows for reflection and feedback. Trying out concepts helps in their own assessment of what works best as well as modifying their approaches if need be. This continued process enhances comprehension of the theory itself as well as effective application.

Finally values make a big difference when shifting from theory to practice but they are often overlooked during discourse. Values play a key role in shaping behaviour; more often than not, they guide decision-making processes alongside moulding attitudes. Thus, when we interpret theories or go about practising them in these manners, our values should be acknowledged so that we can truly understand ourselves. Otherwise, they will act as motivational factors leading to change or an upgrade for better results.

In light of this discussion, it can be said that it is a moving experience to bridge theoretical knowledge with practical applications, for it is a constant quest for new knowledge, adaptation and development. It helps one to understand concepts better, design more operational implementation strategies and enriches the general process of always learning. As lifelong learners in this ever-evolving digital environment, fostering this bridge becomes an integral part of our educational journeys.

Chapter 32

Failures as Learning Opportunities and Developing Grit to Embrace Challenges

***

This chapter takes a deep dive into the meaning of defeat as an opportunity to learn and how grit helps in overcoming challenges. Continuous learning is a lifetime experience that allows us to treat failures as milestones of success, and develop tenacity for success.

Failures should be viewed as a powerful platform for learning rather than hindrance. Change in our mindset can help us learn from our failures, improve on mistakes and eventually grow. This sort of mindset will enable us to bounce back stronger, with the experiences we have had before.

A key feature of continuous learning is grit. It is about persistence, enthusiasm, and toughness that give strength to cope with problems and obstacles faced in life. When we develop grit, we get better at staying motivated even when things are not going well. This determination pushes us towards achieving what we want no matter how challenging it may seem.

Having a growth mindset is one of the most important requirements in continuous learning. We willingly face new intimidating situations because these are investments in our comfort zones, skills development or knowledge enrichment. Embracing challenges instils in us a growth mindset because it makes us believe that effort matters more than talent; thus, anyone can improve their abilities.

We shall look into strategies for continuous learning in this chapter, overcome barriers to progress and discuss resilience as an essential attribute needed while navigating through ups and downs of life's journey. Moreover, we will highlight some personal benefits that accrue from participating in lifelong studies.

Let's proceed down the path of embracing constant education, having grit and turning failures into opportunities for growth together. Prepare yourself to unlock your potential fully and live a satisfying life full of success.

The Power of Continuous Learning

Continuous learning involves personal development throughout one's lifetime career path. It serves as an invaluable tool for enabling people to adapt themselves to changing circumstances as well as grow continuously.

In its simplest terms continuous learning is the process of acquiring new knowledge and skills throughout one's life. It surpasses formal education to embrace a growth mindset where failures and challenges are seen as opportunities for learning and improvement.

Resilience is needed for embracing continuous learning- an ability to get back on track after a setback and stay focused despite the challenges. We believe that our intelligence and abilities can be developed if we approach learning with a growth mindset.

"Continuous learning is the key to unlocking our full potential and achieving success in both our personal and professional lives."

A growth mindset allows us to interpret failures as stepping stones towards success, rather than roadblocks. Therefore, it supports perseverance, overcoming obstacles, and seeking better outcomes at all times. By cultivating a growth mindset, we develop resilience which helps us cope with different environments, changes, etc., and recognize when there are opportunities for personal development.

Adapting to Change

In this dynamic world continuous learning is mandatory in order to remain relevant in the ever changing environment. Constant updating of knowledge together with skills enables individuals to be acquainted with new technologies as well as changes in industry trends or market place expectations.

Individuals who have embraced continuous learning through having a growth mindset become lifelong learners. It ignites the love for knowledge within them; makes them curious about new things hence resulting in personal interest in lifelong professional development.

Growth Mindset and Professional Success

There is a close connection between continuous learning and professional success. Employers respect individuals who are always seeking ways to add to their knowledge and skills, as it shows initiative, flexibility and eagerness to take up new responsibilities.

Individuals with a growth mindset and commitment to continuous learning can unleash their full potential, improve their job performance and open doors to new career opportunities. This keeps us nimble, gaining newer competencies and increasing our worth in the workplace.

"Continuous learning helps us be flexible, creative and successful in everything we do."

Failures as Learning Opportunities

Oftentimes failures are considered obstacles that inhibit progress and achievement. Nevertheless, with appropriate attitude, one can learn from these setbacks. By accepting failure as an opportunity to learn, improve and change for the better, one learns the culture of growth that bolsters resilience and supports continuous learning.

"Failure is simply an opportunity to begin again more intelligently." - Henry Ford

A growth mindset toward failures reframes our perspective where we understand that they are not a full stop but just mere bumps on the way to success. Instead of lamenting this fact, we squeeze out useful information from our failures. Every failure becomes a step towards personal development.

The Power of Reflection

Reflecting on our failures allows us to identify why they occurred and what went wrong. It enables us to delineate those areas that need improvement while at the same time allowing us room for discovering other strategies or approaches towards overcoming challenges. Through honest self-reflection, we open ourselves up for new ideas as well as opportunities for additional learning.

Reframing the Narrative

Failure demands a different narrative approach altogether. Rather than seeing it as indicative of who we really are, it could be perceived as a passing setback. Turning our fiascos into educative experiences changes our focus from negatives into possibilities of growing or developing.

"The greatest glory in living lies not in never falling but in rising every time we fall." - Nelson Mandela

Another reason why we should embrace failures as learning opportunities is that it helps us develop resilience. We learn how to bounce back from disappointments and keep moving ahead despite the challenges that come our way. Our toughness increases with each failure, enabling us to tackle even harder trials.

In addition, failures offer us insights and feedback that may be otherwise missed. They help us identify our strengths as well as weaknesses hence giving a head start to improvement and development. Failures are therefore a stimulus for growth and advancement.

In this manner, by having a growth mindset, accepting our failures as learning opportunities, we shape a mindset of continuous learning. We become more open minded to other possibilities, ready for risks and adventures into unknown territories. The process of continuously learning becomes part of life thus driving one towards personal and professional growth. Remember, failures are not roadblocks but stepping stones towards success. Embrace them, learn from them and see yourself grow.

Developing Grit and Resilience

Grit is an essential quality which encompasses persistence, enthusiasm and toughness while self-motivated. It is what makes people keep on overcoming challenges including setbacks maintaining their focus no matter what happens whatsoever. Grittiness does not only play a key role in the aspect of continuous learning but also in personal life goals attainment both at individual and work levels.

Grit is the capacity to dig deep, push through barriers and keep moving forward even in the face of adversity. With grit, individuals have inner strength to be committed to their goals no matter what challenges they encounter along the way. They know that setbacks are stepping stones for growth and success.

"To me Grit means pushing yourself when you lack motivation. It differentiates between people who quit and those who move forwards."

Developing grit involves cultivating a growth mindset where problems are seen as opportunities for learning and growth. This does not mean giving up but embracing failure as an opportunity to learn, improve and try again.

The Power of Perseverance

Perseverance is a key ingredient of grit. It is about being able to persist despite adversity, setbacks or even failures themselves. Perseverance enables individuals to bounce back, learn from failures and continue working towards their goals.

Perseverance is thus the motivation that keeps the individual focused on his journey of continuous learning.

"Perseverance is when you don't quit because you're tired but you give your all because you got nothing left."

By developing perseverance, individuals build resilience and become better equipped to handle challenges. They learn to embrace discomforts, push past limitations as well as enjoy the ups and downs that come along with unceasing education.

Cultivating Resilience

Resilience is another critical aspect of grit. It is the ability to adapt, bounce back, and thrive in the face of adversity. Resilient individuals view challenges as opportunities for growth and remain flexible in their approach to learning. Resilience allows one to bend without breaking in the presence of obstacles by going head-on with them until finally emerging stronger on the other side.

"Resilience isn't about avoiding hard things; it's about having courage & deep belief in myself."

Cultivating resilience involves developing coping mechanisms, building a support network, and maintaining a positive mindset. Resilient individuals know that setbacks and failures do not mean the end of the road but are stepping stones to further growth and development.

By developing grit, individuals can navigate the challenges and setbacks that come with continuous learning. They embrace the power of perseverance and cultivate resilience, enabling them to stay committed, focused, and determined on their learning journey. With grit as their foundation, individuals can push through obstacles, adapt to changing circumstances, and achieve their goals in both their personal and professional lives.

Embracing Challenges

Embracing challenges is an essential aspect of continuous learning. It is when they face new things or difficult situations that people truly grow. When they willingly step outside of their comfort zones, individuals start expanding themselves beyond belief while acquiring new skills that will be helpful in their personal and professional life.

At the core of embracing challenges is a growth mindset which is an integral part of a growth mindset. Individuals with this type of mindset believe they learn & grow by putting forth effort to learn better or eventually improve in future experiences. Instead of seeing challenges as obstacles to overcome, they view them as opportunities for learning and development fostering resilience that can be achieved through embracing challenges . For instance ,through such a disposition one becomes more persevered as it helps them to persist in spite of setbacks and go on even during hard times.

"The biggest challenge of all is to challenge your own self-doubt and disbelief." - Alicia Vikander

When people face challenges, they are able to become open to new ways of doing things. They come to understand themselves better and gain belief in their capacity to surmount hurdles. And one challenge after another becomes a stepping stone toward personal and professional development.

"The only limits in life are the ones you make." - LeBron James

With this perspective towards challenges, individuals will not only develop new skills and knowledge but also acquire a mindset that is flexible and responsive to change. Such persons become lifelong learners that are always looking for opportunities to broaden their horizons and experience new things.

"The only way to do great work is to love what you do. If you haven't found it yet, keep looking. Don't settle." - Steve Jobs

Then let's embrace challenges with a growth mindset; thirst for learning and development only if we can. Let's see them as chances of becoming our best versions ever as well as unlocking our potential fully. We can overcome any challenge when we work together towards achieving great things. Keep pushing your boundaries and allow your growth thinking to drive you!

Role of Resilience

Resilience plays an integral part in the journey of lifelong learning. It involves facing setbacks, adapting to change, overcoming adversity without losing hope. Whatever challenges may come their way, resilient individuals possess the internal strength needed for recovery and endurance.

In terms of continuous learning, resilience therefore helps individuals manoeuvre through setbacks and obstacles without giving up. Therefore, this trait helps them maintain a positive attitude even when facing adversities hence moving forward regardless of any form of difficulties they confront themselves with. Consequently, resilience allows people to see problems as avenues for growth instead of obstacles.

By embracing resilience, individuals can easily recover from failure, learn from mistakes made so that they can forge ahead with life despite adversaries experienced by them at times. This is because lifelong learning often comes with keeping up with current information regarding one's field or job area which keeps on evolving regularly thereby perpetuating individual growth. It therefore allows a person to be flexible particularly when it comes to embracing new challenges and opportunities for growth.

"Resilience is not just about bouncing back; it's about bouncing forward."

This implies that individuals who are resilient are better placed to embrace continuous learning and succeed in overcoming obstacles. They possess the determination and perseverance needed to overcome setbacks and continue their educational journey. They see that failures are only temporary but learning stones leading to success.

In the next section, we shall look at strategies of developing resilience as well as how individuals can create this vital attribute in their lives.

Strategies for Continuous Learning

Continuous learning is an unending process that requires constant effort and dedication. In order to enhance your learning experience and foster a culture of continuous learning, there are several effective strategies you can implement in your personal and professional life.

Lifelong Learning

Continuous learning starts with accepting the concept of lifelong learning. Lifelong learning is an attitude toward your knowledge that commits you to seeking knowledge throughout your life by always staying curious, open-minded as well as actively looking out for opportunities for self-development.

Embracing Curiosity

Curiosity is one of the main drivers behind continuous learning. Nurturing this natural curiosity will improve how you learn things and help you understand more about what is going on around you. Embrace curiosity by asking questions, exploring different perspectives, and staying open-minded.

Seeking Feedback

Continuous learning is a powerful process that allows individuals to grow and adapt in an ever changing world. It has its challenges though. Our journey towards continuous learning may be hindered by obstacles such as fear of failure, self-doubt, and external pressures. To fully embrace the benefits of continuous learning, we must overcome these stumbling blocks.

"Your thoughts are your own worst enemy."

The fear of failure is one major stumbling block to continuous learning. Many people never venture or take up opportunities for fear of making mistakes or underachieving. Nevertheless, it should be borne in mind that failure is not an impediment but rather a stairway to success. A paradigm shift is required to regard failing as a chance for learning. With this view, we can turn our failures into valuable experiences and opportunities and use them to our advantage.

"Whether you think you can or you think you can't, you're right."

Self-doubt is another obstacle which prevents us from embracing continuous learning. We tend to question our abilities, compare ourselves with others or even underestimate our potential. To overcome self-doubt, we should develop self-belief within us. This entails recognizing one's strengths, building confidence and celebrating even the smallest achievements made in life. Having positive self-belief will enable you to take on new challenges outside your comfort zone.

"In order to reach your highest potential you must tend to your own garden."

External pressures like societal expectations or opinions of others can also limit our journey toward continuous learning. Personal growth should be the foremost priority against all odds while pursuing what one has interest in. In relation to this matter; always endeavour yourself with those who believe in your potentiality and support your ongoing development efforts. Remembering that everyone's path is unique and staying true to oneself is important.

It takes a change in mindset to overcome these obstacles preventing continuous learning from happening for an individual which means it requires reframing failures as valuable experiences, developing self-belief and considering your own growth. We can break these hindrances and maximise our potential if we start seeing challenges as a way of learning, not an absence of progress. However, it is possible to engage in continuous learning although it is not always easy.

Continuous Learning at Work

It is highly important for one to engage in continuous learning in order to be up-to-date with the ever-changing needs of the workplace which is fast-paced and competitive. To be ahead and adjust to the dynamic nature of the professional environment that keeps changing, organisations must emphasise on and promote continuous learning for their employees. This helps them become more adaptable as well as spark up innovation and growth.

Professional development programs represent one of the main strategies employed by organisations to achieve continuous learning. They enhance skills among staff, offer new knowledge thus making them remain updated in their respective careers. Organisations can develop a culture of learning through investment in employee development hence enhancing personal growth and organisational effectiveness.

"Continuous learning is like fuel that arms employees with skills and knowledge needed to overcome today's challenges."

Besides having formal professional development programs, organisations can foster a supportive environment which appreciates and encourages continuous learning. This may include things such as provision of time and resources for learning activities, enhancing collaboration among employees therefore promoting sharing of knowledge or rewarding people who actively participate in ongoing education.

In any organisation, continuous workplace learning is vital so that staff members are still pertinent within a rapidly changing world. It allows individuals to improve themselves professionally by keeping pace with changing trends, technologies as well as jobs in various industries. Continuous improvement enables staff to improve performance outcomes while accepting new responsibilities thereby advancing one's career opportunities.

Advantages

A wide range of benefits are associated with continuous work-based learning both for workers and organisations at large. For workers, it opens up possibilities for self-development on many counts while increasing confidence levels thus leading to job satisfaction. It equips individuals with the knowhow necessary for career growth hence giving them an upper hand in employment markets.

Organisations that embrace a culture of continuous learning are more innovative and adaptable. Continuous learners among employees keep introducing fresh perspectives into organisations' business processes thus maintaining leadership positions even amidst rapidly transforming environments. Additionally, priority given on continuous learning by organisations enables them to attract and retain the best talents since many professionals today are pursuing opportunities for growth and development in their careers.

"Continuous learning in the workplace is the cornerstone of building a talented, adaptable, and future-ready workforce."

When an organisation embraces continuous workplace learning, it sets itself up for long-term success of its employees as well as its competitiveness in the market. This involves creating an environment that cherishes, recognizes, and incorporates learning and development as part of its culture.

Benefits of Continuous Learning

Continuous learning is a lifelong journey and a tool for individual development, better work performance, and more job opportunities. Individuals who choose to adopt the concept of continuous learning are guaranteed numerous benefits that guarantee them success.

"Continuous learning enhances knowledge and improves skills necessary for adjusting to changing jobs and staying ahead in their careers."

Investing in continuous learning enables personal growth through widening perspectives, acquiring new knowledge and honing critical thinking skills. Expanding the understanding will create adaptability to challenges and changes in their professional lives.

Improved Job Performance

"Continuous learning provides the necessary tools and information to excel in their roles hence improved job performance."

Continuous learners actively look for ways to gain new skills relevant to recent industry trends. This keeps them updated with latest developments that can be incorporated into their work place by way of fresh ideas, innovative solutions, and best practices. Highly productive employees portray commitment towards continuous learning which also results in high levels of job satisfaction hence being recognized by both colleagues as well as superiors.

Career Advancement

"Enrolling in continuous programs opens up more career opportunities hence enabling individuals to realise their professional goals."

Employers look favourably upon those employees who display a desire for personal development. By being open-minded learners, they have obtained expertise on how to solve complex problems using cutting-edge technologies as well as leading teams effectively. They become eligible for promotions due to having advanced knowledge levels; thus qualifying them for higher salaries or even leadership positions.

Moreover, it helps widen professional networks and expose people to a greater number of opportunities. Continuous learners involve themselves in various events such as workshops where professionals meet, opening doors to connections, credibility building or even expansion into other fields.

"Embracing continuous learning isn't just about professional growth; it's about the pursuit of personal fulfilment and a lifelong quest for excellence."

Continuous learners find personal satisfaction when they attain set objectives such as pushing beyond boundaries thereby gaining more information about it. They remain relevant and well-equipped to tackle challenges, foster creativity, and make a lasting impact in their chosen fields.

Continuous learning is not just an event but rather a lifelong journey towards personal growth, career development, satisfaction of one's life and fulfilment. By investing in continuous learning, people embark on a transformative path that will unlock their potential so that they can succeed.

Cultivating a Culture of Continuous Learning

Creating a culture of continuous learning is imperative for organisations to be competitive and thrive in today's rapidly changing world. It all boils down to leadership. Leaders who prioritise continuous learning show the importance of ongoing development and create a conducive environment where their teams can engage in continuous learning.

"When leaders prioritise continuous learning their teams will follow suit."

Leaders set an example when they continuously learn by themselves. By constantly gaining new knowledge and skills leaders show commitment to growth and improvement. This encourages others in the organisation to adopt the same approach hence making it a culture of continuous learning.

"A culture of continuous learning is not limited to a select few individuals, but rather extends to all levels of the organisation."

When individuals are allowed to participate in their continuous development and share knowledge, organisational learning becomes ingrained at every level. It is inclusive so that it can get the diverse perspectives and experiences required for enriched learning and innovation.

The culture of continuous learning can be built by the leaders through mentorship programs, cross functional projects, and knowledge sharing platforms. This enables leaders to encourage collaboration and idea sharing that will promote a culture where continuous learning is valued and embraced.

"In a culture of continuous learning, mistakes are seen as opportunities for growth while feedback is appreciated."

Leaders must be able to create an environment where mistakes are cherished because they act as important stepping-stones to growth. In order for these conditions to prevail, leaders should encourage open communication and give constructive feedback.

Ultimately, developing a culture of ongoing learning necessitates commitment from both individuals and leaders. This ability allows them to adapt to changes in their industry as well as other environments, foster innovations there for driving forward or even become market leaders.

Tools and Resources for Continuous Learning

There are many tools available out there when it comes to continuous learning which can help people increase their knowledge and skills. These may include books, online courses, webinars or professional networks among others depending on your preference.

Today's digital era has made online courses quite popular among many people. They cover different topics one may be interested in at any time anywhere. Therefore if you want to learn a programming language like Java or Python may be; improve your marketing skills or just learn better ways of personal growth then such a course is a convenient way of achieving your goals.

Webinars also rank high on the list of best tools used in the process of constant education. They can either be live sessions or recorded ones with professionals leading them on various topics. Get involved in interactive discussion forums, gain insights from other's experiences all this done from your home office while relaxing in your best chair.

"Books are a man's best friend."

Books are timeless resources that offer in-depth knowledge and perspectives. Whether it is a book on self-development or a technical manual, the market is flooded with books on almost any topic. Pick a good book that is well-written and see how this can change your perception of the learning process.

Podcasts are a great way to absorb information while on the move. Subscribe to podcasts featuring recognized thought leaders, industry experts or professionals. The audio platforms contain lots of valuable insights that help people update their knowledge more frequently in different areas.

Apart from individual resources, professional networks are significant for continuous learning.

Professional networks like LinkedIn and other specialised communities provide platforms where individuals can network with others alike, share ideas as well as learn from these experiences. Networking, collaboration and continued growth are facilitated through such interactions with fellow professionals in one's line of work.

Continuous learning has been made easier thanks to numerous tools and resources at our disposal. With this in mind, it means we can embrace online courses, books, webinars or even reach out to podcast platforms among others for our personal growth as well as increased productivity rates.

Embracing Continuous Learning for Success

The key to personal success and professional growth is accepting continuous learning. People who can adapt and come up with new things are the ones who thrive in our world today. By developing a growth mindset and recognizing failures as learning opportunities, people can reach their potential.

Continuous learning is not just about knowledge acquisition but also entails developing resilience and embracing challenges. It refers to being open to new, difficult circumstances that we wouldn't choose to be in. Facing up to challenges in this way improves our skills and gives us deeper insights into how we learn so that we can experience more personal/professional growth.

Continual learning equips us with the ability of adapting to changing situations as well as taking advantage of new chances that arise. It provides us with the necessary tools and information needed for staying ahead in our careers; achieving our objectives; leading a happy life. By adopting constant training, we will succeed, even in an ever changing working environment.

Chapter 33

Cultivating Intellectual Humility and Open-Mindedness: Embracing Diverse Perspectives for Personal Growth
****

The contemporary world is full of different opinions and beliefs hence it is important for individuals to acquire certain qualities that will help them grow personally as well as understand the world more deeply. Intellectual humility and open-mindedness are two essential ingredients that unlock new perspectives and broaden our worldview.

Intellectual humility involves accepting the limitations of one's knowledge and beliefs, being receptive to new information, admitting when one is wrong, valuing other points of view. On the other hand, an open mind refers to an attitude whereby one has the ability to consider ideas or views without allowing his/her preconceived notions about them interfere.

By engaging in intellectual humility and open-mindedness, we can tap into a pool of knowledge beyond ourselves; engage in meaningful dialogues which challenge us as well as promote personal and intellectual growth. These qualities not only benefit us individually but also contribute to a more inclusive and harmonious society.

The importance of intellectual humility and open-mindedness will be explored in this chapter together with a definition of these concepts, their linkages, and their numerous advantages. We will also highlight easy ways we can use to incorporate intellectual humility in our daily experiences while overcoming obstacles impeding openness. Additionally, instances from real life situations as well as resources for continued learning will be given.

Come with us on this journey of self-discovery and intellectual growth where we look at diverse viewpoints for cultivating intellectual humility and open-mindedness. Together let's unlock personal potential!

The Value of Intellectual Humility and Open-Mindedness

Intellectual modesty is a crucial quality necessary for education promotion or making effective communication that hinges on critical thinking. By doing this it allows people to realise that there are limits to what they know apart from opening themselves up for divergent thoughts.

Intellectual humility means recognizing the possibility that there may be things we do not know. It helps us approach situations and conversations with an open mind ready to learn. Having intellectual humility allows people to listen, absorb and embrace ideas as they come along hence broadening our knowledge pool.

Equally, open-mindedness pushes us to consider other perspectives and challenge our own convictions. It encourages us to move outside of what is comfortable, accept different perspectives and engage in meaningful dialogue. Being open minded creates a culture that promotes intellectual growth where people are free to exchange their thoughts.

"Intellectual humility and open-mindedness allow us to transcend our own biases and preconceived ideas about them. They provide intellectual flexibility that lets us seek for diverse perspectives, critically analyse information and make informed choices."

We can develop these qualities by cultivating intellectual humility and open-mindedness, which help not only personal growth but also contribute to a more inclusive society. These qualities enable individuals to bridge gaps, promote understanding as well as find common ground with others. In the world we live today where there are diverse opinions and viewpoints, intellectual humility and open-mindedness are very crucial.

Therefore let's consider embracing these two guiding principles of life, which are intellectual humility and open-mindedness so that it may pave the way for personal growth coupled with intelligence, effective communication while leading into a harmonious society.

Meaning of Intellectual Humility

The most crucial Quality to Achieve and Expand Knowledge is Intellectual Humility which refers to an understanding of one's own limited knowledge and a willingness to accept new information and ideas from others. This is captured in the words of Michael Lynch, "It's about realizing that the beliefs you hold are contingent, they might be wrong."

"Intellectual humility does not involve self-loathing or doubt. Instead, it is an approach to learning that is modest, sincere and open to interaction with others."

Intellectual humility involves admitting mistakes and considering other people's perspectives. It does not mean belittling oneself or reducing one's self confidence but rather accepting that knowledge is dynamic and there remains much more to know. According to Mark Leary, intellectual humility helps people "view others as having thoughts, feelings, and knowledge that may differ from those of oneself."

People can develop intellectual humility by fostering curiosity in their life and having a genuine desire for learning. It means looking for diverse views, speaking gently without any biases and allowing yourself to be convinced by evidence. In doing so intellectual humility can be created.

The Importance of Intellectual Humility

However important it may be in personal development or education, intellectual humility has wider implications for society at large. It nurtures constructive conversations, empathetic listening and bridging divides between people. This fosters the contribution of individuals towards a society that values diverse standpoints.

We will then move on to explore the relationship between intellectual humility and open-mindedness; how these two qualities go hand in hand in encouraging personal growth both academically and personally.

The Link Between Intellectual Humility and Open-Mindedness

Intellectual humility is closely tied with being open-minded. Layman (2013) suggests that intellectual humility creates a space where individuals can embrace new ideas while maintaining an open mind toward them. People who are intellectually humble realise that what they know is not exhaustive of all possible knowledge or beliefs; thus, they are ready to listen and communicate respectfully. In this aspect, acknowledging the fallibility of themselves enables them to be open-minded.

Intellectual humility and open-mindedness support personal growth in different ways. They facilitate continuous learning where individuals expand their knowledge base on various subjects and opinions. This fosters empathy as one becomes more understanding of others. They also enhance critical thinking skills by allowing people to evaluate information critically and make well-informed choices.

Through intellectual humility, individuals recognize their own biases or prejudices and become more aware of new knowledge or alternative perspectives. Such a humble approach cultivates intellectual growth while creating an environment conducive to open-mindedness. This creates a sense of unity and empathy among individuals who embrace intellectual humility as well as open-mindedness since they can share with people who have different cultures or religions from theirs. By engaging in thoughtful conversations and exchanging ideas, intellectual humility and open-mindedness encourage collaboration as well as mutual respect. In the face of complex societal problems that require comprehensive approaches, an inclusive mindset that values diverse opinions is important.

To summarise the connection between intellectual humility and open-mindedness is evident. Intellectual humility gives people a foundation that allows them to accept new ideas and viewpoints with open minds. In this way, it helps personal growth, developing empathic relations and a more inclusive society.

Advantages of intellectual humility and open-mindedness

Cultivating intellectual humility as well as open mindedness presents numerous benefits. These traits enable individuals to improve their critical thinking skills thereby motivating a greater understanding and value of diverse perspectives. When someone embraces intellectual humility, he/she admits the limitations of their own knowledge thus being able to receive new thoughts and information. Being open to different views and questions of one's own assumptions through intellectual humility results in growth intellectually as well as personal development.

Intellectual humility and open-mindedness also contribute to effective problem-solving and better decision-making. By approaching situations with an open mind, individuals are more likely to consider a wide range of possibilities and evaluate them critically. This comprehensive perspective not only increases the chances of finding innovative solutions but also helps prevent cognitive biases from clouding judgement.

Additionally, these qualities build empathy toward others. Through being intellectually humble or receptive, individuals can undertake constructive dialogues by listening actively with consideration for differing opinions. This strengthens relationships based on mutual respect while fostering trust among people.

Embracing Different Perspectives

"By embracing different perspectives, individuals can challenge themselves and gain a better understanding of the world, thereby fostering intellectual development. It helps people to step out of their comfort zones and consider other perspectives that promote empathy with others."

People can gracefully navigate through diverse perspectives and experiences by embracing intellectual humility and open-mindedness. These qualities assist individuals in tearing down walls that divide them, thus contributing to a more inclusive world.

Developing Intellectual Humility

To fully adopt intellectual humility, self-reflection, curiosity, and a desire to learn from others are essential. This means admitting the fallibility of our own knowledge and beliefs as well as recognizing room for growth in understanding.

One way to grow in intellectual humility is through introspection. Reflecting upon our thoughts, beliefs, and prejudices enables us to identify areas where we may be close-minded or resistant to new ideas. By confessing these limitations, we can invite alternative viewpoints into our life journey and realise the opportunity for individual growth on an intellect's level.

"True intellectual humility comes from always questioning what you have believed about yourself."

Furthermore, being receptive to feedback or criticism is another crucial aspect of cultivating intellectual humility. It demands humility as well as distancing oneself from personal involvement or ego in certain concepts or ideas. By actively seeking diverse perspectives and welcoming opposing viewpoints we can expand our own perspective on things while challenging pre-existing assumptions.

Additionally, developing intellectual humility involves being patient with ourselves and committed to growth. Developing this trait is not easy because it requires one to be open-minded at all times so his/her beliefs may change with time based on new information acquired. Consequently, showing that learning is an ongoing process can help breed real humility within a person helping him/her grow even when they move into adulthood.

"Cultivating intellectual Humility implies having a deep desire to challenge what we believe about ourselves which makes us better placed to understand the complexities of today's world."

Promoting Open-Mindedness

In a world that has become more and more diverse and interconnected, fostering openness is vital for personal development as well as intellectual growth. It means being open to considering other perspectives, questioning assumptions, and embracing new information. Like ways in which one can develop a more receptive mind is by actively seeking out multiple points of view through respectful engagement with individuals from different backgrounds.

"To be truly open-minded is to celebrate the full range of human experiences and acknowledge the worth of differing viewpoints."

One way to foster open-mindedness is seeking alternative perspectives. This can be done through exposure to various sources of information such as books, articles or podcasts presenting different sides of an issue. Having conversations with people who have completely different cultural backgrounds from ours as well can give us valuable insight into our own biases.

"Question everything you assume. The beliefs that we hold aren't always reflective of the world we live in."

Another important thing that promotes open-mindedness is questioning assumptions. It means to challenge one's own beliefs and be ready to consider other views no matter if they are opposite to our own perceptions. This can be done by actively seeking opposing arguments and applying critical thinking. In doing so, we can understand the world better by getting into different minds and thereby expanding our own thoughts.

"Approach disagreements with empathy and curiosity, striving to understand rather than to win."

To foster open-mindedness, one should approach disagreements with empathy and curiosity. Instead of looking at disagreements as opportunities to prove oneself right, it is important to regard them as learning and growth opportunities. By listening actively, seeking to understand the other person's point of view, and engaging in respectful dialogue, we can foster open-mindedness and create an environment where diverse opinions are valued.

"Be aware of confirmation bias and the limitations of your own beliefs. Foster open-mindedness by embracing the possibility that you may not have all the answers."

In fostering open-mindedness, it is important to avoid confirmation bias. Confirmation bias refers to our tendency to search for information that will confirm what we already believe while neglecting or dismissing any contradictory evidence. By being conscious of this cognitive bias and purposefully seeking out evidence that challenges our existing beliefs, we can promote a spirit of open-mindedness as well as ensure that our perspectives are grounded on a deeper appreciation of the way things really are.

To foster open-mindedness necessitates intellectual humility wherein one must acknowledge their limited knowledge base. It requires personal development achieved through self-reflection, active involvement with differing viewpoints among others. Therefore through fostering open mindedness I'm able not only learn but also contribute towards building a more harmonious inclusive society.

Overcoming Barriers to Intellectual Humility and Open-Mindedness

In cultivating intellectual humility and openness individuals may come across various barriers that hinder their efforts. These obstacles can include cognitive biases, emotional defensiveness, and social pressure to conform. Overcoming these barriers is critical for individuals to effectively cultivate these qualities and promote their own growth.

"Recognizing and addressing these barriers are key steps in the journey towards intellectual humility and open-mindedness."

Cognitive biases: Our brains naturally tend to look for evidence that confirms our existing beliefs, which is known as confirmation bias. To overcome this barrier, individuals must actively challenge their own assumptions and be open to considering alternative viewpoints. It requires conscious effort to recognize and question our biases in order to expand our understanding.

Emotional defensiveness: Sometimes we let emotions cloud your judgement making it difficult to truly consider other perspectives. Overcoming emotional defensiveness involves cultivating self-awareness and learning to separate our emotions from our intellectual engagement. By acknowledging and managing our emotions, we can engage in more objective and constructive conversations.

Social pressures to conform: Society tends to reinforce specific beliefs or values that are not easily challenged by individuals. Overcoming this barrier requires courage and a willingness to question societal norms. It involves being open to dissenting opinions and standing up for principles that align with intellectual humility and open-mindedness.

Overcoming these obstacles requires commitment to critical thinking and a readiness to challenge one's own opinions. This means the individual must practise self-reflection and be open to new ideas. By acknowledging them, however, people can better develop intellectual humility and open-mindedness, two key facilitators for self-growth and effective engagement with diverse views.

Cases of Intellectual Humility and Open-Mindedness in Real Life

Intellectual humility and open-mindedness are observable in real-life scenarios across different disciplines or contexts that demonstrate how they can effectively contribute towards personal growth and knowledge.

"True intellectual humility involves not just admitting our mistakes but also actively looking for alternative perspectives and considering them with an open mind."

For instance, in the field of science, scientists are aware that an essential part of scientific discovery includes being intellectually humble and open-minded. They are willing to question their own hypotheses as well as entertain other plausible ones even enough to alter or abandon their initial positions.

"Intellectual humility allows us to recognize that we don't have all the answers and that there is always more that we can learn from others."

Lastly, leaders who exhibit intellectual humility together with open-mindedness are also influential individuals. They create space for different perspectives by welcoming input from various sources. In doing so, they foster a culture that promotes collaboration, critical thinking, and innovation.

"Engaging in open and respectful dialogue is a powerful demonstration of intellectual humility and open-mindedness, fostering deeper understanding and empathy among individuals."

Lastly, for instance when people engage in dialogue openly without compromising on respect even when they disagree; this demonstrates an aspect of intellectual modesty as well as open-mindedness. These persons acknowledge their own limitations as well as give room for other possibilities. As a result of their interactions they heal divisions by learning from each other.

These examples show how various situations whether research or leadership might necessitate intellectual modesty e.g. while discussing scientific issues within academia or just talking with friends. If individuals adopt such virtues, they will continue to grow intellectually, emotionally and personally.

Using Intellectual Humility and Open-Mindedness in Everyday Life

Intellectual humility and open-mindedness apply beyond school or work; these can be seen in everyday life. Active listening, seeking multiple perspectives and being willing to change are three ways through which people can develop intellectual humility and open mindedness when relating with their families, friends as well as other members of the community.

In discussions it is important to take part actively by first listening attentively. Instead of thinking about what to say next, listen carefully as the person speaks. This way you get to know what the other person is trying to communicate thus creating respect and empathy.

"Listening is an art of understanding. When we actively listen, we create a space for new ideas and perspectives to emerge."

To encourage intellectual humility and open-mindedness, one must actively seek out different views from various people. Surround yourself with people who have varied beliefs or come from diverse backgrounds. These contrasting viewpoints challenge our own suppositions as well as give us a wider picture of the world.

Moreover, being ready to change one's mind epitomises intellectual humility and open-mindedness further still. It involves admitting that sometimes you may not be right and allowing your beliefs to be re-examined by others. Through this attitude people can grow individually while creating an environment that is conducive for learning intellectually.

The beauty of intellectual humility and open-mindedness lies in being willing to be wrong and having the courage to change.

This application is based on everyday life and the use of humility and open-mindedness which leads to strong connections, a broader understanding of different perspectives, and personal growth. These qualities allow for ongoing expansion of knowledge and constructive dialogue in diverse communities.

Impact of Intellectual Humility and Open-Mindedness on Society

This often goes a long way in developing empathy, respect, understanding between people from different backgrounds. In an era of increased polarisation, these characteristics can heal divisions, promote positive conversations and contribute to solving complex issues affecting societies.

"Intellectual humility and open-mindedness are crucial in creating an inclusive society where individuals are willing to learn from each other through listening."

By making intellectual humility and open-minded societal values, we can make the society more inclusive as well as harmonious. It is through such traits that individuals can stop their echo chambers and have discussions with those who have different opinions or experiences. This exchanges ideas, challenges assumptions, builds mutual respect.

"The impact of intellectual humility and open-mindedness on society is the creation of a space where diverse perspectives are not only acknowledged but also celebrated for the richness and depth of knowledge they bring."

These two attributes enable people to handle complexities arising from globalisation with empathy as well as understanding. By embracing multiple perspectives while questioning our prejudices, we may find innovative remedies for challenges that go beyond individual behaviour patterns thus promoting collaboration across cultures.

"Society flourishes when intellectual humility and open-mindedness are embraced because this forms the basis of collective growth, progress, and social transformation."

In summary, it would be an understatement to say that there is not much effect caused by having intellectual humility combined with openness in any society. Such qualities help build bridges between opposing groups; hence leading to healthy talks about issues facing any nation today. Furthermore, accepting these values makes society more inclusive where differences amongst individuals are not only identified but also celebrated due to the collective growth and transformation they bring.

Resources for Developing Intellectual Humility and Open-Mindedness

Developing intellectual humility and open-mindedness is a lifelong process that calls for continuous learning and growth. Fortunately, there are numerous resources that can be used to foster these qualities thereby expanding one's horizon.

Books

A person's thought process can be greatly influenced by his/her reading material where intellectual humility and open-mindedness are concerned. Some titles you may find useful include Peter Schmid's "Intellectual Humility: An Introduction to Philosophy and Science" or Robyn Jackson's "Open Mind: Unleashing the Power of an Inquisitive Mind." These writings are helpful in framing your mind towards cultivating intellectual humility and open-mindedness.

Online Courses

There are online courses offered by platforms such as Coursera, which allow you to learn at your own pace while focusing on the concepts of intellectual humility and open-mindedness. They range from Developing Intellectual Humility in an Age of Certainty to Becoming an Open-Minded Thinker, among others. Such structured ways of learning enhance understanding and application of these virtues.

Workshops and Conferences

The experience of attending workshops and conferences on intellectual humility and open-mindedness allows for immersive learning experiences and networking with like-minded individuals. Look for functions organised by universities, research institutes, and organisations focused on promoting intellectual growth and critical thinking. These events usually feature expert speakers, interactive sessions as well as collaborative activities aimed at nurturing a sense of intellectual humility and open-mindedness.

Engaging in Dialogue

Open-mindedness is developed through engaging in open and respectful dialogue with people of other backgrounds or perspectives (Brownstein et al 2016). For this reason, it is important to initiate conversations with people who may have differing opinions or beliefs. Paying close attention to others' opinions while asking thoughtful questions about them as one also challenges his own assumptions is a good way to engage in it. In this regard, through dialogues we can develop new insights that can lead us to have a broader understanding concerning these topics thereby enabling us to approach them with intellectual humility and open-mindedness.

By taking advantage of these resources and staying committed to development, you will be able to foster intellectual humility thus opening up a richer, more expansive intellectual experience.

Conclusion

In conclusion, being intellectually humble is essential for personal development in every person as well as the whole society. We can achieve personal growth if we adopt these qualities that are required for effective communication which creates an inclusive environment for all. To cultivate intellectual humility, we must acknowledge the limits of our knowledge as well as embrace new ideas from other perspectives.

Open-mindedness on the other hand involves seeking out new viewpoints or opinions which challenge our assumptions; and approaching disagreements with empathy and curiosity instead (Gray & Wegner 2013). This then implies that these qualities promote critical thinking thereby leading to effective problem solving hence stronger relationships among individuals.

By cultivating intellectual humility and open-mindedness throughout our lives, we embark upon a journey of lifelong intellectual growth and personal development. As we navigate through the intricacies of a changing world, these qualities can help us to understand better, reconcile differences and make our communities better places. Therefore, let us embrace intellectual humility and open-mindedness for us to make the world become more inclusive as well as harmonious where different perspectives are cherished and honoured.

Chapter 34

Handling Changes Effectively through Flexibility and Developing Resilience Skills

****

Flexibility and resilience are paramount in making life-changing decisions. It can be daunting without the right mindset and capabilities. Here, we look at the importance of flexibility and resilience skills in coping with changes, attaining personal development, and leading a successful life. Join us as we discuss practical ways and tips of improving flexibility and building resilience skills to enable you withstand any changes that may come your way.

Recapping What does Personal Development Entail?

Personal development is the process of investing in yourself so that you can turn out to be a unique person. It encompasses self-help, learning, and personal growth which help improve general welfare as well as quality of living. By engaging with ourselves actively and developing our abilities a person obtains more accomplishments, self-acknowledgement, pleasure within countless other objectives. Physical health, mental wellness, relationships, career advancement among others are some of the areas that personal development touches on. In terms of personal development you make an investment into yourself and your future thus creating possibilities for growth and self-discovery.

Self-improvement is an integral part of personal development. This entails steps taken towards enhancing your skills, knowledge or habits towards achieving set goals as well as leading a fulfilling life. It could mean training oneself in new things such as taking care of one's health or practising good communication skills or even caring for oneself personally. On the other hand, personal growth refers to expanding one's emotional mental spiritual capacity thereby increasing one's own self-awareness while being flexible enough to adapt in situations where change is inevitable.

Investing in personal development is a smart move for anyone who wants to become their best selves, have confidence in themselves and live a more satisfying life. By making moves that will better you in various ways also will contribute positive changes to your life thus motivating other people to strive for the same.

Flexibility: Key to Personal Development

Flexibility is the most important attribute towards personal development. It influences positively on personal growth and helps individuals in navigating through the hardships well. Being flexible makes it easier for us to accept changes and learn from new experiences.

Additionally, flexibility enables us to approach problems and obstacles with a growth mindset, which can lead to novel solutions and self-discovery. Through consciously searching for other people's viewpoints, we can increase our level of awareness about ourselves as well as the world we live in.

Significance of Adaptability

Adaptability is one of the essential skills that are required in personal development. It allows us to navigate unexpected situations and cope with adversity. Identifying avenues for improvement and making strides towards achieving personal goals is possible when we are adaptable.

It also helps us remain open-minded and ready to delve into new experiences which ultimately improve our understanding on the private development path. Unleashing one's full potential is therefore possible by embracing change and stepping out of comfort zones.

Ways of Increasing Flexibility

There are multiple ways individuals use to develop their flexibility as well as adaptability. One such method may be practising mindfulness where one remains focused on present moment experience without judgement. This will keep us stable and composed when going through a change or disturbance.

Another way is always to challenge ourselves in trying new things and approaching problems from different angles. When we step out of our comfort zones, we can develop a growth mindset that will greatly help us in becoming more capable. Finally, this searching for feedback from others can be an effective tool for increasing flexibility and personal development. We can ask for feedback and learn from people when we try this; it makes us understand ourselves better, as well as making us adaptable.

Building Resilience: A Key Skill in Personal Development

Personal development requires individuals with resilience to recover from setbacks and face challenges with a positive attitude. Individuals gain the ability to change and manage stress by building their resilience.

There are several strategies that can be employed to build resilience such as self-care practices, keeping a positive viewpoint and leaning on friends and family for support. It is also important to learn from the past and treat mistakes as valuable experiences. Moreover, developing a growth mindset helps one gain resilience by seeing limitations not as fixed but as something that changes into potential growth or learning opportunities. A person who grows his or her mindset will be able to take roadblocks or failures as stepping stones towards personal improvement. All in all, building resilience is an important aspect of personal development that influences how well they manage stress, adapt to change, and recover from failure.

Embracing Change as an Opportunity for Growth

As we know life changes inevitably hence instead of fearing it; we should consider it as an opportunity for personal growth. This means having a growth mindset which sees every change positively viewing it as a platform for learning and improvement. Finally, when we embrace change we allow ourselves to move out of our comfort zones thus enabling us to have different perspectives on different issues regarding life which in turn makes us acquire new skills through learning. As a result one's personality improves because they become more self-conscious therefore they become more confident about themselves than they were before.

It's also good to change this since it allows people to adapt to new situations and have a flexible way of solving problems. This trait is important as it helps us to overcome hurdles that come our way and reach the intended target.

In summary, embracing change as an opportunity for personal growth is a significant element in personal development. It entails adopting a growth mindset and being open to new experiences and challenges. Through this, individuals will nurture their own growth and fully exploit their potential.

Overcoming Challenges through Resilience

Personal development involves overcoming different barriers, confronting challenges head on, and surpassing disappointments. There are life events that are tough to navigate that can benefit from resilience in order to make individuals stronger on the other side.

Resilience refers to an individual's capacity of bouncing back after experiencing some kind of defeat or when there have been changes while still maintaining a positive outlook towards life. Resilience may enable people to face obstacles with greater flexibility as well as a growth mindset such as those who see challenges like opportunities for learning and development hence they can surmount even the most obstinate stumbling blocks.

Another major component of resilience in personal development is looking at the positive side. Rather than dwelling on past failures, individuals can learn from mistakes and move forward with a renewed sense of purpose. Other aspects include developing support systems, seeking guidance from others as well as practising self-care.

Resilience skills development should be the key areas of focus for individuals to enhance personal growth and reach their full potential. It might not always be a smooth sail overcoming challenges, but resilience can help one overcome even the most difficult situations and come out a stronger and more resilient person than ever.

Developing an Open and Flexible Mindset

An open and flexible mindset is an essential aspect of personal development. This enables people to adapt to different circumstances as well as embrace new opportunities for growth.

Cultivating an open mindset involves being receptive to new ideas and perspectives. One must challenge his or her assumptions and prejudices while learning from others.

A flexible mindset must go along with adaptability to diverse scenarios hence adjusting plans accordingly. It requires people to get comfortable with uncertainty as well as change.

To develop an open and flexible mindset, some of the things that individuals can do include practising mindfulness through meditation, engaging in activities that challenge their beliefs, and seeking out diverse perspectives and experiences.

By developing an open mind accompanied by flexibility, individuals could unlock a path of possibilities for personal growth, realise greater achievement as well as lead more fulfilling lives.

Strategies to Enhance Flexibility in Personal Development

When pursuing personal development, it is important to have flexibility skills. Here are some practical strategies that will help you improve your flexibility:

1. Embrace Change

Instead of resisting change, try to embrace it. Recognize that change can bring about growth and new opportunities for personal development.

2. Practice Mindfulness

Mindfulness keeps you present, focused in the moment. Try focusing on what you are doing right now and stay open to unexpected outcomes.

3. Step Out of Your Comfort Zone

Doing something new helps to improve your flexibility and adaptability. Challenge yourself by doing something you are afraid of or outside your usual way of doing things.

4. Learn to Let Go

Being too attached to outcomes can hinder your ability to be flexible. Learn how to let go of your expectations and allow things to unfold naturally.

5. Cultivate a Growth Mindset

A growth mindset is that one that views challenges as opportunities for growth. Concentrate on learning from mistakes and setbacks rather than dwelling on them.

Incorporate these strategies into your personal development program and you will become more flexible, adaptable and grow faster.

Strengthening Resilience Skills for Personal Development

Personal growth involves learning how to bounce back from adversity and develop skills like resilience. However, this ability is gained only through nurturing it over time.

One way of building resilience skills is mindfulness meditation which helps individuals achieve higher levels of awareness and emotional regulation. Another efficient manner is cognitive restructuring where negative thought patterns are changed into positive ones such as through positive affirmations, writing gratitude journals or reframing negative situations in a more positive light.

Additionally, research has shown that physical exercise plays an important role in promoting resilience. Regular physical activities can enhance body strength as well as increase the capability of an individual to cope with stress levels and hence higher levels of resilience.

Lastly, individuals who possess strong social connections are able to develop better resilience because they have people around them who offer support. Social connections create a sense of belongingness thereby helping individuals deal with stress situations effectively. By practising these exercises and techniques, it can make people be more resilient and handle the challenges of life in their personal development journey.

Growth Mindset for Personal Development

A growth mindset is required to develop oneself and learn. It means believing that one's abilities and qualities can be developed and improved upon through effort and dedication.

People with a growth mindset see challenges and failures as chances for learning and improving rather than inadequacy. They are open to new experiences and willing to take risks in order to achieve goals.

Benefits of a Growth Mindset

Cultivating this way of thinking can promote personal development leading to a number of benefits such as:

Embracing new challenges for growth opportunities

Viewing failures as streams of lessons that bring improvements

A love for learning and curiosity about the world

Increase self-esteem as they accomplish set goals.

Developing A Growth Mind-Set

Developing a growth mind-set demands deliberate effort and dedication. Here are some ways that foster a growth mind-set: Challenge yourself to acquire new skills or try out something different. Look at mistakes or failures as ways of developing your character further. Develop an understanding that hard work can promote your abilities and take inspiration from people who have developed this mindset already. Why not practise positive self-talk while focusing on your strengths as well as your progress and celebrate your small achievements along the way.

Self-Reflection in Personal Development

In personal development, self-reflection is an important tool that individuals use to grow personally. By reflecting on what one thinks, feels, and does, an individual gets an insight into themselves. In addition, this practice helps you figure out areas where you need modification or change.

Effective self-reflection involves introspection; looking within oneself honestly. This includes asking oneself tough questions, admitting weaknesses, and rejoicing over strengths. Thus through self-reflection one can gain clarity and make progress towards their personal development goals.

Some techniques for effective self-reflection involve keeping a journal, meditating, seeking feedback from others, and engaging in thoughtful conversations with oneself. By making self-reflection a habit in their daily routine, individuals can speed up their journey of personal development and increase self-awareness.

Seeking Support and Feedback for Personal Growth

Seeking support and feedback from others is important while trying to develop personally. In the face of personal challenges or obstacles, another person's perspective or insight can help provide direction or clarity.

It is necessary that you keep people who encourage personal growth around you. Friends, family members, mentors and coaches can be part of these; they should be the ones who are there for you at all times giving feedback where necessary.

Feedback is an important tool in personal growth because it helps to improve on weak areas as well as enhance strengths. Thus one should take constructive criticism positively as an opportunity to grow rather than a challenge. Even if sometimes it may be hard to listen, it is essential to remain receptive as well as open-minded.

Such courage and vulnerability to seek support and feedback, but the rewards can be incredible. It fosters better self-awareness, enhances skills and builds confidence. Through building a support system and embracing feedback, individuals can speed up their own personal development journey towards meeting their goals and aspirations.

Putting Personal Development into Action

Now that we have explored several strategies and techniques for personal development, it is time to take action. An action plan can help an individual put these approaches into practice in his or her daily life and grow personally.

The first step in creating an action plan is identification of specific areas for improvement. This can be done by reflecting on oneself as well as thinking about oneself, which was discussed in Section 11. Once these areas have been identified, it is important to set achievable goals and timelines to track progress.

Breaking down large goals into smaller tasks that are manageable helps make them less daunting and easier to complete. It is also important to introduce accountability mechanisms in the action plan such as seeking support from others. Implementation of the action plan requires dedication and perseverance. In remaining focused on the end goal, one must remember why they seek personal development in the first place.

To ensure that progress is made and allow any necessary changes to be made along the way, it is essential that the action plan be reviewed regularly. Small victories or milestones should also be celebrated so as to encourage more effort towards personal growth as well as development.

Incorporating personal development strategies into daily life can lead to greater self-awareness, self-confidence, and overall well-being. By creating and implementing an action plan, individuals can take control of their personal growth and achieve their full potential.

Chapter 35

Mentorship: Unlocking Personal
Growth and Sharing Expertise

***

Would you like to develop while having a positive effect on others? Have you considered mentorship? For those who are in need of guidance or mentoring opportunities that can shape their professional lives, mentorship becomes an important tool for learning and growth.

When you look for mentors, they share their thoughts and experiences with you that one needs along the path. This includes giving guidance, support, and advice to navigate through difficult times and achieve your objectives. On the flip side, mentoring is also an opportunity for people to help others grow as individuals. It involves sharing experience and knowledge with others so that outside influence can improve your life and reinforce your own knowledge and leadership skills.

In this chapter, we shall delve into mentorship exploring its benefits, how to find mentors, how to become a mentor as well as successful dynamics of mentor-mentee relationships. We will also explore some of the challenges it poses to personal growth and career progression as well as possible ways of overcoming these challenges. Furthermore, we shall examine mentorship in different contexts including diversity and inclusion issues among other subjects. We shall also consider ethics surrounding mentoring and discuss evaluating success in it and its prospects in the digital age.

What Mentorship Entails

Mentorship is a powerful tool not only to the mentees but also mentors themselves who stand to gain from various valuable benefits. It gives an excellent opportunity for self-realisation at a personal level; enhances professional abilities while encouraging sharing information acquired.

For a mentee, there are many advantages brought by mentorship like insights provided by mentors besides guidance offered by them throughout their journey together. Through relating with mentors, they learn valuable lessons that shape their lives both personally and professionally. They get assistance on how they should deal with challenges, set goals and make informed choices. A mentor is a reliable guide to help mentees discover themselves and their future.

"My own personal growth would not have been possible without mentoring. Having someone believe in me and show me the way made all the difference in my professional life."

On the other hand, mentors also benefit from the mentorship relationship. Mentors gain more insight into their own leadership abilities by sharing about their experiences. They also enhance their skills and knowledge through educating others. It is a rewarding experience where mentors can impact positively on other people's lives while at the same time developing themselves. Mentorship as a culture of learning, sharing and acquisition of knowledge will enable individuals to challenge themselves, broaden horizons and achieve results. It is a mutual trust based system for growing together.

Significance of Personal Growth

One of the key benefits of mentorship is personal growth opportunity. Mentees embrace lessons that they learn through their mentors that transform them as individuals. Mentorship helps them identify areas that need improvement, discover strengths and develop a growth mindset. Additionally, mentorship provides a safe place for mentees to explore different interests and passions thereby helping them find clarity in their career paths and personal aspirations. Mentoring connections not only encourage self-reflection and self-discovery in the mentees but also help them realise their full potentials hence becoming the best version of themselves.

Professional Development and Skill Enhancement

Mentorship is about more than just growing personally; it has significant implications for professional development as well. Apprentices gain access to industry-specific knowledge, insider tricks of the trade, and practical advice from experienced professionals. This can exponentiate their career advancement rate, develop their skills further, and expand their professional networks. As mentors' experiences become real to mentees, they also improve their problem-solving abilities by learning how to think critically. Useful feedback from mentors helps mentees identify their strengths while overcoming any weaknesses they may encounter on their professional way.

Facilitating Knowledge-Sharing and Lifelong Learning

Mentorship is a powerful avenue for knowledge-sharing because this is where mentors are involved. These mentors share what they have been through including mistakes they made along the way thus creating a culture of continuous learning and growth. This mentor's knowledge becomes a valuable resource for the mentee which allows informed decision making as well as calculated risks.

Conversely this exchange of information does not only happen between a mentor and a mentee alone but rather it affects an entire community under them. Depending on circumstances, mentees who look up to their mentors often end up being mentors themselves since they pass on what they know about life experiences as well as advice given by others. In this regard, mentoring would reach out to even more people within other settings that are not confined to just these two persons.

On the whole, mentorship has numerous benefits ranging from personal growth, professional development to knowledge sharing among many others. It is such a mutually beneficial relationship that empowers individuals by opening new doors into the world of opportunities thus improving personal and professional lives.

Finding Mentors

There are different strategies that can be employed to find mentors although it might be a daunting task.

One of these strategies is networking in your industry or field of interest where you may connect with potential mentors. Through active participation in certain professional events and associating with professionals who have similar goals as yours, chances are high that you will come across an individual among them who can guide you on personal and professional growth. This way, relationships with professionals who have been in the field for long will provide insights as well as open doors into new opportunities.

Another great way of finding mentors is attending industry events and conferences mostly attended by seasoned professionals interested in sharing their knowledge about subjects they know best. Engage anyone you meet and express your intention to get a mentor since they offer guidance on how to find one. Many experienced individuals are happy to lend a hand and become mentors for those aspiring to follow their steps.

Online mentorship platforms such as LinkedIn or other professional networking sites can also be useful when searching for possible mentors. By using these platforms, one could search for prospective mentors depending on some criteria like the sector they work, their occupation, or even the place where they live. Such sites link mentees to persons having the right skills needed and who would provide suitable tips taking into account these unique scenarios. Thus use these online resources to increase your pool of mentorship prospects.

"Networking within your industry, attending industry events, and utilising online platforms dedicated to mentorship are all effective strategies in finding mentors who can guide and support your personal and professional growth."

Becoming a Mentor

Becoming a mentor is an opportunity that many find fulfilling both in terms of sharing one's expertise and giving back. It can help someone's life to change for the better, while at the same time having positive impacts on your own personal and career development.

Mentorship programs and volunteer opportunities are ideal pathways to becoming mentors. These mentoring programs offer intensive training and support services so that the mentors have the right tools to guide and assist their mentees. There are mentorship programs available for people of different interests and industries such as those who have many years of experience in a certain field or those who are specialised.

"Being a mentor is one way you can give back what you know to a new generation. That's because it shapes destiny and has some serious implications on someone's life." -Jane Anderson, Founder, Mentorship Matters

Volunteer opportunities create another avenue through which individuals can become mentors. In numerous community-based organisations and non-profit initiatives there are mentorship programs thus enabling individuals to give back to their communities as well as offer support to those who need it most. These opportunities allow mentors to make an impact on others' lives aside from bringing a sense of joy into theirs.

Becoming a mentor also helps people share their knowledge with others but also build upon their leadership skills, improve ability to communicate with others, and grow professional connections with one another. It's a mutually beneficial relationship where both parties in it grow.

Building Successful Partnership between Mentors and Mentees

One cannot get the best out of mentorship without first building good relationships between a mentor and his mentee. It means trust must exist through open communication as well as goal setting for productive cooperation between them throughout the journey. Both parties are key players in creating this bond turning it into a symbiotic process towards growth and self-improvement.

"A successful foundation for every mentor-mentee relationship is trust, where both individuals feel safe enough to share their ideas, experiences and challenges. This creation of a trustful atmosphere stimulates open communication, honest talks and acts as a breeding ground for further growth."

Another important aspect of a successful mentor-mentee relationship is the regular face-to-face or virtual meetings. They serve as opportunities for checking up, talking about progress, setting future objectives, addressing any worries or obstacles. Regular check-ins ensure that both the mentor and mentee are on the same page and working towards the mentee's goals effectively.

"Goal setting is an integral part of the mentor-mentee dynamic, as it gives direction to the whole process of mentoring. The mentor and the student can measure their success together by establishing concrete objectives and milestones."

Every great mentor-mentee relationship is based on effective communication. Both sides should be able to listen actively to one another, give thoughtful insights as well as ask probing questions so that they can develop deeper know-how in this subject matter. This communication should be open-minded respectful non-judgmental guidance-supportive-feedback giving.

"In any successful mentoring relationship between a mentor and a mentee, there has to be room for two-way communications. Because mentees have fresh perspectives, unique ideas and many questions to ask just like mentors share their wisdom alongside other life experiences."

In essence, building a successful mentor-mentee relationship requires commitment from both parties. It is a mutual journey of growth in all aspects of life; it is one that is built on trust, communication, goal setting, and regular meetings which mostly are the foundation for an enriching and impactful mentorship encounter.

Different Contexts for Mentorship

Mentorship can take place in different contexts with each having its own dynamics and requirements. Be it workplace mentoring, educational mentoring or community mentoring, the key principles remain unchanged – guidance, support and information dissemination. They play a central role in assisting their mentees explore their career paths, educational pursuits or personal development.

Workplace Mentorship

Workplace mentorship involves experienced professionals guiding and supporting their less-experienced colleagues. Work mentors enlighten, advise and cheer up their pupils on improving skills, professional development and career problems facing them. This type of program can promote better work environments that are more inclusive and supportive thus encouraging growth while fostering success.

Educational Mentorship

Educational mentorship is meant to guide and support people within academic or learning environments. Mentors in school settings like primary schools, universities/colleges help learners study well, assist them with making career choices as well as helping them develop personally as well as academically. Educational mentorship empowers mentees to overcome challenges and attain their educational goals.

Community-Based Mentorship

Community-based mentorships are aimed at guiding people living in different communities who generally represent specific groups or have common interests. These initiatives link up mentors with mentees coming from diverse backgrounds thereby expanding mentoring outside traditional organisations (workplaces) or education arenas. Community-based mentorship promotes personal growth, skill development, and social engagement among participants.

"Mentorship in different contexts enables customization of guidance and support to meet the unique needs and ambitions of persons within various environments."

Regardless of the context, mentorship promotes personal and professional development, thus enabling mentees to acquire important knowledge, expand their networks and make significant strides towards their goals. The opportunity for mentors to impact the lives of their mentees is enormous; they can share experiences and expertise with them to help them succeed.

The Impact of Mentoring

Mentorship has a great impact on mentees, influencing their career advancement, skill development, confidence building and networking. Through guidance, insights and opportunities provided by mentors, mentees are enabled to make strides towards success.

"Having a mentor can be a game-changer in one's professional journey. They can provide invaluable advice, share their experiences, and open doors to new opportunities," says Sarah Thompson, a marketing professional who credits her mentor for her accelerated career growth.

Career advancement is one of the major areas where mentorship has an effect. Mentors assist mentees in manoeuvring through complexities within their chosen field and offering valuable advice on career planning, job search strategies as well as professional networking. By using their mentor's experience and connections in the industry, mentees can gain the upper hand over others and have access to opportunities that would have otherwise been impossible to get.

Another area where mentorship has much impact is skills development. Mentors identify the strong points and areas of improvement for their mentees. They also guide them on recommended activities they could engage in so as to develop skills further. Therefore, with personalised recommendations and feedback from their mentors; mentees can upgrade their skill set rendering them more competitive in the respective industries.

Mentorship also plays a significant role in confidence building. Mentees often find themselves struggling with self-doubt or uncertainty especially when faced with new challenges or entering into new careers. A mentoring belief and encouragement would help them overcome these obstacles as well as build confidence in themselves. This may come from the reassurance that their mentors give them which gives them power to try new things confidently.

Besides this, mentorships crucially expand a mentee's network of professionals. A number of ways that mentors apply here include introducing students to people they know within the same field who might serve as references among other things (Dobratz & Shanks-Meile, 1997). It is through their mentors' network that students get to meet such experts who can give them insight, collaborate with them or even become potential employers.

"My mentor guided me through different aspects of my career as well as introduced me to influential people in our field. These connections helped me gain exclusive opportunities and broaden my professional network," explains Mark Davis, a former mentee who is now a mentor himself.

The impact of mentorship does not end at the level of the mentee-mentor relationship. Mentees often progress in their careers and become mentors themselves, passing on what they have learned to future generations of professionals. Therefore, the rewards of mentoring cascade down generations, which creates an environment that nurtures growth and learning.

Challenges in Mentorship

However valuable it may be; mentoring has its challenges. The time commitment both for the mentor and mentee can be an obstacle especially when busy schedules hinder regular meetings or dedicated time for mentorship.

It's vital for both parties to put the relationship first by finding ways to effectively manage their time. This may mean setting up specific meeting times or using technology like video conferencing for virtual meetings besides developing alternative means of communication when direct meetings are not possible.

There are also instances where communication flaws pose challenges within a mentoring relationship. In some cases, language differences or lack of effective communications skills might break down information flow leading to misunderstanding.

In overcoming this barrier, open and transparent communication plays a critical role. Therefore, mentors and mentees should work towards establishing clear channels as well as modifying their modes of communicating so as to ensure better exchanges.

Additionally, establishing a relationship between a mentor and mentee can be hindered by personality differences. Each individual brings with them distinctive characteristics, values, and viewpoints into that mentoring connection.

It is crucial to identify these distinctions and appreciate them. Mentors and mentees can transcend their personality differences by creating an atmosphere of empathy and openness. There should be common ground upon which the mentor and mentee can work for effective collaboration in spite of differences in behaviour.

Overcoming Challenges in Mentorship

Dedication, open-mindedness, and willingness to change are all necessary for resolving problems encountered in mentorship. Time management concerns, communication challenges, as well as dissimilarities in character can be addressed so that mentors and mentees enter into successful mentoring relationships.

Overcoming Mentorship Challenges

In mentoring there are situations where there occur difficulties in making it productive. On the other hand, such issues may be overcome through proactive measures for a more fruitful mentor-mentee relationship.

Effective Time Management

One of the main obstacles of mentoring is time management. Both mentors and mentees have tight schedules hence the need to establish priorities within this setup. This calls for dedicating specific times when meetings will be held or discussions made so that there is consistency in meeting objectives. With proper time management skills therefore, mentors and mentees will be able to lay a strong foundation for their relationship.

Fostering Effective Communication

Mentorship relies heavily on communication; thus, barriers should not exist in order to achieve success through this approach. Active listening skills, explicit speech articulation as well as understanding one another's manners of communicating contributes towards better interaction among people. Thus, they help encourage free sharing of ideas where mentors are able to at the same time understand their students' thoughts, worries, or purpose.

Adaptability and Flexibility

These qualities are critical for bridging personal disparities as well as nurturing good mentor-mentee relationships; adaptability and flexibility. With each person having their unique perspective or approach towards things, it is important to understand this. A case in point is that of varying work styles that need to be accommodated for the sake of effective collaboration. Therefore, mentorship thrives upon the ability of mentors to be flexible and adaptable as they pursue a common goal.

By practising effective time management, promoting clear and open communication, and embracing adaptability, mentors and mentees can overcome any challenges that may arise throughout their journey together. By doing so, these strategies will make up a constructive and successful mentoring experience as both parties would have gained knowledge out of it.

Mentorship Programs and Resources

Professional organisations' mentorship programs may provide invaluable resources for finding mentors or accessing mentoring opportunities online. These are structured mentorship programs that match mentees with respective mentors based on shared interests and goals. They foster a supportive environment where mentees can learn from experienced professionals while receiving guidance and support for their personal and professional growth.

Many professional organisations offer industry or field-specific mentorship programs that not only help pair mentors with mentees but also provide additional resources including networking events. This creates communities of like-minded individuals who are interested in learning from one another's experiences through such relationships.

Online platforms dedicated to mentorship provide an easy way of getting connected with mentors as well as accessing numerous resources on mentorship. Such forums include articles, webinars, etc., through which mentees can learn from their peers as well as mentors respectively. Herein lies a virtual environment where people can look for advice in relation to given subjects, share experiences or even obtain insights from experts in such fields.

Online platforms and mentorship programs offer aspiring professionals the chance to connect with experienced mentors who have vast amounts of knowledge as well as other resources.

Through using internet platforms and mentorship programs, mentees can access a large database of mentors who are passionate about growing talents and giving back to society. These programs and platforms create bonds that are effective in bridging the gap between mentors and mentees thus impacting the lives of the latter greatly both personally and professionally.

Mentorship on Diversity

It is not just for growth and development but also promotes diversity in the mentor-mentee relationships. It is important to have diversity among mentors and mentees so as to make it inclusive. Diverse mentors must be sought out across social backgrounds. This ensures various perspectives, experiences, and cultural understandings. Diverse mentors can provide relevant insights and advice on overcoming barriers for mentees resulting from their unique identities.

Diverse mentors bring different experiences that enrich the mentoring process through promoting cultural understanding and empathy. Representation matters a lot hence underrepresented groups should be included in mentorship programs as well as relationships establish this fact. The gap can be filled by actively looking for marginalised demographic groups as our mentors therefore enhancing inclusivity within different industries or fields.

Diverse mentors can act as role models or advocates for those from marginalised communities, thus highlighting their unique obstacles while providing support needed to navigate these hurdles. They may also boost morale helping them surmount hurdles that come along their path towards success

Fostering Innovation and Success Through Diverse Mentors

Ethical reasons alone do not make diversity and inclusion in mentorship important; rather it drives innovation and success. Research has established that problems solving ability, creativity & performance improve with diverse teams and mentoring relationships.

"Diverse mentors bring new perspectives and ideas to the table. Consequently, they challenge the present state of affairs and hence promote innovative thinking."

If we welcome diversity and inclusion in mentorship, positive ripples could be created. In so doing, mentees can become mentors themselves if they continue benefiting from insights and guidance offered by mentors from diverse backgrounds thus expanding the domains of voice and experience.

"To truly have equity and inclusion we must be proactive in seeking out a diverse range of mentors that value everyone's contribution. This way we will create an inclusive, empowered community."

Mentorship for Personal and Professional Development

Mentorship is a powerful tool for both personal and professional growth. Mentoring as such avails guidance required by individuals to accomplish their objectives either on personal development or career advancement grounds.

A mentor is instrumental in shaping his/her mentee's future. They provide an assessment of progress of the mentee, offer constructive criticism as well as help the mentees overcome obstacles that come their way. By imparting knowledge, experiences, and skills to their mentees' lives, mentors motivate them to realise all their dreams and potential.

"Having a mentor can really help someone grow personally and professionally. Mentors are like trusted friends who mentor through life challenges offering informed advice aiding decision making while helping them remain focused on their goals."

Benefit of mentorship is the opportunity it provides for goal achievement. With a mentor's guidance, mentees can set goals that are doable and work towards them. Insights, strategies and resources that mentors offer can help mentees stay on course and make progress that matters. Another advantage of the mentorship relationship is personal growth, as it enables mentees to explore their strengths, areas for improvement and weaknesses in a safe environment. Mentors provide encouragement and support which help boost mentees' self-belief and overcome self-doubt.

Furthermore, mentorship contributes to professional growth as it assists mentees in developing the necessary skills, knowledge required for success in their respective field. Mentors share industry insights, best practices as well as advice on career advancement. In addition they may also help facilitate networking connections or introduce mentees to some valuable professional contacts.

To summarise, mentoring is an influential tool beneficial for both those who are being assisted and those providing assistance. It speeds up personal development and career progression by offering guidance, encouragement, and the tools necessary for achieving goals. Through mentoring programs people can realise their full potential hence flourish both at personal and professional levels.

Ethics in Mentorship

Mentorship has ethics crucial to a healthy relationship between a mentor and a protégé that will drive productivity levels up. Key guiding principles include setting clear boundaries; maintaining confidentiality; demonstrating mutual respect.

Boundaries

Clear boundaries establish scope of mentor-mentee relationships including objectives of each party involved. Healthy boundaries create safe environments preventing any misappropriation or misuse of power in mentorships.

"Boundaries in mentorship are important because they provide structure that directs the relationship towards growth while conserving the well-being and interests shared by both mentors and mentees."

Confidentiality

Confidentiality is one of the pillars upon which trust rests in mentoring. The mentors must uphold confidentiality of any information given by a protege that might be sensitive. This security allows for openness and honesty between the mentor and mentee by building trust.

"Confidentiality is the foundation of any mentor-mentee relationship. When shared information is kept confidential, trust can be built allowing a safe place where mentees are free to express thoughts, fears, and aspirations."

Mutual Respect

Mutual respect is an important aspect of mentoring since it recognizes that both the mentor and protégé value their perspectives, experiences as well as roles. By instilling mutual respect, mentors and mentees create an enabling environment for open communication and learning process.

"Mutual respect is what mentorship is based on because it acknowledges the expertise of mentors while appreciating different experiences and goals that mentees have. This respect ensures a strong basis for growth."

Additionally, mentors should always put the best interests of the mentee first in order to avoid conflicts of interest that could compromise the relationship. Professionalism must also at all times be upheld leading to ethicality in mentorship dialogue which involves integrity, honesty, and fairness. Ethics in mentoring require transparency as far as expectations and boundaries are concerned. This will enable both a protégé or a mentor to know what they can expect from their partnership hence aligning goals/values.

"By making ethics a priority within their interactions with mentees through setting clear boundaries, maintaining confidentiality, fostering mutual respect among other things; mentors can create mentoring relationships that allow for growth, learning and development."

The Mentor's Success Evaluation

The effectiveness and impact of mentorship can be assessed to show success of the relationship for both mentors and mentees. One of the major ways through which mentorship can be evaluated is feedback mechanisms. Regular communication as well as feedback exchange between mentors and mentees results in useful insights which helps in modifying the mentoring process to remain effective and beneficial.

Besides, another aspect that is crucial when it comes to evaluating the success of mentorship is assessing whether mentees have achieved their goals or not. The progress of mentees towards their goals acts as a tangible measuring yardstick on how much mentorship has impacted both their personal and professional growth. On one hand, it provides an opportunity to appreciate positive consequences while on the other hand, identify areas that require more attention.

"Regular feedback allows mentors and mentees to reflect on their interactions, identify strengths, and focus on areas that need improvement. When actively seeking for feedback, mentors and mentees can create a supportive collaborative environment nurturing individual's personal as well as professional development."

Additionally, apart from feedback and achievement of goals, evaluation of impacts also plays a crucial role in assessing the success of mentorship. This could include improved confidence levels; acquiring new skills and getting a wider network in terms of professionalism which may be evident if asked about where they are now compared to initial position. These qualitative assessments provide a deeper understanding of the transformative power of mentorship.

There is more to evaluating successful mentoring than simply counting results; it should also be about making ongoing improvements in the mentoring experience itself. Regular feedback along with goal setting as well as impact assessment helps them identify areas for improvement (i.e., fine tuning or enhancement). It further ensures that the mentoring relationship undergoes an iterative process so that its nature changes with time in order to meet changing needs of the person being guided.

Mentors and mentees who embrace evaluation measures may find themselves part of an impactful and dynamic mentoring experience that leads to personal and professional growth. Mentorship therefore becomes a learning process that is shared, empowering and full of achievements through continuous assessment and improvement.

The Future of Mentorship

The future of mentoring is defined by changing dynamics and technological advancements. Virtual mentoring is increasingly prevalent as we sail through the digital age, and it has transformed mentorship beyond its traditional geographic boundaries. The use of virtual platforms allows mentors and mentees to connect irrespective of their locations, thus creating new possibilities for mentoring in the era of digitalization.

Virtual mentorship provides convenience and accessibility for mentorship bringing together individuals who require different expertise or industry background. Mentorship can be effectively carried out through virtual meetings and communication tools hence supporting purposeful interactions between a mentor and a mentee. This revolution in mentor-mentee relationship enlarges its scope over geographical areas thereby allowing more mentors and mentees from various backgrounds to share ideas for personal development.

As people change and choose what they want in life, mentorship will also develop innovative strategies to meet those wants. Technology integration including artificial intelligence (AI) and virtual reality (VR) can make the mentorship experience much better. AI-driven platforms can give appropriate suggestions about who could be the best suitable mentors based on specific goals set by mentees based on their interests in order to ensure a more personalised learning process among them. VR could also make immersive experiences possible where people can interact with virtual environments that are related to many fields. The future of mentoring entails multiple ways that will enable individuals' empowerment towards growth during this era of technology.

Chapter 36

Unleashing Gratitude– Transforming Your Life & Mental Health

***

Gratitude, often defined as being thankful or ready to show gratitude for kindness, is a powerful tool in building a positive lifestyle. It goes beyond mere thankfulness and becomes a consistent state of mind; it's not just about feeling grateful but always being in a state of positivity and appreciation.

Various studies have shown that deliberate practice of gratitude leads to numerous mental health benefits. These benefits include more than fleeting happiness.

Firstly, expressing gratitude changes our focus from the negative aspects to the positive ones of our lives. This transition from dwelling on what we perceive as negatives to acknowledging the positive can act as an antidote to stressors. By focusing on the good things even amidst difficult times, gratitude helps build resilience and mental strength.

Additionally, engaging in practices of gratitude can serve as an effective strategy to regulate negative emotions such as anger, frustration or anxiety. By changing our mindset, gratitude allows us to think that these feelings are not insurmountable obstacles but opportunities for growth.

For instance, when we genuinely show appreciation for what we already have, we begin shifting our mindset from desires for more towards valuing what is already available. This change promotes contentment and satisfaction – two vital components leading to enhanced psychological well-being.

In addition to individual-level effects, practising gratitude also nurtures stronger social bonds by promoting empathy and reducing aggression. This acknowledgement of the help and kindness one receives leads to positive reciprocity – thus improving relationships with people around them.

"Gratitude helps people feel more positive emotions, relish good experiences, improve their health, deal with adversity and build strong relationships."

The practice of gratitude has significant implications on mental health including: fostering a more positive mind set; reducing stress; deepening social connections; protecting emotional well-being; hence it is beneficial for individuals who are striving towards living positively.

Unravelling the Neuroscience behind Gratitude

To fully appreciate how gratitude impacts mental health, it is important to understand the underlying science behind it. Neuroscience has started uncovering compelling evidence on how gratitude affects the brain.

A pioneering study conducted by neuroscientists found that individuals who regularly engage in the practice of gratitude have more brain activity in the prefrontal cortex, a region associated with decision-making, learning, and emotion regulation. This implies that expressing gratitude activates certain neural circuits that increase the chance of repeating grateful behaviour in future – Hebb's Law.

This increased neuronal stimulation in areas related to positive feelings links directly with physical changes in our brains, termed as gratitude's effects on the brain. In essence, we are training our brains to be more responsive to experiences that bring about thankfulness and positive emotions through regular expression of gratitude.

One astonishing realisation proved that jotting down notes of what you're thankful for can improve our sleeping. Participants underwent 'gratitude intervention' training, having to record some gratitude every night before they sleep for just one week. Brain scans conducted after weeks showed that the experiment had lasting neural sensitivity to gratitude and this was derived from the relationship between gratitude journaling and good sleep.

The process of putting things down for which we are grateful – often referred to as counting your blessings – causes a series of reactions in the brain that lead to the release of serotonin and dopamine; which are neurotransmitters responsible for feelings of happiness and wellbeing. It may therefore be argued that gratitude is not only an emotional but also a chemical gain.

Furthermore, gratitude and neuroscience are interconnected in relation to stress relief. During stressful or scary times, your brain might cause the amygdala, commonly called 'fight or flight' part of your brain, to become active. Nevertheless, it has been observed that practising gratitude reduces amygdala activity and activates brain patterns associated with positive emotions as well- providing an antidote for stress as well as stimulating relaxation responses.

In summation, practising gratitude is more than just saying positive things about life; it is a powerful technique that can actually rewire our brains leading us towards positive neural pathways resulting in optimism, joyfulness and better mental health. On this encouraging note, science continues to explore this exciting frontier where gratitude meets neuroscience thus giving us invaluable advice on how we could nurture our minds towards healthier living through daily acts of appreciation.

Practical Ways to Build Daily Gratitude Habits

Now that we have understood what gratitude entails both theoretically and scientifically, let us see ways through which we can make it part of our daily lives. Cultivating consistent habits around gratefulness can bring profound transformations in one's mental well-being and overall contentment with life.

Journaling is one simple yet effective way to cultivate gratefulness. Keeping a mental health journal gives us an organised manner to reflect on our everyday life experiences and identify their positive aspects. So, what should you write in your gratitude journal? You could record anything that made you smile or warmed your heart; these could be moments with people we love, unexpected gifts or just small pleasures such as a cup of hot cocoa on a cold night.

Gratitude journaling is not about merely noting what caused us joy though—it also involves showing appreciation for those experiences. For instance, instead of simply stating "Watched sunset after ages," go deeper into the emotional response you had. This might lead you to say "Feeling deeply grateful for having witnessed such a beautiful sunset today—it was soul-soothing after an exhaustive week."

Apart from writing in journals, there are other ways to show gratitude. Mindfulness is one good example. It means staying completely present where we are and enjoying everything that is happening right now. This can involve taking time to appreciate your morning coffee, admiring the wonders of nature during a walk or treasuring a shared joke with friends.

Another powerful way to cultivate gratitude is through meditation. Numerous online resources offer guided meditations specifically on thankfulness. These practices often incorporate visualisation techniques where you imagine scenarios that fill you with joy and express inner fulfilment and appreciation for those experiences.

It is also an amazing practice to give thanks directly to other people. For example, writing a heartfelt thank-you note to someone who was kind or expressing your gratitude for a colleague's hard work not only uplifts others but also improves our emotional well-being. "Expressing appreciation" therefore has two meanings—it strengthens our relationships as well as enhances personal happiness levels.

Small acts have great power too. Even small moments of gratitude throughout the day can alter things considerably over time—for example, saying grace before meals or appreciative prayers said upon waking up and while retiring—these small practices often lead to bigger shifts towards more positive attitudes.

Actually, there are several ways to foster gratitude in everyday life. Thus, different persons may choose different methods according to their own tastes and preferences.

Coping with Stress, Depression and Loneliness through Gratitude

However, gratitude may have its biggest impact when you are feeling stressed or depressed. In addition to heightening pleasure during good times, being grateful helps us traverse more difficult emotional terrains with toughness.

Several studies have established that regular expressions of gratitude can significantly decrease depression rates among people. The active engagement of gratitude interferes with distorted thinking patterns which is a common manifestation of depression. Gradually over time we evolve from a negative frame of mind on what is not good or has gone wrong in our lives into a positive one by focusing on what is right.

The idea of "gratitude and depression" at first seems contradictory—how would one be grateful amidst feelings of despair? Nevertheless, it can be the first step towards getting better when we seek out areas of thankfulness in the midst of being overwhelmed by sadness—a ray of hope that gently guides us out of the darkness.

For instance, when feeling down or lonely, keeping a thanksgiving diary may be very therapeutic. It gives an avenue for expressing oneself freely—a medium through which pain can be given expression in words. Simultaneously, it helps one to weave together a fabric of hope because as we note down positive things amidst pain—such as brief moments of joy or acts of kindness that touch us—we are constructing a tapestry. This is the very essence of "journaling for mental health", so that instead of just venting out our negative feelings, we grow an attitude of appreciation.

Applying gratitude techniques also has other significant implications on stress reduction within our brains. As mentioned earlier, gratitude results in the release of brain chemicals responsible for happiness like serotonin and dopamine. These changes make it possible to deal with stress more effectively, and thereby reduce its negative impact on our mental well-being—"gratitude and stress reduction" are thus intertwined.

Apart from individual psychological states, there is a great potential in gratitude to fight against loneliness and isolation. Recognizing others' contributions towards our lives and appreciating them makes us feel part of something bigger and hence improves our social connectedness. By softening the blow of "isolation", it reminds us that we are not alone—that there is love, kindness and support in our world if only we choose to look for it.

When you are met with life's difficulties, adopting thankfulness can be an amazing choice. It doesn't deny hardships nor promise that there would be no times of adversity; rather , it prepares us better to face these challenges—meaning that we have an inner sanctuary of serenity and cheerfulness even when the storms rage around us.

Augmenting social connections through giving thanks

Most of our daily lives revolve around interactions with others. We live a life full of complex relationships, from quick encounters with strangers to profound love for someone close. Interestingly, practising gratitude can significantly enrich these bonds, making them stronger and more involved.

Gratitude and social connection have a deep interconnection. To exemplify a thankful spirit requires appreciating others' good impacts in our lives. As we mention or silently acknowledge such acts of kindness, we subconsciously instil greater appreciation of those around us. This transition usually results in friendlier dealings and more cohesive associations.

One single act of giving thanks may make someone feel visible, acknowledged as well as respected. It implies that their efforts were not vain – they actually helped another person's welfare improve. This forms a strong bond between them based on mutual respect and affection thereby increasing the quality of interpersonal relationships.

This is not just abstract; scientific research has substantiated it as well. A study called "The benefits of expressing gratitude: expressing gratitude to a partner changes one's view of the relationship" indicated that people who expressed gratitude felt more content about their associations and considered them to be meaningful.

Besides this expression is not limited to intimate partners or close friends alone; even acquaintanceships or workplace relationships can hugely profit from expressions of gratefulness.

Within professional settings appreciating team members' contributions bolsters their self-worth while spurring higher productivity—proof that "expressing appreciation" really works. For example, according to a Harvard Business Review study 76% respondents mentioned they found fulfilment in their jobs when they felt appreciated.

In addition, gratitude has been linked to compassion and decreased aggression hence further enhancing positive social contexts. This realisation inadvertently supports healthier social dynamics by promoting more empathetic understanding and less aggressive responses. In a world that is divided such as ours, this revelation shows how something as simple as giving thanks can go a long way in bridging the gap between miscomprehension and understanding.

Therefore, it's apparent that expressing gratitude is not only about mental health but also determines the kind of relationships we form with others. Be it thanking the barista for your morning coffee or writing a heartfelt note to an old friend, these acts of appreciation have the potential to change our lives and those around us for good.

Chapter 37

Welcoming Experiences
Which Make Life Worth Living

****

The intention of this piece is to enlighten individuals on the fact that embracing new experiences is important in one's journey towards a more fulfilling life. This, however, can be a difficult thing to do since it involves stepping out of one's comfort zone and challenging oneself. This chapter will explain how breaking free from limitations and seeking new opportunities for growth and happiness can be possible by going out of our comfort zones and challenging ourselves.

Embracing experiences mean stepping outside the box. Staying within your comfort zone may feel safe but it prevents personal growth as well as excitement. Comfort zones have their limits and there is a need to embrace discomfort in order to enjoy new experiences.

Fear and uncertainty hold us back from embracing new things. However, it is important to note that embarrassment or feeling uncertain are natural reactions when trying something different. Thus, embracing discomforts and finding humour in the process can help one overcome fear that hinders meaningful experience.

Positive experiences have the ability to change our well-being and resilience. In a world where negativity tends to overshadow everything else, taking stock of positive experiences consciously can have far-reaching consequences in our lives. We can build positive neural pathways by mindfully noticing and absorbing positive experiences thereby increasing our overall happiness and resilience.

Cultivating positivity in the mind is always healthy for mental health. Shifting attention towards the positive entails giving yourself credit for what you have done right, accepting compliments, and countering negative self-talk with positive ones. Engaging in contemplative experiences such as nature walks or attending cultural festivals are among other ways through which we can foster positivity in life.

Embracing new experiences helps an individual's personal development. Each experience that involves learning something new; solo travels abroad; volunteering abroad; learning foreign languages; conquering fears; among others usually offers valuable lessons about oneself. Another way of embracing experiences lies in finding time for what truly makes us happy. Being creative helps in nurturing our talents and making a difference in life. For instance, through writing, painting, playing music or even doing what we love most, we can be able to ignite our creativity which will give us happiness in life.

To fully embrace experiences, we must find some appreciation for cultural diversity. This can be achieved by attending cultural festivals, trying out different foods and engaging in various cultural practices among many more things that enlighten an individual's perspective on the world. By embracing cultural diversity, empathy and respect are promoted while fostering connections among people.

Embracing experience could also mean getting into other forms of entertainment that people usually do not try like online casinos. Online casinos have a vast collection of games and entertainment options that allow individuals to bet on the comfort of their homes.

Nature is a great way for refreshing the mind, body as well as spirit. Whether it is hiking, camping or just sun bathing outside one will get a break from the digital world so as they can reconnect with the natural one.

Not only is embracing new experiences important but it should become a lifestyle. If we deliberately seek out opportunities for growth and development we truly come alive. These new experiences are what give meaning to our lives hence let's take advantage of this wonderful journey called life by consistently embracing new experiences.

The Problem with Comfort Zones

Though remaining within your comfort zone may feel secure and easy, it can impede your personal development and prevent you from experiencing new, exciting things. Comfort zones are stagnating and they inhibit individuals from taking risks as well as trying new things. Missing out on personal growth opportunities and the chance to create lifelong memories are done when one remains just where he or she is.

Comfort zones restrict you, trapping you in familiarity and predictability. It makes you feel safe but keeps you from venturing out of your boundaries to explore new horizons. By accepting experiences that go beyond our comfort zones, we open ourselves to growth, learning, and self-discovery.

However, breaking free from a comfort zone isn't an easy task. Consequently, many people remain trapped by fear of failure or rejection when venturing into the unknown. Nevertheless, recognizing the confines of comfort zones alongside the great possibilities outside them permits one to overcome these barriers with confidence and enthusiasm for new experiences.

Embracing experiences beyond your comfort zone allows you to expand your horizons, discover new passions, and build resilience. You will have to abandon your beliefs in order to broaden your perspectives on life and develop survival tactics for your future endeavours. When we try something different than what we're used to doing it brings about change in ourselves hence personal growth.

Stepping into the Unknown

By stepping out of our comfort zones we embark on a journey of self-discovery and personal transformational process. You get used to dealing with uncertainty issues as well as adapting yourself with unfamiliar surroundings. Every experience becomes a lesson that is useful in order to let us know more about our world.

These experiences can involve solo trips or learning something completely new such as hobbies or skills that push you far beyond what you believed were limits before. The pursuit should be for opportunities which challenge us instead of letting us stay within our boundaries. When we embrace these experiences outside our comfort zones we create a positive feedback loop of growth and self-improvement. It is through these new experiences that we progress in our journey towards a more fulfilling and enriching life.

Overcoming Fear and Uncertainty

Often, fear and uncertainty prevent us from fully engaging with new experiences. However, it's worth remembering that feeling embarrassed or uncertain is completely normal when trying something new. Humour can be a great way to overcome these fears by embracing discomfort. We can start to let go of the hold of fear on us when we recognize it as a natural part of growing up and make the experience fun.

It is important for us to identify our fears and understand them directly. By taking calculated risks starting with small steps, we can slowly build our confidence as well as expand our comfort zones. Remember, embracing new experiences is a process, and it's okay to feel uncertain at times. Opening ourselves up to incredible personal growth opportunities by facing our fears and stepping into the unknown. Take risks! Start something different today so that you can own your future!

Our well-being and resilience is greatly affected by positive experiences. Consciously accepting and embracing the good things in our life can compensate for our brain's natural inclination towards negativity since the world tends to be more pessimistic than optimistic. By being fully present, attending to, and soaking up pleasant experiences into ourselves, we can generate more constructive neural pathways and amplify our total joyfulness as well as ability to last.

Feeding the Brain

Teaching your brain positivity may be difficult but it is immensely rewarding. When you intentionally direct your attention to positive things, you are likely to have a more positive mentality which further enhances happiness and resilience. In short, so many people today have chosen a path of positivity that has had an incredible impact on their lives.

Shift Your Focus

Acknowledging your accomplishments is one of the main ways through which you can foster positivity in yourself. Instead of dwelling on mistakes or failures that occurred previously, recognize and celebrate any achievement no matter how small it might be. This way, your mind will slowly get used to knowing only the bright sides of your life. Similarly, taking compliments gracefully is another way of training your brain for positivity. Do not dismiss kind words but accept them humbly thus allowing yourself to enjoy some moments of merit. Compliments are essential to nurturing self-confidence and self-love when they are allowed in; this sets a stage for receiving many other compliments.

Refuting negative self-talk is also crucial if you want to grow positivity in you. Any time negative thoughts come up, challenge them with new affirmations and statements aimed at encouraging oneself rather than beating oneself down 84). As we choose what we think about daily, we have the power to change our thoughts from negativity towards positivism; hence a renewed hope in life.

Encouraging Experiences

Engaging in meditative practices like mindfulness or meditation can be utilised as potent tools for developing positivity (30). These activities enable one to cultivate a deep sense of presence and gratefulness that allows them to experience the beauty and goodness in every moment. It is from this that you can train your mind to always think positive things about life.

Connecting with nature helps to nurture positivity (10). This might involve being outside whether it's hiking, a walk in the park or simply sitting under a tree where you will have your mindset transformed as well as feel wonder and awe coming over you. Nature has a way of calming our moods and brightening our souls; therefore, spending time amidst natural beauty can be therapeutic for our emotions.

Moreover, attending cultural festivals can be another great way of embracing positivity (55). These events celebrate diversity, creativity and human connections thus providing an opportunity for people to learn more about different cultures. By engaging into these festivals' vibrant atmosphere one may end up having his memories for life along with inculcating a sense of self-confidence, oneness and gratitude towards the world.

Fostering Positivity through Positive Experiences

Promoting positive experiences enhances not just the quality of life but also improves neural pathways for happiness and resilience. Thus, by shifting one's focus consciously and partaking in activities that breed positivity one is able to create a virtuous circle within his brain leading a more satisfying fulfilled life that is full of excitement.

Embracing new experiences is a necessary trigger for personal growth. We have to dare ourselves and step outside our comfort zones to know who we really are and extend our horizons. Travelling alone, volunteering abroad, learning languages, confronting fears or doing extreme sports develop us as people. When we embrace new experiences, we expose ourselves to rich learning opportunities.

Every trip is an opportunity for you to learn new things, broaden your viewpoint and understand the world more deeply. In the process of adapting to new cultures and environments as well as problem-solving, we grow.

Further still embracing experience encourages self-discovery too. As we negotiate these paths, we discover hidden talents within ourselves that inform our perception of who we are in essence. We challenge what we think we believe in, face our limits and come out stronger than before.

The Power of Personal Transformation

This shows how much embracing experiences can change a person's life; it becomes the source of lifelong thirst for personal growth affecting various dimensions such as relationships, professional life and general wellbeing. We become adaptable, open-minded and empathic individuals through looking for fresh experiences all the time.

So make a conscious decision to step outside of your comfort zone and embrace new experiences regularly. Whether big or small, each experience holds potential for a personal development journey involving self-discovery, resilience and greater understanding of the world. Embrace the unknowns; face challenges; welcome opportunities.

Unleashing Creativity and Passion

Embracing experiences does not only require us to leave our comfort zones but also dive into our passions where creative juices flow. By dedicating time to activities that give us joy and satisfaction there is no limit to what can be possible.

Embracing our passions could be visual arts paintings filled with vibrant colours; books with captivating stories; tunes from musical instruments that touch one's soul or other ways of making art that bring us happiness. It gives meaning to life by enabling unique expression.

When we immerse ourselves fully in our passions, be it for a moment or over an extended period of time, we unleash our creativity and open ourselves up to new ideas and perspectives. Our passions make us think outside the box, go into uncharted territories, and challenge the limits of what is feasible.

By embracing our passions, we are willing to take chances and embrace new experiences. This makes us more robust, flexible as well as open-minded. Our passions feed the flame of our motivation thereby moving forward towards personal growth and self-discovery.

So therefore let us embrace both bold brush strokes in paintings, heartfelt words in writing songs that resonate with our souls or immersing ourselves in hobbies which bring us joy so that they can guide us into boundless creativity and happiness.

Embracing Cultural Diversity

To truly embrace experiences, it is important to appreciate cultural diversity and celebrate it. Around the world, cultures are a treasure chest of customs, traditions and perspectives that need to be discovered. By immersing ourselves in diverse cultures we tap into new possibilities and deepen our understanding of the world.

One way to embrace cultural diversity is by going to cultural festivals. These events depict various customs through vibrant parades and captivating performances. You can see, hear or taste other people's culture, something which will provide a memorable experience as well as widen your knowledge.

Exploring different cuisines is another avenue towards embracing diversity in culture. Each meal represents its root meaning the flavours and methods that have been passed down over many generations. In this way one can enjoy various tastes that are related to a particular culture's past. For instance, trying Indian cuisine gives you the feeling of being in Mumbai through its aromatic spices or trying out Japanese sushi entailing umami flavours which make one think of serene cherry blossom gardens.

By embracing cultural diversity, we cultivate empathy, respect, and a sense of interconnectedness. It allows us to recognize and appreciate the beauty in our differences while finding common ground that unites us all as humans. When we embrace cultural diversity rather than fear it, we create a richer, more harmonious world full of endless opportunities for growth and understanding.

Embrace Nature's Healing Power

Nature has an intrinsic power that can rejuvenate and heal our mind-body-spirit. In today's digitalized society where screens and notifications are an integral part of our lives, connecting with the natural world offers a much-needed respite.

We can find solace in the outdoors either by hiking through lush woods, camping under the stars or simply basking in the sun's warmth. The serene and beautiful nature has an immense effect on one's well-being because it allows us to relax and heal; such feelings leave us invigorated physically and mentally while also deeply connected to ourselves and others.

Scientific studies have shown that embracing nature can reduce stress levels, improve mood, and enhance mental clarity. The natural environment rouses our senses with its colours, sounds and scents, as we develop a sense of wonderment for the world around us. It is soothing for our souls when birds sing melodiously, trees sway gently under a breeze or when even blooming flowers give off a sweet fragrance in nature- reminding us about simple pleasures in life.

Thus, next time you feel overwhelmed or in need of some kind of healing, walk outside and embrace nature as a remedy. Let the earth below your feet, the vastness of sky above you and rhythms of nature's cycles be a constant reminder that you are as tough as they come and that you are connected to the world around you. Embracing the healing power of nature is both restorative and humbling because it reminds us that we are part of something bigger than ourselves.

Embracing novelty as a way of life

Life is an amazing adventure that presents different opportunities for growth and self-discovery. However, embracing new experiences should be more than a one-time event; it should be a way of life. By actively looking for and accepting new opportunities, we can open ourselves up to excitement, learning and personal growth.

From trying out exotic dishes to immersing in various cultures, every new experience has served to deepen our lives. We have allowed ourselves to look beyond normalcy so that we can catch the exceptional things within it. Today, solo adventures may be embarked on hobbies taken up or languages learned but whatever it is it gets us closer towards embracing life at its best.

Embracing new experiences is not merely about making memories but rather about developing an attitude of curiosity and open-mindedness. It means viewing this planet as an infinite playground where every opportunity for learning or advancing oneself must be taken with both hands. This is how we create opportunities for personal growth, self-expression and lives that are more satisfying.

Okay let us make a conscious decision to seek out those new experiences whether big or small which will infuse our lives with adventure, wonderment and joy. This suggests that adopting such a lifestyle would create moments spiced with flavours that would make our hearts jump in happiness. After all there's more to life than familiar boundaries let alone living by them everyday; hence embrace what lies beyond them towards an enriched, more vibrant and limitless life.

Chapter 38

Advanced Volunteering
for Personal Development

***

Volunteering is not just about giving back to society; it involves personal long-term development that can be transformative. Engaging in voluntary activities contributes to personal growth, skill acquisition, and overall well-being. In this chapter, we will explore the various benefits of volunteerism and its positive impact on personal development, from building meaningful connections to advancing professionally and experiencing personal satisfaction.

Advantages of Volunteering

Volunteer work not only positively impacts others but also brings considerable advantages to those who participate. Here are some key benefits:

1. A Sense of Purpose and Achievement

Volunteering provides a sense of purpose and fulfilment by actively participating in activities aligned with one's passions, bringing deeper meaning into life.

2. Stress Reduction and Depression Fighting

Engaging in voluntary activities has been found to be helpful in stress reduction and managing symptoms of depression, promoting mental well-being.

3. Mental Stimulation and Growth

Volunteering keeps the mind active, providing continuous mental stimulation and opportunities for learning new skills, gaining knowledge, and broadening horizons.

4. Connection and Belonging

Volunteering brings together people with common goals, fostering a sense of belonging and increasing overall happiness through social interactions.

5. Better Health and Happiness

Volunteering is associated with improved mental and physical health, leading to greater well-being and satisfaction with life.

In summary, volunteerism goes beyond altruism, serving as a major driver for personal growth, mental well-being, physical health, and a sense of mission in life.

Volunteering Bonds You to Others

Volunteering not only allows individuals to give back to their communities but also facilitates the creation of new friendships and the enhancement of existing relationships. Through volunteer work, one can meet like-minded individuals, broadening horizons and developing important social skills such as communication, teamwork, and leadership.

Creating new relationships through volunteer work is not only satisfying but can also enrich personal life, leading to lasting connections and support systems. These friendships extend beyond the volunteering period, contributing to personal growth and skill development applicable in various contexts, including career building.

Volunteerism for Wellness

Beyond helping others, volunteering has numerous benefits for mental health and physical fitness. Engaging in volunteer activities can significantly lower stress levels, fight against depression, and contribute to an overall sense of well-being. Research indicates that volunteering is linked to reduced mortality rates and decreased chances of heart disease.

By dedicating oneself to meaningful activities, individuals not only improve the lives of others but also enhance their own quality of life, fostering confidence and emotional well-being.

Volunteering for Professional Growth

Volunteering is a powerful tool for shaping future career paths. Through volunteer work, individuals gain valuable experience, acquire essential skills, and explore different sectors of the economy. Volunteering demonstrates commitment, hard work, and a willingness to contribute, attributes highly valued in the workplace.

Volunteering can serve as a platform to showcase and sharpen skills for potential employers or customers. It provides practical experience in areas relevant to personal or professional interests, such as event planning, project management, and community outreach.

Obtain Experience & Develop Abilities

Volunteerism offers a unique opportunity to acquire practical experience in areas resonating with personal or professional goals. Skills developed through volunteerism, such as event planning or project management, provide a strong foundation for career success.

Additionally, volunteering allows for the exploration of new fields, expanding knowledge and improving skill sets. For example, volunteering in a non-profit organisation can offer an opportunity to learn new skills, such as graphic design, while making a positive impact.

Create Professional Network

Volunteering is an excellent means of expanding one's professional network in terms of scope and diversity. Collaborating on volunteer projects brings together individuals from diverse backgrounds and professions, creating valuable connections.

Building professional networks through volunteering opens doors to advice, mentorship, and potential collaborations. These connections can be instrumental in navigating one's career path more efficiently and tapping into the hidden job market, where many opportunities arise through word-of-mouth recommendations.

In conclusion, volunteering offers a wealth of benefits, ranging from personal development and well-being to professional growth and the creation of lasting connections. Engaging in volunteer activities is not only a contribution to society but also a transformative journey that positively influences various aspects of life.

Personal long-term development and not just giving back to society is what volunteering entails. A person's participation in voluntary activities can be a life-changer in the sense that it contributes to personal growth and the acquisition of skills. Volunteering also helps people to connect with others, develop themselves mentally and physically, grow professionally, and enjoy their lives.

Volunteering offers an exceptional platform through which individuals can learn more about themselves and develop their full potential. Meaningful bonds are formed when you give your time and expertise to a specific cause or organisation, thus improving society. While volunteering, one gets to build important skills, create new networks, and discover new hobbies.

In this chapter, we will look at various benefits of volunteerism and how it positively influences personal development. From engaging with others to advancing in a career and enjoying personal satisfaction, volunteering can be a transformative experience. So, let us get into it now and see how this amazing volunteering journey unfolds!

Advantages of Volunteering

By doing volunteer work, we get to impact other people's lives positively while also being part of worthy causes that strengthen societies. There is more than being selfless or acting altruistically, given that these actions bring considerable advantages to those who participate.

A Sense of Purpose and Achievement

The sense of purpose provided by volunteering and fulfilment arises from impacting other people's lives. It allows you to actively participate in activities for which you feel passionate about, thus bringing deeper meaning into your life.

Stress Reduction and Depression Fighting

Mental health greatly benefits from engaging in voluntary activities. Such efforts have been found helpful in stress reduction as well as managing depression symptoms. When such acts are directed towards others instead of ourselves, it helps us believe again.

Mental Stimulation and Growth

Volunteering keeps your mind active all the time, which provides continuous mental stimulation. It creates chances for learning new skills, as well as gaining knowledge in different fields and broadening your horizons. By daring to be different and pursuing things that are outside of your comfort zone, you stand a chance of evolving both mentally and personally.

Connection and Belonging

Volunteering brings together people with various backgrounds who have a common goal of achieving something positive. Such relationships enable one to find a sense of belonging through interacting with those who share similar interests. Apart from making us more socially inclined, they also increase our level of happiness overall.

Better Health and Happiness

Among other benefits associated with volunteering is improved mental and physical health. Most volunteers find themselves happier, satisfied with life generally, and tend to enjoy greater well-being through getting involved in positive activities or thinking processes. Our emotional states improve by engaging in voluntary work such as assisting others without seeking monetary compensation.

In summary, the advantages of volunteerism go beyond impacts on others. It is a major driver towards personal growth, mental well-being, physical well-being, and a larger sense of mission in life. By dedicating yourself to bettering humanity with your expertise, there are so many ways through which this can transform your own life as well as those around you positively.

Volunteering Bonds You to Others

Volunteering offers a unique opportunity to give back to your community, and it also helps you connect with people and make a difference. This means that volunteering allows for the creation of new friendships, enlarges your social network, and enhances your existing relationships.

While volunteering, you have an opportunity to meet others who are like-minded in making a difference. This is because helping at a local soup kitchen or participating in community clean up will expose you to other volunteers who are passionate about improving lives.

Creating new relationships through volunteer work is not only satisfying but can also enrich your personal life. You will meet individuals from diverse backgrounds and experiences, which will broaden your horizons and create bonds that last forever. Such friendships continue beyond the volunteering period itself, leading to support systems and groups of people who share common values with you.

It is also through volunteering that one can grow personally and develop important social skills. By taking part in diverse volunteer activities, you will be able to enhance your communication, teamwork, and leadership abilities. These skills are crucial not only during the volunteer work but can as well be applied in various contexts such as career building.

Therefore, if you want to make new friends, grow your contacts, and improve on your social skills then consider volunteering. This way, apart from making significant contributions towards the welfare of society, you will also create lasting connections plus memories.

Volunteerism for Wellness

Volunteering goes beyond helping others; it has numerous benefits on mental health as well as physical fitness levels. Getting involved in volunteer activities can significantly lower your stress levels and help fight against depression. Thus, by dedicating yourself to something that interests you most, you contribute positively towards creating a better world hence enhancing one's overall state of well-being.

Research has shown that volunteering leads to reduced mortality rates as well as decreased chances of getting heart disease. Volunteering always results in feeling fulfilled, hence raising confidence levels which, in turn, boost one's mental as well as emotional well-being. By serving others, their lives are improved and your quality of life will be enhanced.

Volunteering for Professional Growth

Volunteering means much more than just doing good for society; it can also be a tool to shape your future career path. Through volunteer work, one gains rich experience and acquires necessary skills that can be employed in various job settings. This allows you to try out different sectors of the economy, gain insight into potential careers, and make contacts with professionals from various backgrounds.

When you volunteer, you show that you are committed, hardworking, and willing to contribute something that is highly valued in the workplace. Volunteering is a highly regarded attribute when such promotions or leadership positions are considered. Thus, volunteering serves as a way to sharpen and demonstrate your skills for possible employers or customers.

Obtain Experience & Develop Abilities

Volunteerism provides a unique opportunity for one to acquire practical experience in areas that resonate with them professionally or personally. For instance, event planning, project management, and community outreach are some of the areas where necessary skills can be developed and sharpened to benefit a person in their work life. This is so because the experiential knowledge obtained through volunteerism serves as a strong foundation for eventual career success.

Additionally, volunteerism allows you to explore new frontiers and enlightens your knowledge base, which improves your skill set. For example, if you currently work in marketing but want to explore graphic design, volunteering for a non-profit organisation can provide you with an opportunity to learn designing skills while making a positive impact.

Create Professional Network

Volunteering is also an excellent means of expanding one's professional network in terms of scope and diversity. Through joint volunteering projects aimed at achieving common objectives, individuals of diverse backgrounds and professions come together to form networks. These linkages could be important in terms of future employment opportunities, mentorship or even collaboration.

By forming relationships inside your volunteering community, you gain access to professionals who can offer you advice, counsel, and guidance on how best to navigate through your career path. These persons may have information and experiences that may be helpful in more efficiently steering your path towards career goals or opening doors that lead to unforeseen opportunities.

In this way, building professional networks through volunteering becomes one means of tapping into the hidden job market as many jobs are often filled through word-of-mouth recommendations. Your volunteer connections may let you know when there is a vacancy in your dream job or refer you to potential employers or clients.

Chapter 39

Optimising Your Physical and Social Space for Lasting Positivity

****

This chapter is dedicated to optimising your physical space and building a supportive social network as a means of creating a positive lifestyle. We will shed light on how one can be happy in his/her daily life and share some expert recommendations as well as strategies to make a positive environment around oneself and meaningful relationships.

The state of your environment matters so much with regard to your own happiness, mental health in general, and how you feel on any particular day. By removing clutter, incorporating nature themes, and personalising one's space, an atmosphere that inspires positive thinking can be created, which is also visually appealing.

The friends you keep are not less important either. There are emotional support channels, opportunities for personal growth, and belonging that come with building strong social connections. This guide is going to direct you on how you can enhance already existing links between people, make new ones, as well as promote an enabling grounded communal society.

We will explore this connection between the environment we live in and our friends, hence making it possible to unlock these secrets towards having the best life anyone would wish for. So let us embrace the journey together, unpacking the transformative power behind optimising our physical environments while forging a supportive social network.

Why Does Your Physical Environment Matter?

It has been found out through research that your physical environment counts in terms of your well-being. Lighting, colours, organisation, cleanliness, among other factors, are known to affect your moods, productivity levels, and overall mental health. Optimising your physical space creates an inspiring atmosphere.

Practical Tips for Optimising Your Physical Space

Optimising your physical space is what makes up a positive lifestyle. During this process, decluttering; organising; adding natural elements would help convert it into visually appealing yet functional spaces that support holistic wellness.

Below are practical tips for optimising your physical space:

1. Decluttering and organising: First, identify the things that you do not require anymore and get rid of them. For instance, there should be spots for different items such as clothes, novels, books, and various household items. By decluttering and organising your space, you can achieve a relaxed feeling.

2. Incorporating natural elements: Plants are great additions to any interior space because they provide a breath of fresh air. They purify the air within the room and enhance the general appearance of the environment. Also, maximise on natural lighting by leaving your window curtains open in daylight hours to create an appealingly bright atmosphere.
3. Creating specific areas: Create different zones within one's living space. This involves having an area that is specifically set for work productivity purposes; a comfort corner for stress-reducing activities and maintaining an exercise section for physical health purposes. With these different sections created, you will concentrate better without any form of disturbances.
4. Personalise with meaningful decor: Meaningful décor adds personality to any space. Display photographs or artworks that evoke happy emotions or other personal mementos. By surrounding yourself with meaningful decorations, you are able to create an environment that reflects your individuality while at the same time bringing joy to your heart.

By utilising these practical tips, one will be able to optimise their physical space to facilitate positive living. Remember that aesthetic appeal and orderliness in our surroundings can greatly influence our daily motivation levels as well as our overall well-being.

"A serene place betrays a serene frame of mind. Make sure that your surroundings are such that it lifts you up and encourages you."

The Importance of Social Connections for a Positive Lifestyle

Being able to form, maintain, and develop robust social connections is vital for living positively. Such a social network can provide emotional support, personal development opportunities as well as the feeling of belongingness. Recent studies indicate that individuals who have strong social bonds enjoy better mental health and overall well-being.

Human beings are social animals, and therefore our relationships with others are crucial for our well-being. Constructive social connections may offer a support system when times are rough, increase self-esteem and self-confidence, or even improve our physical condition. Thus, be it friendship, family, or community, meaningful relationships add value to life in general.

When we lack social connections, we tend to feel alone, lonely, and isolated. This can be detrimental to both our mental and physical health, leading to increased stress levels, anxiety disorders, and depression. On the other hand, having a robust social network can improve our resilience, help us cope with stress, while giving direction in life.

The Power of Emotional Support

"Having anyone who listens and supports you could make all the difference in your world."

Supportive networks also provide emotional protection to those who need them. Having someone who listens and supports you can make a world of difference in your life. Whether you need someone's shoulder to lean on or advice or celebrating successes with someone at the end of the day; it gives comfortability and positivity to each single day.

Opportunities for Personal Growth

"Interacting with different people from diverse backgrounds exposes us to varying perspectives, thoughts and experiences."

Developing ties through interaction with diverse groups provides new chances for personal growth (Hoffman). For instance, interacting with different people from diverse backgrounds exposes us to varying perspectives, thoughts, and experiences. Other people teach us things about ourselves that challenge us on what we believe. These enriching experiences help us grow as individuals and become more open-minded, empathetic, and tolerant.

A Sense of Belonging

"Membership in a community or group gives us a sense of identity, meaning, and connection."

We feel connected when we belong to a group of people. Membership in a community or group gives us a sense of identity, meaning, and connection. It serves as our support network, where we can find people who share similar interests with us and have similar value systems or just be ourselves without judgement. Therefore, self-esteem and confidence, among other things, are boosted by this sense of belonging.

In conclusion, nurturing social ties is important for maintaining positive lifestyles. By seeking out opportunities to connect with others, building meaningful relationships, and putting time and effort into preserving them, we create a social support system that contributes to our health and happiness.

Building a Supportive Social Network

In today's fast-paced world, building connections and fostering a supportive social network is essential for overall well-being and happiness. Surrounding yourself with like-minded individuals who understand and uplift you can provide emotional support, encouragement, and a sense of belonging. Here are some effective strategies to start building a supportive social network:

1. Join Community Groups

Engaging in community groups or organisations enables one to connect with people who have the same interests, likes, or objectives. Book clubs, sports teams, and local charities are examples of these, and they offer platforms for meeting new people as well as establishing relationships based on commonalities.

2. Volunteering

What is more, volunteering allows an individual to become part of a giving community that shares your values and altruistic mentality. This could involve helping at a nearby shelter, participating in environmental cleanup drives, or assisting with education programs. It is through volunteering that one can enlarge their social circle and bring good effects.

3. Show up to Social Events

Also, attending social events such as parties, networking gatherings, or professional conferences can provide opportunities to meet new friends and create valuable contacts. To be able to achieve this aim; you will need to make conversations happen, pay attention to what others are saying, and learn from different perspectives. Such social interactions form a basis for long-term friendships.

4. Social Media Platforms Can be Used

Similarly, the use of social media platforms such as Facebook, LinkedIn, or Instagram can also aid in building networks. You could join relevant groups or online communities, engage in discussions or talk to persons with similar hobbies who are located elsewhere, thus broadening your network.

5. Preserve Present Ties

The development of a supportive social network does not only mean forging new connections but also preserving existing ones. Regularly checking on each other's lives by choosing a specific time for it shows how much you care about them; while rendering assistance when required goes a long way towards deepening friendship bonds. These endeavours go towards enhancing links which eventually link up individuals into unending friendships.

6. Work hard at making new acquaintances

Furthermore, going out of your way to meet strangers can result in amazing relationships later on in life. Attend gatherings with friends whom you didn't know so well before today; talk to new people on streets that are suitable and be ready to undertake unfamiliar tasks. In order to create a robust social network, it is necessary to establish various types of rapport.

"Surround yourself with only people who are going to lift you higher" Oprah Winfrey

Remember, developing a supportive social network is a gradual process that requires time and effort. Just be calm, be yourself and always keep to your own words. Properly networking will support and lift you at different points in your life.

Maintaining Healthy Relationships

To keep healthy relationships in your social network, one must prioritise communication, respecting boundaries, saying thanks and supporting others. Positive friendships can make a huge difference in how happy and well you feel.

Any successful relationship begins with communication. By actively listening and speaking honestly and respectfully about your thoughts and feelings, meaningful, open connections can be built. Try to keep in touch with them on a regular basis to find out how they are doing.

"A true friend is a person who is always there for you through thick and thin."

Equally important towards maintaining healthy relationships is respecting boundaries. Get to know your friends' personal space, privacy, and limits. It is crucial to appreciate that every person has unique needs and limits.

In order to create strong bonds of friendship, expressing gratitude and appreciation is one of the most effective strategies. Take time to recognize as well as thank friends for their support, kindness, or just being in existence. A heartfelt "thank you" can do wonders in fostering positive connections.

The Power of Supportive Relationships

Supportive relationships provide a sense of belonging, encouragement, and understanding. Friends who care about your well-being can also uplift your spirits when things become difficult.

"Surround yourself with people who push you up."

Be empathetic and compassionate when offering support to others. Show your friends that you are there for them whenever they require someone to listen or lean on. These acts will go miles in constantly establishing stronger bonds of friendship.

The Benefits of Positive Friendships

Positive friendships have numerous benefits for your overall well-being such as:

Providing emotional support hence reducing stress levels

Increasing happiness and life satisfaction

Enhancing mental health as well resilience

Driving personal growth plus self-confidence

Enhancing social connectedness while promoting the feeling of belongingness

"A true friend is priceless."

Spending time on nourishing healthy relationships is crucial for having a positive living style. Be around friends who inspire and motivate you, and who are there for you too. Remember, positive friendships go both ways; both sides must engage to build the relationship.

Creating a Positive Social Environment

Developing a positive social environment is critical in enhancing your well-being. Creating a supportive and uplifting social atmosphere can be achieved by surrounding yourself with individuals of similar values and interests, promoting kindness and inclusivity, and engaging in activities that foster positivity and personal growth.

When trying to create a good social network, it is important to surround yourself only with people who share your values, dreams, and aspirations. Find friends and associates who inspire you as well as genuinely support your personal growth or wellbeing.

"Surround yourself only with people who will lift you higher." - Oprah Winfrey

Promotion of kindness and inclusivity should be the key qualities to consider within your social circle for the establishment of a positive society. Friendliness, openness, plus empathy among friends will go a long way in achieving this goal. A culture of kindness and inclusivity creates an environment where everyone feels valued and supported.

To cultivate a good social environment, it's also essential to indulge in activities that promote positivity and personal growth. You might consider getting involved in community service projects, volunteering for causes you are passionate about, or joining clubs that match your interests and passions. Through these activities, one not only grows as a person but also finds like-minded individuals whose values are similar to yours.

"Surround yourself with positive people who believe in your dreams, encourage your ideas, support your ambitions, and bring out the best in you." — Roy Bennett

Physical Space and Social Relationships

The physical space you occupy has a great effect on your social connections and relationships. The layout and ambiance of the space can either impede or facilitate social interactions and determine how frequently one will communicate with others. By creating an inviting and welcoming environment, you can foster positive interactions and build stronger social connections.

When your physical space is well-designed, it provides a comfortable and inspiring backdrop for socialising and bonding with others. An aesthetically appealing setting which features cosy furniture such as seats covered with cushions; warm lighting plus fascinating ornaments creates an enjoyable place where people meet around. It becomes, therefore, a stage set for meaningful conversations through shared experiences.

Think about how your space is arranged. Open floor plans or designated gathering areas can improve interaction and collaboration so that people can more easily engage in conversations or participate in various activities together. Spaces that promote movement or flow such as outdoor spaces or common rooms may also offer opportunities for chance contacts.

Moreover, the ambiance of the physical environment can impact social interaction moods as well as energy levels. A well-designed space incorporating natural elements like plants or natural light encourages relaxation hence creating a sense of peace within its users. It is possible for this to contribute towards genuine bonds being formed.

"The physical environment plays a significant role in shaping our social connections. A space that is comfortable, inviting, and aesthetically pleasing can enhance social interactions and foster deeper connections." – Dr. Jane Thompson, Environmental Psychologist

"Surround yourself with only individuals who will lift you higher."

Always surround yourself with people whose minds are always filled with happiness and who make you feel like being at your best every moment. With these influences, one may possess optimism for a long time, develop oneself personally as well as uphold healthiness.

"To maintain a positive lifestyle, it's important to build a strong support system."

Within your social network, regularly engage in activities that breed positivity and self-improvement whether it involves attending social events or participating in group activities such as common hobbies since meetings contribute to bonding thereby facilitating meaningful connections among the attendees.

Remember that creating and sustaining a positive lifestyle is never an end but rather an ongoing journey that needs constant efforts. Keep around you people who add up worth to your life; join growth communities or forums when necessary. By concentrating on social support, we can have optimistic ideas towards life as we live a wholesome existence full of joy.

Balancing Physical and Social Elements in Your Lifestyle

Striking an equilibrium between having the best physical space for optimum use and cultivating supporting friends is essential for maintaining positivity in our lives. These two components fuse perfectly together allowing individuals to lead fulfilled lives. You create a foundation for overall well being

Optimising Your Physical Space:

The condition of your physical environment affects how productive you become, how happy you are, what mood you carry around; indeed it is all about wellness generally. Take some time out of your schedule to check the state of your space and see which areas can be improved upon to promote ease, inspiration and calmness. This may involve decluttering and re-arranging the room, use of natural elements like flowers or sunlight as well as personalising your décor according to what has a meaning for you. Your design should be visually appealing and functional in order to support a positive life.

Cultivating a Supportive Social Network:

However, also forming and nurturing strong social bonds contributes significantly towards our overall happiness. Therefore, stay close with those who lift you up or join activities that foster connection. This may mean joining groups, clubs or communities that focus on shared interests and passions. Be active during social events where genuine relationships can be established. Through developing a supportive social network, we create an environment of belonging in which personal growth is enhanced thereby leading to overall happiness.

The fulfilment of human life lies in balancing these two competing aspects which are physical and social; one should realise they are not mutually exclusive but rather they are intertwined with each other. In order to maintain a positive lifestyle one must invest time in optimising the physical space around them while at the same time prioritise friendships.

The Positive Impact of Lifestyle Optimization on Mental Health

Lifestyle optimization – improving upon one's physical space as well as cultivating an encouraging social network – has been shown to have major benefits on mental health conditions such as stress, anxiety, and depression. According to research studies, individuals who prioritise self-care, meaningful connections and a positive physical environment have lower rates of stress, anxiety disorders and depression symptoms.

The creation of a lifestyle in favour of mental well-being involves the holistic approach that encompasses different aspects of your life. Optimising physical space and nurturing social connections can help you to establish an environment that generates positivity, sustains overall well-being, and contributes to mental health improvement.

"A healthy physical environment and strong social support are key to good mental health."

Dr. Sarah Johnson

When you think about lifestyle optimization, you intend your surroundings and experiences to be supportive of your mental well-being. Here is how improving on physical space and developing supportive social network can impact positively on your mental health:

Improving Your Physical Surroundings

Your physical environment plays a vital part in your psychological welfare. A sanctuary for relaxation and positive feelings can be created by making a visually appealing, organised and functional space for oneself. Consider the following ways to optimise your physical space:

1. Clean up as well as rearrange things in order to feel calm and at peace.

2. Add green plants that will improve air quality as well as provide soothing effects.

3. Use lighting colours that elicit passion, happiness, or excitement into your room.

4. Make the interior design personal by adding meaningful items that make you happy.

5. Developing Supportive Social Networks

Mental health requires strong relationships with other people. A supportive group of friends offers emotional encouragement, company, and membership sense.

A well-designed friendly physical space accomplished through a good support system from friends and family is what forms the foundation for sound mental health. When lifestyle optimization becomes your priority, it means that you have decided to take charge of your own wellbeing so as to improve your life generally.

Embracing a Positive Lifestyle for Long-term Well-being

Embracing a positive lifestyle is the key to long-term well-being. By consciously striving to optimise your physical space and nurture your social connections, you create a solid foundation for sustainable happiness and fulfilment in life.

Begin by cultivating a positive mindset. Approach each new day with intentionality, focusing on gratitude, positivity, and self-growth. This mindset will permeate all aspects of your life, allowing you to navigate challenges with resilience and maintain an optimistic outlook.

In parallel, make it a priority to optimise your physical space. Declutter and organise your surroundings to create a visually appealing and functional environment that supports your well-being. Incorporate natural elements such as plants or natural light, and personalise your space with meaningful decor. These actions will foster an atmosphere of harmony and inspiration.

Equally important is building and nurturing a supportive social network. Surround yourself with like-minded individuals who uplift and inspire you. Engage in activities that promote positive interactions and personal growth. By fostering meaningful connections, you cultivate a network of support that enhances your overall happiness and well-being.

Chapter 40

Celebrating Achievements and Maintaining Commitment to New Habits

****

Celebrating your achievements is a crucial aspect of personal growth. By recognizing the progress and accomplishments you have made along the way, this will raise your self-esteem, inspiration, and promote both personal and career growth.

When we appreciate our achievements we give ourselves the recognition that we deserve. It shows that we recognize the effort we put into it, motivating us to continue growing and climbing higher.

We can find any reason to celebrate whether it's big milestones or small victories. It lets us know what we are able to overcome so that we can appreciate how far we have come. It helps us understand that challenges can be overcome and goals can be achieved.

In addition to all these, celebrating your achievements also creates a positive mindset. We increase confidence in our abilities as well as self-confidence by focusing on successes. A shift takes place where one sees themselves as good enough for success thereby prompting them towards higher performance levels.

Moreover, celebrating your achievements spills over into other areas of your life too. It increases overall well-being, improves relationships and even enhances productivity. When you take pride in what you've achieved, always an aura of positivity surrounds you, influencing others around you.

So, let us bask in the glory of celebrating our accomplishments; let's acknowledge that our journey is ongoing, will boost our faith in ourselves while enabling personal development for us all.

SMART GOALS - Remember Them!

Setting clear and effective goals is critical when it comes to achieving success. This is where SMART goals come in; SMART being Specific, Measurable, Achievable, Relevant and Time-bound which acts as a guide for setting goals.

Specific: SMART objectives should be specific meaning they are clearly defined on what exactly you intend to achieve hence giving yourself a clear focus and direction.

Measurable: On this note, SMART goals can be measured through which you can monitor your progress and ascertain whether you're on the right track. Measurable goals also make you accountable and keep you motivated.

Achievable: These are goals that are attainable for you, hence they are realistic. Goal setting within your limits helps to sustain motivation while discouraging despondency.

Relevant: Relevant means that the SMART goals align with the general objectives and priorities of an individual. When your goals are relevant, they have meaning and significance thus making one remain focused and committed.

Time-bound: SMART goals have a specific deadline or timeframe. A time limit is created by setting deadlines which give vent to urgency thereby providing direction.

By understanding and implementing the principles of SMART goals, you can set yourself up for success. They help clarify intentions, maintain motivation, and allow meaningful progress towards desired outcomes to be made.

Importance of Celebrating Progresses and Successes

Celebrating your progressions and successes has implications beyond being nice; it impacts your motivation, confidence, happiness at large. The act of acknowledging where we have come from in terms of how much work we've put into our journeys cannot only be rewarding but also reinforces positive thinking patterns while boosting self-worth.

Your celebration routine should include self-care rituals. Take time to indulge yourself, do activities that make you happy and be mindful of your needs. These activities can range from visiting a spa, practising mindfulness and meditation to taking up hobbies; they help you refuel your energy levels and keep a positive attitude throughout the journey of personal development.

The relationship between celebrating achievements and progress is quite strong in terms of motivation, confidence and happiness. Personally tracking your progress visually, setting milestone rewards for yourself, sharing your accomplishments on social media platforms, keeping a personal growth journal, or incorporating self-care rituals are some ways to create an exciting and rewarding personal development journey. Therefore, start recognizing them today as well as being excited about growing up!

Celebrating Successes during Hard Times

Celebrating your progress and successes during challenging times can be very difficult. But no matter what setbacks, crises or failures come our way we can still find reasons to celebrate. By having compassion for oneself as well as being grateful for what one has got while reaching out to others for support one can celebrate even in difficult times.

During this juncture it may be hard to maintain positivity when facing challenges which may cause setbacks on your path towards celebrating your achievements. Also remember setbacks are part of the journey so do not get discouraged from acknowledging and celebrating them. In fact such celebrations act as boosts towards motivation in tough times thus restoring resilience back into you.

Dealing with Setbacks

In moments of setback it pays off to treat oneself kindly since failure is part of the learning process. Understand that every failure is temporary hence use it to learn more about how you could have approached things differently. It is because viewing setbacks from an optimistic perspective will keep you moving forward with enthusiasm.

Moreover, seek solace from loved ones and friends when things get tough. Being surrounded by a strong network provides comfort, encourages one's soul along with different views needed during challenging periods. Share the hardships and celebrate the progress made along the way as an aggregate effort and encouragement contribute towards a sense of belonging and motivation.

Healing and Moving On

Celebrating your progress in hard times can be healing. This means that you give yourself permission to be happy amidst all the struggles and just appreciate all that you have achieved. Celebrations serve as reminders of how resilient one is, gives them strength, consequently making them optimistic.

Regardless of how small it may appear, take time to reflect on your journey and what you have achieved thus far. In addition, celebrate every milestone no matter how insignificant it may look because each tiny step represents your determination as well as dedication. Heed the call to heal with joyous celebrations that shall propel an enlightened future ahead.

Therefore, celebrating progress, even in hard times shows resilience in terms of strength. It is always good to show compassion for oneself, find support and value accomplishments when facing setbacks so as not to lose focus while trying to stand up from difficulties after recovering from them later on. Find a way of celebrating either big or small achievements then allow such functions lead you through personal growth processes plus conquering obstacles.

What Not to Do While Celebrating

Despite the importance of celebrating your progress and accomplishments, you must also be aware of common pitfalls that can hinder your journey towards personal growth. By knowing what to avoid, you can ensure that your celebrations are valuable and useful.

Stop Comparing Yourself to Others

Comparing yourself with other people is one of the greatest mistakes people make. Remember that everyone's journey is unique; comparing yourself with others only causes feelings of inferiority or doubt about oneself. Instead, concentrate on how well you have done as an individual and take time to rejoice over your personal accomplishments.

Do Not Get Too Comfortable or Proud

Never let complacency or hubris set in when you celebrate your achievements. Personal development is a continuous process that requires hard work and dedication. Therefore, it is essential to keep up momentum and aim at greater achievements.

Avoid Guilt and Selfishness

Do not feel guilty or selfish when acknowledging your accomplishments or practising self-care. Celebrating success in personal growth should be cherished as a means of maintaining your health and drive rather than being considered a blameful or self-centred act.

While understanding these possible pitfalls will allow you to celebrate personal growth in a healthy manner full of productivity; this will help you remain focused, motivated and committed towards reaching out for your goals of personal development.

Reflecting on Your Progress

In order to acknowledge success as well as stay motivated, it is imperative to track progress while noting achievements made. Keep records indicating actions performed, results obtained and feedback given along the path one takes through life just like in a diary or journal planner spreadsheet app among other things used to document different events experienced during one's quest for personal growth.

Breaking down goals into smaller chunks helps achieve milestones while assigning time frames for each milestone keeps one focused and motivated. In so doing we can celebrate little successes thereby creating a sense of accomplishment which further fuels our determination.

This way regular reflection enables us to evaluate how much we have achieved and identify areas that need improvement and also see how far we have come thus urging us to continue investing in our dreams. Celebrate every achievement, small or big, and be happy about the progress you have made, motivating yourself to adopt a positive attitude.

Through keeping records and reflecting as one moves along the journey of personal development, there is a way of mapping achievements which not only validates efforts but also gives a sense of pride in one's own accomplishments. Also, these records will serve as encouragement for you when you are down, reminding you of what you can achieve and therefore making you work even harder to attain higher goals and ensure that growth does not stop.

Importance of Acknowledging Achievements

Acknowledging your success leads to validation, motivation, and encouragement. It fosters positive thinking and enhances self-esteem when individuals take time out to accept progress made and successes registered. As a result, by celebrating such achievements, there is an attachment of meaning as well as purpose to what you do leading to the motivation required in setting new targets for yourself for further personal and professional growth.

Sharing Success Empowers

Sharing your success with others is one way of celebrating that achievement in order to reiterate it. When friends, parents, mentors or society at large learn about your success they can validate your achievement in addition to enhancing your emotions positively hence relating more closely with each other.

You can develop a group that constantly backs and cheers you up by saying thank you and appreciating other people's input. By sharing your success, others are encouraged to push ahead in their dreams as they get to see a proof of concept.

Sharing the success one has encountered creates a sense of affiliation and community. The support and encouragement from others will help move you on in life making your journey more meaningful. It enhances appreciation so that one does not just have self-awareness about their own achievements but also gets to acknowledge how others have contributed towards their successes.

Support and Gratitude

When you share your successes, you tap into the strength of support and gratitude. You can use this as an opportunity to thank those who guided, advised or encouraged you along your path. Strengthening family ties through recognition of the role played by supportive persons around us builds unity within society.

Moreover, by sharing your success, you can also offer support and encouragement to others who might be on their own personal development journey. These accomplishments can encourage others to believe in themselves and take up challenges they thought impossible.

External Validation and Motivation

Celebrating achievements with others may result in external validation which can influence one's motivation levels positively as well as build self-belief. This validation confirms that the road taken is correct and reminds where they came from before reaching this point. Such external validation serves to propel one through obstacles, keep them focused on their goals thereby enabling them to realise continual growth even when faced with setbacks.

By sharing your success, you open yourself up to praise, encouragement, and admiration from others. This assertion bolsters personal confidence while also driving its owner forward. External validation leads to increased understanding about the process itself as well as its overall significance for an individual's life.

So take a moment to share your success with your community. Express your gratitude, inspire others, and let the power of support and external validation propel you even further on your personal development journey.

Strategies for Self-Care and Enjoying the Journey

As you celebrate your progress on your personal development journey, it's crucial to prioritise self-care and enjoy the process. Reflecting on the accomplishments made will help you appreciate how much distance has been covered as well as rejuvenate your energy for the future. Additionally, practising self-compassion is essential for maintaining a positive mindset and staying motivated.

Begin by dedicating moments of reflection to recognize your achievements. Find time every day or week to take a break and assess how far you have come. Reflect on the challenges you've overcome and the lessons you've learned along the way. Through engaging in this practice of self-reflection, one gets a deeper insight into their own growth which in turn amplifies pride and gratitude for one's successes.

Recharging your energy levels is equally important. Engage in activities that bring you joy and relaxation. It could be anything from being outside in nature, hobbies or just taking a few minutes off from daily routines to recharge yourself; all these make up moments of self-love that refuel one's strength thus preventing them from burning out. Remember, self-care is not selfish but essential for your overall well-being

When you are on your personal development journey keep practising self-compassion. Be good to yourself and accept all that comes with it. Understand that all failures and troubles are part of your progress in life and chances of learning. With a self-compassionate mind, you will gain the strength to rise above setbacks and go forward.

Finally, always keep a positive mind throughout your journey. Even little achievements ought to be celebrated, not only ending goals. Have a positive attitude towards the process that allows you to see improvements and stay motivated for further progressions. Maintain awareness that self-development is not just about getting there but enjoying every bit of transformation into another person.

Through these techniques as you walk through your personal development journey, celebrate your success, prioritise self-care, and fully enjoy the transformative process of growth. Reflect, recharge, practice self-compassion, and stay positive as you continue on your path towards personal development.

Avoiding Comparison and Embracing Individuality

One of the key aspects of celebrating your achievements is avoiding comparison and embracing your unique journey. We have different paths with different circumstances and goals for everyone's lives. By focusing on what you have achieved alone this will help in appreciating yourself without lowering others efforts.

Using Achievements as Fuel for Growth

Your achievements have the power to fuel your progress and contribute to sustainable success. Celebrating accomplishments enables us not only to acknowledge our work but also to set higher targets for ourselves thereby enhancing our performance level.

Celebrating achievements goes beyond just the initial joy and sense of accomplishment; it becomes motivation to press forward harder in order to achieve even greater victories. It becomes a catalyst for consistent growth and development.

Chapter 41

The Synergy of Strategies: Combining Different Approaches to Personal Development
****

In life, our growth as we journey is not random. This process is continuous and relies on the coordination of various diverse approaches. That is what strategic synergy entails. Therefore, this comprehensive guide concentrates majorly on Chapter 41: The Synergy of Strategies: Combining different approaches to personal development.

Sometimes, it's important to blend several strategies for one to succeed in any area of their lives; be it career, relationships or personal goals. By combining multiple growth strategies concurrently we can make use of the collective power of their impact. It is a principle that is commonly referred to as 'synergy of strategies'. Think about music production –although each instrument alone makes a great sound, the symphony from an orchestra will sound much nicer and stronger.

The Necessity for Growth: The Synergy of Strategies

Personal development comes in different forms that cannot be generalised. For example, it has both objective and subjective components which are very different from each other. Consequently, a single rigid strategy may not show much significance when employed in this case. On the other hand, mixing different methods allows one to benefit from the unique outcomes that come with each approach.

Through this synthesis your decision making abilities improve and you maintain the momentum towards achieving your desired goals with efficiency and rapidity . One interesting thing about these interdependent strategies is how they enhance each other- often producing effects that go beyond their individual capability.

A Powerful Tool for Personal Development: Strategic Synergy

Strategic synergy plays an important role in personal development. Instead of focusing on a single developmental method or philosophy there should be more emphasis on collective action. Diversifying our strategies facilitates cross-pollination leading to creativity and innovation while pursuing growth.

Continuous improvement underlies this synergy where small adjustments over time can produce significant improvements. At the same time this kind of synergy supports effective decision making which represents another aspect of personal development for an individual hence promoting long term change and growth.

Personal Development Strategies are Diverse

The field of personal development is quite broad and offers a variety of strategies that can be used to guide us. By combining them, we not only grow smarter but also come to recognize ourselves better and become more adept at dealing with life's problems. Such diverse strategic approaches ranging from multilevel interventions to strategic positioning where one may better align themselves with their goals make personal development more holistic and robust.

Further into this guide, we will see how one can mix these various strategies to generate productive growth, resilience and ultimately success.

This means that the next sections will go into greater detail on these ideas by offering practical tips and real-life examples on how you can harness the power of strategic synergy in your personal development journey. Keep watching as we trace the path towards a fuller, richer life characterised by continuous improvement and effective decision making processes.

Concept Analysis

The first step in any journey of personal development is self-discovery. Before trying out different strategies or approaches, it is necessary for an individual to know his/her strengths as well as weaknesses which is what Exercise of Authority brings into play.

Commanding others and self-governance are the main ways of exercising authority. It is essentially about getting to know oneself (strengths, weaknesses, values, beliefs, biases, etc.) and using this knowledge to guide actions before influencing others. Additionally, it has a significant impact on personal development through refining decision-making skills and strategic positioning improvement.

Strategic Positioning is recognizing where one stands with his or her goals and aligning oneself with things that will help achieve them strategically. Simultaneously integrating different strategies can make it even stronger. This concept closely relates to multilevel interventions and continuous improvement which promote holistic growth.

Multilevel Interventions

In the personal development sphere, Multilevel Interventions refers to enhancing growth over multiple domains at once. Instead of concentrating on one aspect at a time, it makes individuals strive to improve their skill sets across various areas simultaneously. This kind of diversified approach to learning often results in quicker progress and ensures that growth is balanced.

Develop Ways to Combine Strategies

Developing Ways to Combine Strategies may empower individuals by adding depth into their growth plan while allowing customization per changing circumstances or needs. Flexibility comes from strategic synergy which is capable of being customised continually as well as coordinated for instance.

Cross-Domain Planning and Joint Force Development

One aspect of how you can develop ways in which to combine strategies refers to Cross-Domain Planning. In other terms, create a roadmap for yourself that covers different areas for development. Good cross-domain planning coupled with joint force development can lead to strong outcomes; this means that personal growth can become more rewarding and freeing.

Joint Force Development

Joint Force Development is a concept from military strategy where power in numbers is sought after. Here it involves combining different strategies leading approaches as well as interventions into a powerful and far reaching personal development plan.

Also, the introduction of something like the Three-Step Development Strategy can add some structure but also allows individuals enough flexibility to personalise it. Such an approach also helps with better risk management by breaking the task of personal growth into simpler parts so that one can easily see what possible downfalls can happen in the course.

To conclude, understanding these concepts provides a strong foundation for customising our individual development journey as per our needs and aspirations. Truly leveraging strategic synergy involves being open to combining various approaches and learning methods - each offering unique insights and tools to foster continuous improvement on all fronts.

Case Study: Practical Examples of Synergy of Strategies in Personal Development

These ideas will be illustrated through a case study of Susan who is a perfect example of strategies' synergy.

Susan was a diligent worker who found herself stuck in a management position with no clear path for promotion. Her efforts were not yielding results as she expected. Upon realising that she needed to revise her personal development strategy, Susan decided to adopt strategic synergy.

Employing Multilevel Interventions

Susan first incorporated Multilevel Interventions in her personal growth plan. Susan, who realised that there was a need to make simultaneous changes in several aspects of her career development, took this integrated approach. This involved improving her technical skills while, at the same time, undergoing leadership training and emotional intelligence education. All these activities contributed to Susan's professional success in various ways.

Incorporating Cross-Domain Planning

Another strategy that Susan employed was Cross-Domain Planning. She drew up a holistic plan addressing various aspects of her personal development; from enhancing communication skills to positioning herself strategically for promotions at work. She also attended professional courses, read influential business books and engaged her seniors and peers to continuously improve.

Developing Ways to Combine Strategies

Developing Ways to Combine Strategies was another vital move on Susan's part. She designed a portfolio of powerful competencies that improved both job performance and life satisfaction by deliberately incorporating different growth techniques including time management approaches alongside stress reduction exercises.

Leveraging Joint Force Development

The principle of Joint Force Development too was factored in by Susan. For example, she grouped strategies such as mentoring and networking that supercharged each other's effectiveness thereby making it possible for her to increase visibility among peers and establish new contacts expanding opportunities for promotion.

The Role of Risk Management in Susan's journey

The way risk management helped shape Susan's journey is shown herein below: In developing her growth plan, Susan also included Risk Management as an essential component wherein she meticulously identified possible hindrances towards meeting his personal objectives while planning how to counter them in advance through coming up with risk scenarios for every major step she intended to take as well as planning ahead. By engaging in this kind of forward thinking she went through the course of her development with more certainty enabling her to grow upwards professionally at last.

In conclusion, Sarah's story is a powerful reminder of what can be achieved by integrating multiple methods into an individual's own personal growth journey, offering a tangible example of the potential of strategic synergy. The combination of various approaches expanded Susan's competence, fortified her skill set, and amplified her overall success.

What was striking about this case study is that personal growth could be more effective if we use different strategies together in contrast to relying on a few tactics. We will now go through these sections elaborating on them as a way by which you can practically apply these concepts to your own personal development journey dynamically.

The 'How-to' Section: Implementing Strategic Synergy in Personal Development

After learning how strategic synergy can be used to enhance personal growth, let us see how you can effectively tap into it. This section will outline practical steps towards implementing diverse strategies for comprehensive development - from decision-making skills to risk management.

A Three-Step Development Strategy

Initially, use A Three-Step Development Strategy to build your personal development plan. The steps include planning, execution, and evaluation. During the first stage identify what aspects you want to develop. Leadership skills and emotional intelligence are some examples of these areas that one might choose from. Carry out your plan as planned in step two. Finally, evaluate your progress periodically in step three and make adjustments where necessary.

The Role of Exercise of Authority in Planning

During the planning phase of the self-development process Exercise of Authority is crucial for one's success. This kind of self-governance makes it easier for an individual to make the right choices regarding which strategies they should adopt during their quest towards their self-improvement endeavours; not only that but taking this path also means clearly stating one's objectives as well as aligning them with what they value most in life.

Utilising Strategic Positioning

In every step of your journey, consider Strategic Positioning. Assess where you stand concerning your desired outcome at all times. This understanding empowers you to reposition yourself in activities that bring you closer to your goals or even change those goals if necessary.

Holistic Growth through Multilevel Interventions

Instead of concentrating on only one aspect, full-fledged growth involves tackling several aspects simultaneously – a principle referred to as Multilevel Interventions. You can look for ways of enhancing different factors concurrently. For example, it may mean signing up for leadership courses as well as taking up a new hobby so as to broaden our horizons or even working on some habit that we want to develop while acquiring a new skill.

Create Mechanisms to Merge Strategies

The next stage is about creating mechanisms to merge strategies. Remember this is not just about growing but growing efficiently. It would be ideal if there were complementary techniques that may be implemented concurrently without overwhelming you. Suppose for instance, using mindfulness exercises during your daily commutes could enhance mental clarity and reduce stress thus maximising your downtime value.

Effective Risk Management: Mitigating Risks

Risk management is an essential part of personal development because the process inevitably involves risk-taking. In addition, you need to be proactive and identify obstacles that are likely hinder your growth plan and come up with strategies on how to overcome these barriers. One of the things that risk management skills would help us achieve is making smoother passageways in our own personal developmental plans hence walking through the journey with ease in case any unanticipated challenges occur.

Finally, strategic synergy realisation requires careful planning, execution and adjustment of various self-growth strategies. By embracing this multipronged approach towards personal development, better results will definitely be realised – tapping into the potential inherent in synergy towards transformative self-improvement.

Nurturing Leadership Through Management Development Programs

Traditionally companies have used management development programs as a way of breeding leaders. This kind of program often focuses on cultivating a set of characteristics like strategic thinking, decision-making capabilities, communication skills, resilience or empathy. Such teachings when incorporated into our personal developments can be a force to reckon with and open ways for better opportunities and experiences.

Combination Prevention: Proactive Growth Management

Just as public health strategies use combination prevention methods to deal with different aspects of disease control together, so should we embrace combination strategies in our journey for personal growth. For example, this could entail integrating stress management techniques with time-management approaches or even matching physical fitness goals against mental health benchmarks. This preventive approach fosters balanced development that's sustainable over time.

Personal Development Hand-In-Hand: Tailoring and Coordinating

Tailoring and Coordinating go hand-in-hand when talking about strategic synergy – it's the art of customising plans based on individual needs while ensuring all strategies interrelate effectively. In any personal development plan, long-term participation is facilitated by this versatility keeping it effective overall.

In conclusion, applying these seemingly unconventional concepts in a broader perspective can provide fresh insights for your personal development journey. Remember, every discipline carries innate wisdom that could be aligned towards enhancing self-growth – all we need is an open mind to connect the dots.

Chapter 42

Creating Your Personal Blueprint Designing a custom action plan for continued self-development

***

A boost to morale is achieved through self-improvement. A personalised action plan is hence needed for constant self-improvement which will allow you to unlock your potential and continue growing. In this chapter, you will find steps that can help you make a plan as per your goals and objectives. You will be able to determine the skills you have right now, set targets that would lead to taking the right actions for the growth of both you and other people around you. This would involve things like figuring out ways of building a support network, identifying appropriate growth strategies among others. This way, one can be in charge of their personal development both in their professional and daily life.

Key Takeaways:

A customised action plan helps in continuous personal development

Evaluating your current skills and areas for improvement is necessary when creating an individualised plan

It is important to create SMART objectives to keep focused with your action plan

It is good to identify several growth strategies as well as having a supportive community around

The key to sustainability of continuous self-improvement lies within progress tracking, milestone achievement celebration and making necessary adjustments.

Understanding the Importance of Self-Development

There's an old saying that goes "If you're not growing, you're dying." This applies to personal growth too. Investing in oneself is important because it influences different aspects of one's life leading to success and fulfilment.

By developing yourself, it means acquiring new skills, knowledge or insights that occur from time to time. Additionally, if an individual develops himself/herself he/she becomes more confident since such a person can overcome obstacles and challenges more easily. Furthermore, engaging in self-development enables one to indulge into personal interests hence increased satisfaction with life. When there is investment in personal growth and lifelong learning then one becomes a multifaceted person.

Ultimately through personal development individuals become better versions of themselves and this has a positive impact on society. Becoming a source of motivation and inspiration to others is one result of growth and improvement in oneself. Why wait then? Start your journey of self- development today and realise your potential!

Assessing Your Current Skills and Areas for Improvement

To develop a customised action plan for ongoing self-improvement, it is essential to evaluate your current skills and identify the areas that require improvement. Self-reflection and self-assessment provide an opportunity to understand your weaknesses as well as strengths.

The first step in this process is conducting a skills assessment that involves evaluating what you can do at present in terms of skills as well as identifying where you need to grow. Honesty during this process is very important since it will enable you not to overestimate yourself.

After finding out both the strong points and weak points, this would help you direct efforts towards improving different areas. This means that one has to really go into those aspects they are weak in order to find ways of enhancing them. Therefore, these goals should be precise enough and attainable.

Self-reflection plays a vital role in assessing your abilities but it may be hard doing it alone; hence, try seeking feedback from colleagues, mentors or any other trusted person who can give an objective view on things that need change.

Remember, assessing your skills and identifying areas for improvement is an ongoing process. Consistently reflecting on oneself helps keep one on track while working towards such objectives.

Setting SMART Goals

To be successful in your self-development journey, it is important to set SMART goals. These are goals that are specific, measurable, attainable, relevant and time bound. You should separate the bigger goal into smaller actionable objectives that will help you to remain focused and motivated.

When setting SMART goals ensure that they are realistic and make your action plan more detailed by defining what actions will help you achieve them. Establish benchmarks that can be measured as well as reasonable timeframes for each action. It is also vital that your overall personal development philosophy matches with the goals and they are feasible but not easy.

One essential thing to note when you set SMART goals is that there must be flexibility in case of any changes. Whenever new information comes up or something changes around us we should be ready to shift our targets while considering the main objective throughout.

Choosing Self-Development Strategies That Work

Finding effective approaches for your needs and preferences can go a long way towards achieving self-growth. This is why it is necessary to check out different modes so you can establish those that match you best.

One productive approach would be to combine multiple learning techniques in your personalised roadmap. This might entail reading materials on self-help or motivational literature attending seminars or workshops or taking online courses.

Another helpful method involves focusing on personal growth using mindfulness practices like meditation and yoga. They enhance mental health as well as emotions making it possible to consider further improvements.

Thirdly, one can choose a specific area of personal growth such as communication, leadership skills or decision-making processes upon which they want to work on. A person may seek mentorship/coaching, practise new techniques including strategies through reflecting periodically about their progress/achievement.

By exploring different strategies and methods for self-development, an individual can realise which ones they fit into better by incorporating these techniques into their customised action plans.

Setting Up Support Network

Sometimes embarking on a self-development journey may feel daunting thus having a support system helps to keep one motivated and accountable. This could involve finding someone who has a wealth of knowledge and experience in the same field that can give you guidance or connect with people who are walking on the same path as you.

While selecting a mentor, look for someone with experience in your chosen area of self-development whose values and approach resonate with yours. An accountability partner is anyone who commits to helping you achieve your goals and holding you responsible for implementing your action plan.

Remember that building a support system takes time and effort, but it is worth it. When the going gets tough, those you have surrounded yourself with will be there to encourage you to move forward toward success.

Making a Reasonable Timeline

In order for self-development to be effective, it should have a realistic timeline that takes into account proper time management and prioritisation. The first step is identifying specific goals stated in your action plan and estimate the length of time it will take for each task.

Once you have a ballpark figure of the time expected, it is important to rank each activity according to its level of significance and urgency. This will enable you to organise your timetable in a manner that optimises output while reducing disturbances.

Remember too to make time for rest and relaxation as burnout can hamper long-term success. Properly managing your time and setting achievable objectives can guarantee steady growth in self-development.

Implementing Action Steps

Now that you have a concrete plan in place, it's about time you put it into action. Execution of the plan is the most crucial part of achieving self-development objectives. To succeed, one needs to break down their plan into actionable steps.

Begin by identifying the first actions that you need to take. Ensure that they are specifically achievable and if necessary set priorities. Getting started with small steps that are easy to achieve is better as this builds momentum and motivation. As progress occurs, you can gradually heighten the difficulty of your action steps.

Create new habits that support your plan in order to retain consistency. Habits take time to develop so be patient while starting small. Concentrate on one habit at a time until it becomes automatic. Each successful step should be celebrated so as to boost confidence and motivation along the way.

Remember that there may be challenges on the way but always stay committed and adaptable. If there are any setbacks, assess the situation and adjust accordingly in your action plans. Persistence and dedication can overcome any hurdle leading towards self-development goals achievement.

Tracking Progress and Making Adjustments

As one begins their path towards self-improvement, it is important for them to track how they are progressing while adjusting their plans accordingly. Current monitoring provides an opportunity for celebrating little victories, finding out where one's strengths lie as well as releasing areas for further progress.

For tracking purposes think about using things such as self-reflection journals, habit trackers or performance metrics among others which show progress made over time. Periodic self-assessments will help you in determining the gaps between your current situation and the desired one, and this may lead to necessary adjustments. This means that growth is part of becoming the best person one can be; hence, changes are not usually bad.

Remember self-development is a journey, and there may be challenges along the way. But tracking progress and making adjustments can keep you motivated, overcome setbacks and achieve personal and professional goals.

Celebrating Milestones and Achievements

Congratulations! You have taken steps necessary to create and implement a custom action plan for further self-development. Throughout your journey, it's essential to recognize and celebrate your milestones and achievements to stay motivated and inspired.

Whether it's completing a course or conquering an obstacle or mastering a new skill, take time to acknowledge your progress by appreciating your own hard work. Celebrating with others can also trigger self-motivation for more of the same.

Think about rewarding yourself with something special, buying yourself a new book or spending time with friends after reaching some milestones. It is said that self-development is not a destination but a journey which calls for celebration of each milestone so as to maintain enough momentum in seeking continuous growth as well as improvement.

Perpetuating Sustained Improvement of One's Self

To make your self-improvement a lifelong practice, it is necessary to develop the growth mindset that is personal. It means that you have to move beyond your first plan of action and embrace the idea of continuous progress. This involves learning and being open to new avenues for growth.

Acquiring knowledge throughout life is a useful skill that will help you in your personal and professional life. Continually seeking new knowledge and skills will enable you to keep up with current trends and remain relevant in a changing world. Remember, learning does not have to be in classrooms or expensive. You can read a book, attend workshops, watch documentaries or listen to podcasts.

Personal growth mindset centres on process not outcome. It also implies that one has to accept setbacks as well as mistakes being part of the normal course of learning. Do not let these things pull you down or discourage you but embrace them as opportunities for growth. Developing a positive attitude enables one to maintain focus through motivation when working towards achieving his objectives.

Finally, keeping up continuous improvement requires commitment and discipline. It is important to stay responsible for your actions, monitor your progress and change your plans when necessary. Make sure you celebrate milestones achieved along the way as well as use them as stepping stones towards greater achievements. By maintaining a personal growth mindset and striving for continuous improvement, all aspects of life may be successful.

Staying Committed to Your Journey Maintaining momentum and staying true to your path of growth

****

Chapter 43: "Holding to The Course of Growth and Keeping Momentum Going"

Staying true to the path of growth is very vital when it comes to achieving your goals and pursuing dreams. Maintaining momentum in your journey of growth is not always a walk in the park. There could be stumbling blocks or challenges that may cause you to feel like quitting. That's why there's a need for a plan on how to stay committed and focused towards your goals.

This chapter provides practical tips on staying true to your path of growth while keeping momentum. For instance, setting clear goals and building discipline, seeking support and celebrating progress; these are some of the approaches that we will examine, aiming at getting you back on track.

Therefore, if you want to go further in your personal or professional development journey, join us now and learn how you can remain committed and keep the pace of development!

Keywords: Staying with Your Journey, Maintaining pace, path to follow

The Power of Commitment

Commitment is what keeps us going forward on our road to maturity. It is an inner force that makes it possible for us to deal with obstacles, keep our eyes fixed on our targets, keep moving ahead even if things do not go smoothly as expected. When one has commitment towards his/her trip one becomes more determined than ever before in his/her life with no obstacles in his/her lifetime.

Discipline, patience and embracing discomfort are some elements that can help you stay committed to your trip. This means having clearly defined objectives matching up with values and aspirations then working towards them consistently even when it gets tough. By being dedicated enough you realise the fact that you have been living under masses of self-limiting prejudices.

Although travelling is not always smooth sailing but with commitment one can withstand any storm experienced along their way. So whenever road blocks come across your ways and hurdles confront you one should lean onto commitment by rebuilding resilience within oneself, being open to new ideas and adjusting accordingly.

Ultimately, commitment is about honouring your inner compass and staying true to your path. As a result, continue developing strong bonds of commitment and one day you will experience fulfilment in your journey of life. Consequently, it makes sense to keep on moving forward as you are experiencing this beautiful journey which is even making each step worth it.

Setting Clear Goals

In order to maintain the momentum of growing up, it is important that you set clear and effective goals that align with your values and aspirations. To begin with, state your long-term objectives and break them down into smaller portions that can be accomplished easily. Make sure they are specific, measurable, attainable, realistic and time bound then write them down so as to enhance the commitment.

Keep tabs on yourself by monitoring how far you have gone towards reaching your targets on a regular basis this will enable you to make any required adjustments according to changes happening in the course of life. The person who holds their objectives in mind is more likely to continue being committed than others who do not. Finally you can also consider engaging someone whom to hold accountable for any shortcomings experienced while trying to work on the identified goals.

Remember that this is your personal journey of growth; hence setting well-defined aims that match up with values and aspirations will ensure that you remain faithful and satisfied throughout it.

Cultivating Discipline

Your growth journey will require you to be disciplined. Consistent practice and self-control are needed if one is to keep going and reach the set of targets they have. You can develop routines and habits for personal and professional success through discipline.

Creating goals and developing a plan to achieve them is a way of nurturing discipline. Divide your goals into smaller manageable tasks that you can accomplish on a daily basis. Even when there are obstacles or setbacks, stick to your schedule.

Another way to nurture discipline is holding yourself accountable for your actions. Keep track of your progress and regularly assess how you are doing. Seek ways to better it if necessary.

Discipline does not mean being perfect or denying oneself pleasure. It means making a promise to yourself and staying by it. If you remain committed to your growth journey, you will overcome challenges on your way towards achieving your objectives.

Motivating the Inner Self

Motivation keeps growth moving forward in spite of obstacles or reversals that occur along the path; somehow, this motivation must be sustained. The main thing here is to remind yourself what started motivating you in the first place; this could be anything from passion for writing or aspiration towards becoming a rock-star artist.

To sustain motivation, take some time off so as to prevent burn out, as well as introduce some changes into normal routine activities. A change of environment or trying new things may create excitement or curiosity about life's possibilities. Set up systems that hold you accountable for objectives as well as recognize milestones achieved along the way. Both short-term achievements leading to long-term goals act as motivation boosts throughout this process.

Eventually, self-care influences motivation most profoundly of all factors mentioned above. Make sure that you care about both mental and physical health since these will determine how productive you can be at any moment in time. By putting yourself first before anything else, and by committing fully towards personal development, one can foster motivation needed for continuous advancement along their growth pathway.

Overcoming Hurdles and Resilience

In the process of personal growth, there are many hurdles and roadblocks that you will encounter. This is vital because it helps in remaining dedicated to your journey despite the challenges that may come on the way.

One approach is to see obstacles as opportunities for growth. Instead of regarding struggling with obstacles as setbacks, you need to look at them as learning opportunities or ways to adapt. This perspective can help you stay motivated and focused on your goals.

Building resilience also requires a strong support network. Be around people who have faith in you and your vision; those who will encourage you along the way when it gets tough.

Finally, even in difficult times, don't give up on your path. Always remember why you started and keep your eyes on the final goal. By being resilient and staying focused, no barrier can block your way.

Support and accountability

Starting a personal growth journey is exciting and rewarding though sometimes challenging. Thus, it is important to look for support and accountability so as to maintain momentum as well as commitment towards personal objectives.

Getting encouragement from a support system that can consist of close friends, families or even mentors may be useful in keeping you on your track to self-improvement. This can be done by finding a mentor to consult, talking to relatives and other close people, or joining a group which has people with the same goals as yours.

Another important aspect of being accountable is having an accountability partner. An accountability partner may be a family member, friend or teammate who will help you stay focused and keep moving forward. This way, you will maintain momentum on your journey of improvement by checking in regularly, setting goals and tracking progress.

Do not hesitate to ask for support and accountability. Remember that it shows strength rather than weakness. Build a support system and find an accountability buddy to make sure you reach your goals always.

The embrace of growth

Remaining true to the path of self-realisation requires embracing change and welcoming growth. To do this one must have the appropriate mindset, and attitudes required for welcoming new opportunities as well as managing ambiguity. In order to achieve this, you must be willing to learn and adapt as you move forward in life.

Later when change occurs, approach it with a mindset ready for growth. Reframe change as a chance for learning, developing oneself and becoming better instead of seeing it as a threat. Therefore one does not need fear but should instead embrace it confidently as they strive towards their goal.

In the same way, embracing growth demands going beyond one's comfort zone and trying something new. It can be quite difficult but it is necessary for sticking to your path of development. Always remember that when growing you need to take risks and overcome your phobias although this is tough but worth it.

By embracing growth and change; this implies that you are ever evolving hence staying committed in your journey of self-realisation. Amazing results are achievable if only we can adopt an open mind together with a positive attitude.

Recognizing milestones and progress

You should take time to acknowledge your accomplishments as you proceed on the road of self-improvement. Reflecting on your progress and milestones can help keep you motivated and inspired to keep going.

Different people have different ways of celebrating milestones. One might choose to go for a special dinner or even take a day off just to relax. The important thing is that whatever it is, it must be appreciated that one has really worked hard in order to be where he or she is now.

Recognizing progress is also a key aspect of continuing with the journey. Sometimes, progress may be slow or not clearly seen but it's important to appreciate and celebrate even small wins along the way. Consequently, this will help you remain focused and continue making strides towards your goals.

Always remember to stick to your path of growth while still celebrating all the milestones and progress made so far. This will ensure that you keep up momentum and stay motivated on your personal and professional growth journey.

The development of continuous growth commitment

Staying committed towards one's journey for self-improvement takes an entire lifetime. This means consciously seeking self-improvement, learning new skills as well as pursuing one's passions consistently describing their desire for improvement.

For one to develop a continuous commitment to growth, adopting the mindset of growth is essential. This is just viewing the challenges as learning opportunities rather than obstacles that are supposed to be avoided.

What's more, is that you have to welcome change and be open to new things. Life keeps on calling for transformation, and your devotion for growth has to also be evolving. Look for new chances and do not stop sampling or acquiring knowledge.

Another element which would make you hold onto development in yourself are long term objectives. These targets ought to match your aspirations and principles and they must be specific as well as measurable. Separate them into steps which can be accomplished then monitor your process accordingly.

Lastly, make growth become a habit. Consequently, include activities that promote development in one's daily routine such as reading or learning new skills. In addition, find people around you who are growth oriented so that they too can contribute towards your goal.

Remember it takes a lifetime to remain committed to your own personal development journey. However, with the right attitude, habits and support system; you can constantly improve and excel both personally and professionally

Thus, continue with this commitment towards your developing personality since changes are inevitable and always appreciate every stage you accomplish in life while moving along this path. Therefore, by remaining focused on growth throughout your life will bring you an indefinite number of opportunities that will enable you to achieve both personal satisfaction as well as professional fulfilment.

Chapter 44

The Ripple Effect of Your Transformation Understanding how your personal changes can positively influence others and the world

***

Has it ever crossed your mind what kind of effect your personal transformations could have on people around you and even the world at large? Your actions, decisions and choices have the potential to catalyse change in others, both those within your immediate vicinity as well as the global community.

In this chapter, we will look at how personal growth is related to influence and why self-improvement projects should not be limited to our own lives only. We can be agents of change in a big way by appreciating the power of personal changes and realising their positive implications. Let us therefore examine some aspects of personal growth that transform lives and show ways you can positively impact other peoples' lives and the globe.

The Dividends of Personal Growth

In today's fast paced world, personal growth may seem like a luxury or something that can wait until another day. Nonetheless, such an investment into personal development can lead to significant positive changes in life. Learning new skills, self-reflection practices or setting goals are some ways through which self-improvement brings about profound personal change.

Additionally, working on oneself does not help only you but also those who surround you. This may be through showing others their ability to grow or imparting knowledge learnt from one's experience. It is possible to transform yourself without noticing how much this has influenced a whole lot more than it seems.

Just understanding that there is a great deal at stake when one undergoes personal development is key. The next step involves taking action and committing oneself to a growth process. One of the most important decisions one might make is investing in themselves whether it's by reading books, attending classes, hiring coaches or simply dedicating time for self-reflection and exploration.

Embracing Mindset Shifts

Do you feel like you are stuck with your current mindset? Embracing mindset shifts can be a powerful tool for personal growth and positive influence. A positive, growth-oriented mindset can benefit not only yourself but others as well.

Instead of seeing limitations and obstacles, start to think positively about such issues. Begin by believing in yourself and that you have the capacity for success in your personal development and growth. Challenges could be learning opportunities you embrace and acknowledge the small achievements made as you proceed.

By having a growth mindset, one becomes a change agent whose impact is felt even beyond them. Other people can also benefit from your positivity whose mindsets could also be changed leading to a more supportive and growth oriented environment for everyone.

Therefore, if you want to change your attitude towards life and think with a progressive perspective, get started by believing in yourself and the level of potential within you.

Building Empathy and Connection

Empathy is an essential aspect of influence. Through empathy, one creates an avenue for understanding other people's experiences as well as their point of view Thus it forms the basis for establishing authentic connections with others.

When you connect with others genuinely, you establish a support network that fosters personal growth and positive change. This means that when people are heard and understood they are more likely to reciprocate, thus creating a cycle of empathy and connection.

Empathy also allows you to positively influence others. Once you can feel how another person is feeling, responding in a way that acknowledges their feelings creates an environment for constructive dialogue. By adopting this approach, we will be able to create an atmosphere of trust and collaboration that promotes better understanding among group members and results in better outcomes.

To build empathy and connection, approach others with an open mind and heart. Listen carefully, try to get their point of view and let them know their feelings matter. In return this shall help you in building a safe space for other people so that they can end up exposing themselves truly. Therefore being open about your own struggles too would enable others to feel free enough to share their experiences thus fostering mutual understanding.

In summary, developing empathy and connection with others breeds personal growth, positive change and genuine relationships. Consequently, it lets other people develop self-growth within a friendly environment whilst being positive towards others.

Leading by Example

When it comes to influencing others, leading by example is important. When you live the changes you desire worldwide; then individuals around will consider you as their best examples. Your behaviour or what you do makes them want to be like one of your followers as well as changing themselves through the same actions.

Being positive and proactive in your own life can positively affect those around you too. For instance, someone close may see where you have come from through a personal growth journey hence be inspired into having his or her own journey as well. Also someone may just observe when you commit yourself in collaboration with other co-workers thus copying the same method used in his job area.

By taking responsibility for how much influence they have over other people's lives by acting as role models, they are able to make the world a better place. This means that if you make personal changes in life, it may inspire others to take a step and also cause positive impact hence leading to positive growth and change.

Spreading Positivity and Kindness

Have you ever thought of how simple things like smiles or a kind word can create an impact? By spreading positivity and kindness, other people will be motivated to do the same, therefore creating an atmosphere of empathy and support.

Acts of kindness need not be grand gestures; even small everyday actions can have a huge effect. These little things such as keeping doors open for someone or giving someone your ear might seem insignificant but they do generally tend to influence people in a better way.

But the ripple does not stop here because when people experience these acts of kindness and positivity they will in turn want to extend them to others thus starting a series of activities that can change the world.

Therefore next time you have an opportunity to spread positivity and kindness, grasp it with both hands. Never underestimate the power hidden behind the smallest act because at times it might turn out to be very influential and you yourself might not know who should credit you with this.

Choose to be a catalyst for change by intentionally spreading positivity and kindness in your daily life, and watch as it creates a ripple effect that extends beyond yourself.

Recognizing the Domino Effect

Ever paused to consider the cause and effect of your action? Simple actions and choices that we make can have a ripple effect that ultimately leads to a huge shift. The domino effect is important in acknowledging how big our own influence may be upon others and the world.

Inspiring people around us through making small changes creates a chain reaction of positivity. This influence can lead to greater change and even ignite global movement towards unity.

So next time you want to make a change, remember it's like a domino. Whatever you choose or do will affect other people even beyond their classrooms hence, you are working as part of the whole world.

Embracing Collaboration and Cooperation

Cooperation and collaboration are indispensable for any positive change worth having. An aggregate impact achieved by bringing together different individuals with diverse skills cannot be overemphasised.

Jointly focusing on one objective enhances unity among us motivating collective efforts which surpass individual ones. We can thus ease our burdens by sharing them out thereby gaining from each other's experience as well as insights.

When people embrace collaboration and cooperation, some level of trust is built between them. Here, all voices matter while every perspective counts leading to safety of space where dialogue can occur meaningfully. Such an approach encourages a decision-making process that is inclusive as well as strengthens the determination towards a peaceful planet formation.

Therefore, whether you are involved in a personal growth journey or trying to make some positive difference in the world, always remember this power of collaboration and cooperation.

By unifying with others who equally have ideas and strengths like ours, we are able to increase our influence resulting in longer lasting positive transformations than we could ever imagine.

Taking Responsibility for Your Influence

There is power in influencing those who surround you but also there comes along with some responsibility attached to it. Understanding its significance is therefore essential if we want it changed positively and used for good purposes rather than bad ones since we're all aware that nobody lives alone in this world. Personal responsibility in turn helps one to become aware and mindful of his or her own actions and choices, hence making influence more deliberate and meaningful.

By being responsible about your influence, you take it upon yourself as to whether it is positive or negative. By understanding where you can make a difference, you are able to act in ways that facilitate growth and improvement.

Therefore, taking personal responsibility means acknowledging the potential ripple effects of whatever we choose to do. This also implies that once people know they can go beyond their private lives with their deeds, it will activate them for making changes favourable for all people no matter where they live

Ultimately, taking responsibility for your influence is a powerful tool for personal growth and positive change. When you deliberately decide which action makes an impact on others' life, you position yourself as an agent of good towards the neighbours.

Inspiring Change Through Sharing Stories

Nothing else can do what storytelling does: it has the power to inspire change. Deeper connections are made with people through personal narratives and experiences. By admitting our weaknesses, difficulties and victories we call on other people to do the same.

In this way, empathy and comprehension may be initiated by storytelling thus allowing others to see beyond themselves. Through these instances of life, individuals could be stimulated into making positive changes in their own lives.

Personal stories also demonstrate the potential of personal development and transformation in an individual. To other people, we show that change is actually possible when we share our journeys towards self-improvement. We become evidence that if a person grows personally their life will only get better and motivate others to set goals for themselves.

This means, through storytelling one can create a narrative that is inspirational, motivational and calls for personal growth. With personal stories shared by us, others can lead positive lives while creating a better future for all.

Collective Progress

When one is pursuing self-development and positive change, it is important to appreciate where everyone has reached including oneself. Celebrating collective progress goes a long way in giving someone a sense of accomplishment which further motivates them towards growth. Knowing how far you have come will inspire you to keep making a difference.

Also recognizing growth allows you to track progress effectively and evaluate which methods have been successful so far. In this way, you can learn from those strategies and further refine your approach, ultimately leading to more impactful and sustainable change.

Furthermore, celebrating success is not just about acknowledging your triumphs alone but also recognizing similar achievements made by others as well. This fosters an environment that supports continuous positive change because collective progress becomes the source of motivation for everyone concerned.

What's more important; celebrating collective progress is the key to creating an environment where individuals grow personally and positively transform the world around them Recognizing the positive changes made by oneself or anyone else contributes immensely to building a more harmonious world, and ultimately making a lasting legacy in order to inspire future generations.

Maintaining and Enhancing Impact

In fact, creating positive change is not one act but a long-term commitment that sustains it. The following are some of the strategies to sustain and amplify your impact over time:

Set targets that can be achieved: Divide your long-term view into small goals which are achievable on a daily basis.

Monitor your progress: Keep track of the achievement of the objectives you have set, this will always encourage you to work harder.

Work with others: Join hands with other like-minded individuals or organisations that share your vision in order to magnify your influence and contribute towards a common objective.

Be a role model: Always act accordingly, for other people to follow you as an example in doing what is right.

Keenly observe new developments: It is important for you to stay connected with what is happening around the world concerning your purpose so as to adjust your approach accordingly.

Keep learning: Continue improving yourself through personal growth thus enabling yourself to become equipped with knowledge and skills for responding adequately to challenges as well as opportunities.

Celebrate success: Don't forget appreciating what you have done for yourself and others by admitting the changes; it is worth noting that this should motivate further growth.

Create a legacy: Think of the contribution you would like to make and start working towards creating lasting and meaningful changes that will keep on benefiting others for a long time even after you are gone.

By doing this, your personal changes can have a sustained and amplified impact, thus making the world a better place for everyone.

Chapter 45

Life Upgrade: Your Ongoing Revolution Embracing a lifelong commitment to growth, learning, and self-improvement

***

Welcome to a Life Upgrade! This article is about a lifelong commitment to self-improvement. Whether you start today or have been on this road for a while, there is always space for growth and transformation. The expression "Life Upgrade" says it all – upgrading your life in all possible ways. This means that every part of your life should be getting better by the day, from personal growth to habits and relationships. It requires a lifelong commitment to self-development, which we shall cover in this article. Let's dive into it and see how you can Upgrade Your Life!

The Power of Growth Mindset

When one embraces the growth mindset, they open up themselves limitlessly. The growth mindset is the belief that you can always improve, learn new things, and develop new skills. It enables you to see challenges as opportunities for growth rather than being afraid of them, maintaining a positive attitude. Instead of being intimidated by novel experiences, they are seen as chances to expand knowledge and abilities.

In particular, on the way to self-improvement, a growth mindset is greatly important. It means that you are ready to take risks and learn from your mistakes since failure is part of the learning process. You are able to step out of your comfort zone and engage in new challenges because you know that such an experience brings you closer to your goals. In short, cultivating a growth mindset sets one on a lifelong journey of learning and enhancement.

Setting Clear Goals for Personal Development

Your personal development starts with setting clear goals that can be easily achieved. Without goals, it's quite difficult to track your progress; so one may not know where he/she is going without goals in place; therefore, they give us something to work towards.

It's necessary when setting personal development goals to make them specific as well as measurable because intentions such as "be healthier" or "get better at public speaking" are too vague and make it hard to measure progress. Instead, have targets like "exercise for not less than thirty minutes daily on five occasions" or better still "deliver a five-minute speech before a small group by the month's end."

Moreover, putting time frames for your goals helps you be responsible and focused. Ensure that your goals align with your objectives for personal development and do not feel afraid to change them as you grow.

One of the frameworks through which goals can be set is the SMART criteria. SMART stands for Specific, Measurable, Attainable, Relevant, and Time-Bound. These criteria make sure that your goals are clearly defined and realistic.

Just remember that setting goals is only one step in your journey of self-development. Stay committed and spurred on, always being proud of the strides you take.

Cultivating Positive Daily Habits

Developing positive habits may seem trivial and insignificant, but they are vital aspects of the self-improvement process. Beginning the day with a healthy breakfast, exercising regularly, taking frequent breaks throughout the day, among other practices, builds a routine that lays a foundation for leading life well.

Indeed, positive habits help inculcate discipline, self-control, and self-confidence; all of which are crucial in achieving your personal growth goals. Eventually, they become deeply embedded routines that impact your life tremendously.

On top of creating orderliness and inculcating discipline, positive daily practices promote good health by reducing stress and increasing emotional resilience. This will enable you to deal with challenges and setbacks positively as well as proactively, overcoming barriers with success.

Well then, if you want to improve yourself, begin by forming positive daily habits that are consistent with your long-term goals for personal development. Small but consistent alterations in your everyday routine can have a huge impact on you, helping you get closer to your dreams and lead a more satisfying life.

The Importance of Continuous Learning

Continuous learning is necessary for one's personal growth and development since it widens the knowledge base and equips individuals with new skills that benefit them both personally and professionally.

Integrating continuous learning into your life can be as simple as dedicating specific time to read books, registering for online courses, attending conferences, or even looking for fresh experiences that will push you out of your comfort zones.

By consistently seeking knowledge about changes in your industry while at the same time enhancing new attributes and abilities within yourself, you would be capable of excelling in both professional and personal life areas respectively.

So why wait? Embrace the power of continuous learning today and take steps to ensure your personal growth and development never stagnate.

Developing Emotional Intelligence

Developing emotional intelligence is highly important on one's journey towards self-improvement. Emotional intelligence refers to the capacity to recognize how we feel as well as how others feel so that we may adjust our behaviour accordingly. You can develop higher levels of emotional intelligence through improved awareness of yourself emotionally as well as others around you; this aspect has been found to lead to better relationships, decision-making processes, general health status, among other things.

One way to develop emotional intelligence is through mindful practice; this involves being present in the moment and observing your thoughts and emotions without judgement. This helps you observe how your feelings affect your actions and how to control them.

Seeking others' feedback and being open to constructive criticisms can also improve your emotional intelligence. This way, you will identify those areas that you may not have realised were interfering with a better understanding of self or others.

By developing emotional intelligence and self-awareness, one can understand oneself and others better, enhancing communication, empathy, as well as personal growth.

Nurturing Relationships and Building a Support Network

On your quest for self-improvement, it is important to remember the significance of developing meaningful relationships and creating a strong support system. Surrounding yourself with individuals who are supportive, positive, and encouraging can make a significant difference in your progress.

A strong support network includes those who inspire you, hold you accountable for your actions, and believe in the greatness within you. These kinds of relationships will help motivate you further by giving advice on how to overcome challenges that come your way.

Building relationships and having a support network is key towards achieving personal growth. Whether it is friends, family members, or mentors; these ties offer different perspectives as well as resources for enhancing personal development.

Developing strong relationships and creating a support system can help one feel they belong to a community. A sense of belonging and community is essential for personal growth; no man can reach his goals alone, having the assistance of a supportive community can make all the difference.

Mindfulness and Self-reflection

Using mindfulness as well as reflecting on oneself are some of the most powerful tools on your way to achieving self-improvement. Mindfulness refers to staying in the present moment and observing your thoughts and feelings without judgement. By doing this, you will be able to understand more about your emotions and behaviours so that you can change them for good. On the other hand, self-reflection involves taking time to think about your experiences, thoughts, and deeds so that you may understand them better.

Together, mindfulness and self-reflection can help us identify unhealthy areas of our lives, discard negative attitudes or behaviours, and cultivate a thankful attitude. You become more aware of yourself by taking consistent stock-taking moments while analysing your experiences, thus making it easier for you to overcome challenges on your life path while striving towards the realisation of your dreams.

For instance, try using mindfulness practices like meditation or deep breathing as part of your everyday activities, as well as allocating time for reflection on whatever might have happened around you or inside of you at any particular moment. The transformative power of mindfulness and self-reflection will be felt when they become routine in one's lifestyle – helping with personal development and the journey towards Life Upgrade becomes achievable.

Overcoming Challenges & Resilience

Self-improvement is not usually straightforward; there are moments where tests arise along the way. Remember that setbacks do not define who we are but how we handle them does.

One way to overcome these challenges is looking at what they have taught us. Think about what went wrong or what could have been done differently? Use this knowledge to change your approach so that going forward is easier.

Building resilience is also crucial considering the inevitable high tides encountered in self-improvement. Keep a positive attitude and show yourself some love, as that is expected of any human who wishes to advance in life. Stay motivated by focusing on your progress and celebrate small wins along the way.

Everyone experiences their own set of challenges when trying to improve. But not everyone finds a way to conquer them; this, therefore, makes the difference. You can only move forward; you will emerge stronger and resilient on the other side.

Celebrating Milestones and Small Victories

As you continue your journey towards self-improvement, it is important for you to pause sometimes and celebrate the milestones that you have made no matter how small they may be. Setting goals for oneself that are later achieved is considered part of personal growth, and appreciating one's effort counts too.

You can also get motivated to keep progressing when you recognize and appreciate little achievements that take place throughout your life. These minor victories could be completing any task successfully or making progress towards any long-term goal.

Sometimes we focus so much on the outcome that we forget about what it takes us to achieve it. Therefore, pause a moment to reflect on how far you have come and utilise that positive energy into moving forward looking forward to achieving the next milestone in your journey.

However, celebrating your accomplishments, whether they are small or large, can remind you of how much progress you have made and give you the confidence to move forward in seeking personal development.

Conclusion: Begin Your Life Upgrade Journey Today

Undoubtedly, dedicating oneself to self-improvement through a Life Upgrade is a significant step towards personal and professional accomplishment. Throughout this article, you have learned about the power of a growth mindset, the importance of setting smart goals, the advantages of positive daily habits, among many others.

Remember that your Life Upgrade experience is unique to you. Self-help is not one-size-fits-all, and it is normal to face roadblocks on the path to transformation. Nevertheless, by working hard at what we want to do and remaining committed, we can always get there.

So what are you waiting for? Begin your Life Upgrade today, remembering to mark every milestone and small achievement along the way. It may be tough, but it will be worth it.

Thank you for reading this summary on "Life Upgrade" and good luck on your journey towards self-improvement.

"Embrace the challenge of self-development as the key to unleashing the extraordinary upgrade your life deserves. In the quest for becoming a greater form of who you are, you re-script the possibilities and light up the way leading to a life unmatched."

Life Upgrade FAQ

Q: What is Life Upgrade?

A: It means a lifelong commitment to improving oneself.

Q: Why is it important to embrace a lifelong commitment towards self-improvement?

A: By embracing a lifelong commitment towards self-improvement, one realises their potential, achieves personal growth, and leads a fulfilling as well as purpose-driven life. It enables continuous learning, the ability to face challenges, and achieve goals.

Q: What's a growth mindset?

A: A growth mindset refers to the notion that abilities, talents, or intelligence are developed through effort and a desire for learning. As such, it embraces challenges, perseveres in the face of setbacks, and sees failures as opportunities for growth.

Q: How can I develop a growth mindset?

A: The development of a growth mindset requires identification of fixed beliefs, then adopting an attitude that focuses on effort and resilience-based learning. Instead of saying "I cannot," shift towards "I can learn and improve."

Q: Why is setting clear goals important for personal development?

A: Setting clear goals gives direction, motivation, and a sense of purpose in your personal development journey. It helps you prioritise your actions, gauge your progress, and stay focused on what outcomes mean the most to you.

Q: How can I set clear and achievable goals for personal development?

A: To set clear and achievable goals, start by identifying areas in which you need improvement, reflecting on your values and aspirations, and breaking down objectives into smaller, more actionable steps. Make sure that your goals are specific, measurable, attainable, realistic, and time-bound (SMART).

Q: What are positive daily habits?

A: Positive daily habits are behaviours or routines that contribute to your well-being, personal growth, or overall happiness. Examples include exercise, reading books for self-empowerment purposes, meditation, journaling, practising gratitude, and self-reflections.

Q: How do positive daily habits contribute to self-improvement?

A: Developing good daily habits helps you cultivate discipline, create order, and bring stability to your life. These habits can increase your productivity, improve your physical and mental well-being, and help you grow personally.

Q: Why is ongoing education important for personal growth?

A: Learning continuously keeps your mind working, increases your knowledge and skills base to match an ever-changing world. It promotes curiosity, innovation, and open-mindedness as catalysts for personal growth and development.

Q: How do I incorporate continuous learning into my life?

A: To inculcate continuous learning into your lifestyle, seek new knowledge through a variety of sources (e.g., books), acquire new skills by enrolling in online courses or attending intensive workshops, read inspiring blogs, or listen to podcasts that address topics related to personal development, and engage in helpful conversations with experts. Form a habit of studying throughout one's lifetime, exploring subjects related to what one loves doing and planning to achieve.

Q: What is meant by emotional intelligence?

A: Emotional intelligence refers to the level at which you are able to manage your own emotions effectively and show empathy towards others' feelings. It involves self-awareness, self-regulation, social awareness, and relationship management.

Q: How does developing emotional intelligence contribute to my goal of self-improvement?

A: Developing emotional intelligence raises one's self-awareness, empathy levels, and interpersonal relationship abilities. It also improves communication competence, helps navigate conflicts more easily, and fosters positive relationships with others – an important aspect of personal development.

Q: Why is it important to build relationships and establish a support system?

A: By cultivating meaningful relationships and building support networks that provide emotional support systems for yourself during the process of improving oneself, motivation can be provided at an individual level through encouragement as well as accountability on their journey of self-improvement. In addition, it creates belongingness among people which promotes collaboration as well as enriches overall well-being.

Q: How can I build relationships and establish a support system?

A: To establish a support network and nurture relationships, one should invest time into building meaningful connections with relatives, friends, mentors, and people of similar interests. Try to meet people where they are in life by engaging them in meaningful conversation beyond just talking to them. This involves planning for dialogue, listening actively, counselling others, and being open to advice from others.

Q: What is mindfulness?

A: Mindfulness is when you intentionally focus on the present moment without judging your experience. It includes being aware of your thoughts, feelings, sensations

Epilogue: The Future You..

You've now come to the end of this book, but in many ways it also marks a new beginning. The insights and strategies shared over the past chapters have hopefully sparked reflection on what really matters most to you and how you want to spend your one wild and precious life. By taking the time to better understand your core values and clarify your sense of purpose, you now have a North Star to guide your decision making. And through learning how to break big goals into achievable daily tasks, you have a roadmap for purposefully directing your energy and effort.

While the road ahead may not always be clear, stay focused on constantly moving in the right direction through small, focused steps each day. Remember that living with intention and purpose is a journey, not a destination, and progress often happens gradually through commitment to the process over instant gratification or results. There will undoubtedly be challenges along the way as well as days where motivation waivers, but your broader reasons for pursuing your passion can sustain you through difficulties.

Have faith that your daily drops of effort, like raindrops forming streams and rivers, will lead somewhere meaningful if you don't lose sight of your priorities and commitments to yourself. And don't be afraid to course correct when needed - listening to feedback and making adjustments shows wisdom, not weakness. What's most important is that you continue walking confidently toward who and what gives your life significance.

With purpose and passion lighting your path, I know your light will help guide others along their journeys as well through your actions and the ripples of your impact. Remember that in showing up as your best self each day, however imperfectly, you have the power to positively change lives and make this world just a little bit brighter. Now go start your journey - the world awaits your unique contribution. Stay determined, follow your truth, and know that you have the strength within you to live fully and purposefully. I wish you all the very best as you embark on this exciting new chapter.

"Life might be a box of chocolates, but remember you get to pick the box.."